Farsi
(Persian)

lonely planet

phrase...
an...

Civic Center

Dr Yavar D...

Farsi (Persian) phrasebook
2nd edition – November 2008

Published by
Lonely Planet Publications Pty Ltd ABN 36 005 607 983
90 Maribyrnong St, Footscray, Victoria 3011, Australia

Lonely Planet Offices
Australia Locked Bag 1, Footscray, Victoria 3011
USA 150 Linden St, Oakland CA 94607
UK Media Centre, 201 Wood Lane, London W12 7TQ

Cover illustration
Dreaming from Tehran to Esfahan by Yukiyoshi Kamimura

ISBN 978 1 74104 060 9

text © Lonely Planet Publications Pty Ltd 2008
cover illustration © Lonely Planet Publications Pty Ltd 2008

10 9 8 7 6 5

Printed in China.

Although the authors and Lonely Planet try to make the information   ity
for any   ne
using th

31232009784960

acknowledgments

about the author

Dr Yavar Dehghani was born in Iran. After completing a Bachelor degree in speech pathology and a MA in linguistics, he taught at universities in Tehran and Tabriz while writing several books on speech disorders and related areas. He has also translated several books from English into Persian.

Yavar completed a PhD in linguistics in Melbourne, and has published his thesis, *A Grammar of Azari Including Comparisons with Persian* (published by Lincom Europa), as well as *Persian Grammar, Azeri Grammar* and a Persian learner's dictionary. He is a NAATI translator and currently Head of Iranian Languages at a language school in Melbourne.

from the author

Yavar gives his thanks to his parents and uncle, Bahram, who gave their support during his years of studying Persian. He also thanks his Iranian friends in Melbourne for their encouragement while he wrote this book, with special thanks to Dariush Salehi who helped edit the Persian script. Thanks also to his dear friend John Saliba for his continued help and support.

Yavar dedicates this book to his wife Mojgan, who helped with writing and proofreading, and who has always been an inspiration.

from the publisher

Peter D'Onghia and Karin Vidstrup Monk co-ordinated; Dariush Salehi helped edit the script; Haya Husseini proofread, researched and dreamed of the desert; Natasha Velleley and Wayne Murphy produced the map; Yukiyoshi Kamimura excelled in design while smoking his hubble bubble; Vicki Webb edited and scoffed plenty of *ghahve*; Yukiyoshi Kamimura drew the cover, Andrew McLeod the inside illustrations, and Fabrice Rocher oversaw design. Thanks to Patrick Marris for his zen-like act of creation, Pat Yale for his suggestions, and Branislava Vladisavljevic, David Kemp, Laura Crawford and Annelies Mertens for their assistance with this book.

make the most of this phrasebook ...

Anyone can speak another language! It's all about confidence. Don't worry if you can't remember your school language lessons or if you've never learnt a language before. Even if you learn the very basics (on the inside covers of this book), your travel experience will be the better for it. You have nothing to lose and everything to gain when the locals hear you making an effort.

finding things in this book

For easy navigation, this book is in sections. The Pronunciation and Grammar chapters are the ones you'll thumb through time and again. The Getting Around and Accommodation chapters cover basic travel situations like catching transport and finding a bed. The Meeting People and Interests chapters give you conversational phrases and the ability to express opinions – so you can get to know people. Food has a section all of its own: gourmets and vegetarians are covered and local dishes feature. The Health and Emergencies chapters equip you with health and police phrases, just in case. The Sustainable Travel section will help you travel responsibly. Use the comprehensive Index to find everything easily. Otherwise, check the traveller's Dictionary for the word you need.

being understood

Throughout this book you'll see coloured phrases on each page. They're phonetic guides to help you pronounce the language. Start with them to get a feel for how the language sounds. The Pronunciation chapter will explain more, but you can be confident that if you read the coloured phrase, you'll be understood.

communication tips

Body language, ways of doing things, sense of humour – all have a role to play in every culture. The boxes included throughout this phrasebook give you useful cultural and linguistic information that will help you communicate with the locals and enrich your travel experience.

CONTENTS

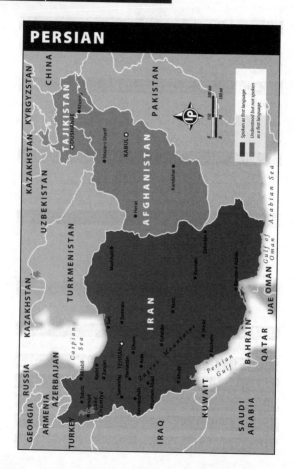

INTRODUCTION

The Persian people were once part of a tribal family known as Iranians, nomadic tribes whose original homeland was the Eurasian plains of Southern Russia. Persians began their migration into the Middle East around 2000 BC, and within 1500 years had created the first world empire which stretched throughout the entire Middle East, with Old Persian as the common language.

For centuries, Persian – also known as Farsi (see page 10) – has remained the language of this civilisation. It belongs to the Indo-Iranian group of languages, which forms part of the large Indo-European language family.

Today, Modern Persian is spoken by around 70 million people in Iran. It's an official language in Afghanistan and Tajikistan. Persian is understood in parts of Armenia, Azerbaijan, Georgia, India, Iraq, Kazakhstan, Pakistan, Turkmenistan, Turkey and Uzbekistan. A large number of Persian speakers have also emigrated to the US and Europe.

Persian was written in Pahlavi script until the introduction of Islam in Iran in 637 AD, when Arabic script was adopted. Although it uses the Arabic system of writing and has borrowed a large amount of its vocabulary, Persian has no grammatical similarities to Arabic – it belongs to a different language family.

Pahlavi Script

Persian script is written from right to left and, unlike its appearance suggests, is quite easy to learn. As the six vowels in Persian are represented by only one letter – ĩ, called '*alef*' – in most cases you can only tell how to pronounce a vowel by its context.

Persian has several dialects, including Esfahani, Shirazi, Tehrani and Yazdi, which all are mutually intelligible. This phrasebook is based on the Tehrani dialect, which is considered to be the standard dialect and is spoken by most Persian speakers.

INTRODUCTION

WRITTEN & SPOKEN STYLES

Persian has two styles – a written and a spoken style. The sounds and grammar of the written style haven't been changed for at least a century, and thus is more conservative. On the other hand, the spoken style has changed dramatically, especially in its system of sounds. The spoken style is more economical in its sounds and in the units, such as suffixes, used to represent meaning:

	WRITTEN STYLE	SPOKEN STYLE
I want to go.	mikhāham beravam	mikhām beram

If used in everyday conversation, the written style can seem artificial to the native speaker. Transliterations in this phrasebook reflect the spoken style, while the accompanying Persian script is given in the more formal style, so you'll be able to learn practical, everyday Persian.

Learning some Persian will give you a chance to learn more about the culture and the history of 3000 years of Persian civilisation, and to communicate with speakers of related languages like Tajik, and Afghani Farsi. As most Persian speakers don't speak English, any attempt made by foreigners to speak in Persian is welcomed.

PERSIAN OR FARSI?

The language of Iran is alternately called 'Persian' and 'Farsi' in the West.

At the time of the introduction of Islam in Iran in around 600 AD, the Arab name for Persia was 'Farsi', and this is the name they gave to the language. Due to the long-lasting influence of Arabs and Arabic, the language is still called Farsi in Iran today but is commonly known as Persian elsewhere.

ABBREVIATIONS USED IN THIS BOOK

adj	adjective
com	command
n	noun
pl	plural
pol	polite
sg	singular

HOW TO USE THIS PHRASEBOOK
You *Can* Speak Another Language

It's true – anyone can speak another language. Don't worry if you haven't studied languages before, or that you studied a language at school for years and can't remember any of it. It doesn't even matter if you failed English grammar. After all, that's never affected your ability to speak English! And this is the key to picking up a language in another country. You don't need to sit down and memorise endless grammatical details and you don't need to memorise long lists of vocabulary. You just need to start speaking. Once you start, you'll be amazed how many prompts you'll get to help you build on those first words. You'll hear people speaking, pick up sounds from TV, catch a word or two that you think you know from the local radio, see something on a billboard – all these things help to build your understanding.

Plunge In

There's just one thing you need to start speaking another language – courage. Your biggest hurdle is overcoming the fear of saying aloud what may seem to you to be just a bunch of sounds. There are a number of ways to do this.

The best way to start overcoming your fear is to memorise a few key words. These are the words you know you'll be saying again and again, like 'hello', 'thank you' and 'how much?' Here's an important hint though – right from the beginning, learn at least one phrase that will be useful but not essential.

INTRODUCTION

Such as 'good morning' or 'good afternoon', 'see you later' or even a conversational piece like 'lovely day, isn't it?' or 'it's cold today' (people everywhere love to talk about the weather). Having this extra phrase (just start with one, if you like, and learn to say it really well) will enable you to move away from the basics, and when you get a reply and a smile, it'll also boost your confidence. You'll find that people you speak to will like it too, as they'll understand that at least you've tried to learn more of the language than just the usual essential words.

Don't worry that you're not getting a whole sentence right first time. People will understand if you stick to the key word. And you'll find that once you're in the country, it won't take long to remember the complete sentence.

Ways to Remember

There are several ways to learn a language. Most people find they learn from a variety of these, although people usually have a preferred way to remember. Some like to see the written word and remember the sound from what they see. Some like to just hear it spoken in context (if this is you, try talking to yourself in Persian). Others, especially the more mathematically inclined, like to analyse the grammar of a language, and piece together words according to the rules of grammar. The very visually inclined like to associate the written word and even sounds with some visual stimulus, such as from illustrations, TV and general things they see in the street. As you learn, you'll discover what works best for you – be aware of what made you really remember a particular word, and keep using that method.

Kicking Off

Chances are you'll want to learn some of the language before you go. The first thing to do is to memorise those essential phrases and words. Check out the basics (page 35) ... and don't forget that extra phrase (see Plunge In).

Try the sections on Greetings or First Encounters in Meeting People, pages 36 and 38 for a phrase you'd like to use. Write some of these words and phrases down on a piece of paper and stick them up around the place: on the fridge, by the bed, on your computer, as a bookmark – somewhere where you'll see them often. Try putting some words in context – the 'How much is it?' note, for instance, could go in your wallet.

Building the Picture

We include a grammar chapter in our books for two main reasons.

Firstly, some people have an aptitude for grammar and find understanding it a key tool to their learning. If you're such a person, then the grammar chapter in a phrasebook will help you build a picture of the language, as it works through all the basics.

The second reason for the grammar chapter is that it gives answers to questions you might raise as you hear or memorise some key phrases. You may find a particular word is always used when there is a question – check out Questions in Grammar and it should explain why. This way you don't have to read the grammar chapter from start to finish, nor do you need to memorise a grammatical point. It will simply present itself to you in the course of your learning. Key grammatical points are repeated throughout the book.

Any Questions?

Try to learn the main question words (see page 30). As you read through different situations, you'll see these words used in the example sentences, and this will help you remember them. So if you want to hire a bicycle, turn to the Bicycles section in Getting Around (use the Contents or Index to find it quickly). You'll see the words for 'where' and 'bicycle' a number of times in this book. When you come across the sentence 'Where can I hire a bicycle?', you'll recognise the key words and this will help you remember the whole phrase. If there's no category for your need, try the dictionary (the question words are repeated there too, with examples), and memorise the phrase 'How do you say ...?' (page 47).

INTRODUCTION

I've Got a Flat Tyre

Doesn't seem like the phrase you're going to need? Well, in fact, it could be very useful. As are all the phrases in this book, provided you have the courage to mix and match them. We have given specific examples within each section. But the key words remain the same even when the situation changes. So while you may not be planning on any cycling during your trip, the first part of the phrase 'I've got ...' could refer to anything else, and there are plenty of words in the dictionary that, we hope, will fit your needs. So whether it's 'a ticket', 'a visa' or 'a condom', you'll be able to put the words together to convey your meaning.

Finally

Don't be concerned if you feel you can't memorise words. On the inside front and back covers are the most essential words and phrases you'll need. You could also try tagging a few pages for other key phrases, or use the notes pages to write your own reminders.

PRONUNCIATION

The pronunciation of Persian is fairly straightforward, with a strong consistency between pronunciation and spelling.

VOWELS

The vowel system in Persian consists of just six vowel sounds, all represented by the letter ī, called *alef*. The vowels ā, u and i are longer than the other vowels. However, pronouncing them short won't change the meaning of a word.

ī	*alef*	a, ā, e, i, o, u

CONSONANTS

Most Persian consonants are pronounced like their English counter parts. All consonant sounds are sometimes doubled, in which case they're always pronounced distinctly, such as the 'tt' in 'hot tea', not as in 'kettle'.

ب	*be*	b	ض	*zād*	z
پ	*pe*	p	ط	*tā*	t
ت	*te*	t	ظ	*zā*	z,
ث	*se*	s	ع	*eyn*	'
ج	*jim*	j	غ	*gheyn*	gh
چ	*chim*	ch	ف	*fe*	f
ح	*he*	h	ق	*ghāf*	gh
خ	*khe*	kh	ك	*kāf*	k
د	*dāl*	d	گ	*gāf*	g
ذ	*zāl*	z	ل	*lām*	l
ر	*re*	r	م	*mim*	m
ز	*ze*	z	ن	*nun*	n
ژ	*zhe*	zh	و	*ve*	v
س	*sin*	s	ه	*he*	h
ش	*shin*	sh	ی	*ye*	y
ص	*sād*	s			

PRONUNCIATION

TRANSLITERATIONS

The transliteration system in this phrasebook reflects the pronunciation of spoken Persian, which is much more economical than the more formal written style (see page 10). The equivalent Persian script is in the written form. Transliterations of examples in the Grammar chapter reflect the written style.

Vowels

a	as the 'a' in 'father'
ā	as the 'a' in 'far' (longer than a)
e	as the 'e' in 'bed'
i	as the 'i' in 'marine'
o	as the 'o' in 'mole'
u	as the 'u' in 'rule'

Consonants

Consonants not described here are pronounced as they are in English.

ch	as the 'ch' in 'cheese'
g	as the 'g' in 'goose'
gh	a guttural sound like a heavy French 'r', pronounced at the back of the mouth
h	as the 'h' in 'hot'
j	as the 'j' in 'jar'
kh	as the 'ch' in Scottish 'loch', pronounced at the back of the mouth
'	a glottal stop, pronounced in the throat, marking a break in the flow of speech. As the sound made between the words 'uh-oh' or the 'tt' in Cockney 'bottle'.
r	trilled
s	as the 's' in 'sin'
y	as the 'y' in 'yes'
zh	as the 'zh' in 'Zhivago'

A hyphen between two letters in the transliteration indicates that they have two separate sounds. In the word:

religion   **maz-hab**

z and h are pronounced separately. In:

Japan   **zhāpon**

they're pronounced as the 'Zh' in 'Zhivago'.

STRESS

Stress is generally placed on the last syllable of a word:

bakery   **nā-ne-vā-*yi***

However, the stress on proper names is always on the first syllable:

Darius   **d*ā*-ri-yush**

PRONUNCIATION

HIP TO BE SQUARE

Because the subject of a sentence is indicated in the verb, subject pronouns are optional. In this phrasebook, subject pronouns appear in square brackets.

PRONUNCIATION

ACCENTS & DIALECTS

There are several dialects in Persian, including Esfahani, Kermani, Shirazi, Tehrani and Yazdi. The main difference between these dialects is in intonation, word stress and in the reduction of syllables. Speakers of these dialects can understand one another well.

Other languages spoken in Iran which belong to the Iranian language family are Baluchi, Gilaki, Lori, Kurdish, Mazandarani and Talysh. They all differ extensively from modern Persian, and can't easily be understood by speakers of Persian. An unrelated language spoken in the north-west of Iran is Azeri, a Turkic language. Most Azeri speakers can also communicate in Persian.

GRAMMAR

This section provides a basic grammar of Persian, although it can't cover all aspects of the grammar in these few pages. You'll find that Persian grammar is regular, making it relatively easy to remember.

In Modern Persian, each verb changes its form according to person (I, you, she, and so on) and number (such as singular 'I' as opposed to plural 'we'). As you can tell who or what the speaker is referring to by the form of the verb, the subject can usually be left out of a sentence.

I went home.
man be khāne raftam   **be khāne raftam**
(lit: I to home went-I)   (lit: to home went-I)

WORD ORDER

The basic word order in Persian is Subject-Object-Verb. However, this order isn't fixed, especially in the spoken style where the verb can come before the object – Subject-Verb-Object – as in English.

As verbs indicate the subject of a sentence, even if you can't remember the word order, Persian speakers will understand you no matter where you put the verb in a sentence.

ARTICLES

Persian has different ways to express articles like 'the', 'a' and 'an'.

- Placing the word **yek**, meaning 'one', before a noun gives the meaning of the indefinite articles 'a' and 'an'.

I went to a hotel yesterday.   **diruz be yek hotel raftam**
(lit: yesterday to one hotel went-I)

- Placing the sound-i after a noun also makes the noun indefinite:

  I saw a boy in the street.   pesari rā dar khiyābān didam
  (lit: boy-a in the street saw-I)

- Nouns not marked byyek or-i are definite:

  I saw the museum.   man muze rā didam
  (lit: I museumrā saw-I)
  (See page 21 for an explanation ofrā .)

NOUNS
Plurals

Nouns are made plural by adding the suffix-hā to the end of the noun:

| book | ketāb | books | ketābhā |
| car | māshin | cars | māshinhā |

In spoken Persian,-hā is reduced toā :

books ketābā

However, nouns aren't pluralised when they appear after a number or a quantity noun such as 'some':

one house	yek khāne (lit: one house)
two houses	do khāne (lit: two house)
ten houses	dah khāne (lit: three house)

A few nouns borrowed from Arabic don't follow this rule of pluralisation:

festival eyd   festivals a'yād

Case

Case shows the function of a noun or pronoun in a sentence, (see page 22 for an explanation of grammatical terms). English shows these relationships between nouns by word order – 'the dog bit the man' means the dog did the biting, while 'the man bit the dog' means the man did.

Persian has five cases. It uses prepositions (before the noun) and postpositions (after the noun) as labels to indicate the role of a noun within a sentence.

- **NOMINATIVE CASE**

    The Subject of a sentence – who or what is peforming the action – is never marked with a preposition or postposition

    The bus left.   **utubus raft** (lit: the-bus went-it)

- rā **ACCUSATIVE CASE**

    Placing **rā** after a noun shows that the noun is directly affected by the action of the Subject

    I saw Shiraz.   **man shirāz rā didam**
    (lit: I Shiraz rā saw-I)

- be **DATIVE CASE**

    be shows that the noun is the receiver or goal of an action

    I went to Tehran.   **man be tehrān raftam**
    (lit: I be Tehran went-I)

- dar **LOCATIVE CASE**

    dar before a noun to shows where an action takes place

    Can I meet you in   **mitavānam shomā rā dar**
    the hotel?   **hotel bebinam?**
    (lit: can-I you rā dar the-hotel see-I?)

- az **ABLATIVE CASE**

    az indicates from where an action originated

    I came from Tabriz   **man emruz az tabriz āmadam**
    today.   (lit: I today az Tabriz came-I)

GRAMMAR

ON THE CASE

In English, we're able to recognise the 'role' of a noun in a sentence (whether it's Subject, Direct Object or Indirect Object) by its position in the sentence and/or by the use of prepositions. Persian has five cases. It uses prepositions and postpositions to indicate the role of a noun and its relationship to other words within a sentence.

1. The **nominative** case refers to the Subject of a verb in a sentence, and is also the form you'll find in a dictionary. It indicates what or who is performing an action:

The singer came from Kentucky to give presents to his friends in New York. (*the singer* 'gave')

2. The **accusative** is the Direct Object of a phrase or sentence. It indicates what or whom a verb refers to. Here it indicates what was given:

The singer came from Kentucky to give *presents* to his friends in New York.

3. The **dative** case is the Indirect Object, or the person to whom something is given or shown:

The singer came from Kentucky to give presents to *his friends* in New York.

4. The **locative** case describes where an action takes place.

The singer came from Kentucky to give presents to his friends *in New York*.

5. The **ablative** case shows from where an action originated.

The singer came *from Kentucky* to give presents to his friends in New York.

PERSIAN CARPETS

The Persian carpet is more than just a floor covering – it's a display of wealth and artistry. Carpets or rugs form an integral part of religious and cultural festivities, as well as in everyday life, such as prayer mats. Carpets have long been used as a form of currency, and weaving new carpets is a kind of savings account, which can be sold off in times of need.

Some carpet names and varieties:

gul-i-bulbul carpets feature birds and flowers.
heriz and mehriban carpets feature hunting scenes and tales
gabbeh carpets usually contain sporting and hunting scenes, local monuments or mosques.

ADJECTIVES

Adjectives in Persian appear after the noun they describe. The vowel e, known as *ezafe*, appears between a noun and an adjective, to indicate that an attribute 'belongs' to the noun. If the noun ends in a vowel, it takes the form ye. (See Possession, page 29, for other uses of *ezafe*.)

good book	ketāb e khub (lit: book e good)
good books	ketābhā ye khub (lit: books ye good)
the pretty house	khāne ye zibā (lit: house ye pretty)

Comparatives

Comparatives (better, hotter) are formed by adding the sufffix -tar to the end of an adjective, which appears after the noun it modifies.

the prettier house   khāne ye zibātar (lit: house ye prettier)

Superlatives

Superlatives (best, hottest) are formed by adding -tarin to the end of an adjective. Superlative adjectives appear before a noun.

the prettiest house   zibātarin khāne (lit: prettiest house)

PRONOUNS

Because all Persian verbs show the person and number of their subject in a suffix attached to the verb (see page 25), subject pronouns can be omitted from a sentence. In this phrasebook, subject pronouns have been put in square brackets to show that they are optional.

There are both informal and polite forms of the singular pronoun 'you'. The polite form, shomā, has the same form as the plural form of 'you'. The informal form to is only used among close friends and relatives.

The third person singular (he, she, it) has two forms – u is used to refer to animate nouns (such as people and animals), while ān refers to inanimate objects (things).

PRONOUNS			
SG		**PL**	
I	man	we	mā
you (inf)	to	you	shomā
you (pol)	shomā	they	ānhā
he/she/it (animate)	u		
(inanimate)	ān		

VERBS

Verbs in Persian change their form according to the person and
number of the Subject as well as for tense. Subject and tense are
indicated by the type of suffix which appears on a verb root.
Verb roots are formed by deleting the suffix -dan from an infinitive.

INFINITIVE
to read   khāndan

VERB ROOT
read   khān

KEY VERBS	
to agree	movāfegh budan
to come	āmadan
to cost	arzidan
to depart	tark kardan
to know (someone)	shenākhtan
to know (something)	dānestan
to like	dust dāshtan
to make	sākhtan
to meet	molāghāt kardan
to need	niyāz dāshtan
to prefer	tarjih dādan
to return	bargashtan
to say	goftan
to see	didan
to stay	māndan
to take	bordan
to understand	fahmidan

GRAMMAR

Present tense

The present tense is formed by adding:

- the prefix mi- before a verb root; and
- a personal suffix to the end of the verb root.

Present-Tense Personal Suffixes			
I	-am	we	-im
you	-i	you (pl)	-id
he/she/it	-ad	they	-and

eat	khor	
I eat.	mikhoram	(lit: mi-eat-I)
You eat. (sg)	mikhori	(lit: mi-eat-you)

Simple Past Tense

The simple past tense is formed by adding a personal suffix to the end of a verb root.

Past-Tense Personal Suffixes			
I	-dam	we	-dim
you	-di	you (pl)	-did
he/she/it	-d	they	-dand

eat	khor	
She ate.	khord	(lit: ate-she)
You (pl) ate.	khordid	(lit: ate-you)

Continuous Past Tense

To form the continuous past tense (was doing something), just add the prefix mi- to the past-tense form (see page 31).

I ate.	khordam	(lit: ate-I)
I was eating.	mikhordam	(lit: mi-ate-I)

Future Tense

In the future tense, the verb root khāh, 'want', takes a present-tense personal suffix (see page 33). It appears before the main verb in a sentence. The main verb is always in the past tense form for the third person singular – that is, it takes the suffix -d.

She will eat.	khāhad khord	(lit: want-she ate)
We will eat.	khāhim khord	(lit: want-I ate)

In colloquial speech, the present tense can also be used in place of the future tense – if context makes it clear that you're talking about the future.

I will eat tomorrow.　fardā mikhoram　(lit: tomorrow eat-I)

IMPERATIVES

To give an order or command, the prefix be- is added to a verb root.

khordan (eat)	khāndan (read)
Eat!	Read!
bekhor! (lit: be-eat!)	bekhān! (lit: be-read!)

To order someone not to do something, add the prefix na- before the verb root.

Don't eat!	Don't read!
nakhor! (lit: na-eat!)	nakhān! (lit: na-read!)

TO BE

The verb 'to be' is irregular in Persian. The present tense form is
hast, 'is', and the past tense form is **bud**, 'was'. Like other verbs,
hast and **bud** take a personal suffix. These verbs can be used with
nouns, adjectives or adverbs.

I'm thirsty.	**teshne hastam** (lit: thirsty am-I)
You were thirsty.	**teshne buddi** (lit: thirsty were-you)

In colloquial speech, **hast** can be omitted (except with 'he, she, it'),
but the personal suffix still remains.

I'm thirsty.	**teshne am** (lit: thirsty I)

TO HAVE

The word **dāshtan** has a similar function as the verb 'to have'.
It always takes a personal suffix (see page 32) at the end of its
verb root **dār**, and appears directly after a noun in a sentence.

have (**dār**)

I have a book.   **man ketāb dāram** (lit: I book have-I)

COMPOUND VERBS

Persian has a large number of compound verbs. They are formed
with a verb, noun, adjective or adverb followed by a simple verb
form like **kardan**, 'to do', **shodan**, 'to become', or **raftan**, 'to go'.
The simple verb takes a suffix to indicate tense, person and
number.

I cried.	**gerye kardam** (lit: cry did-I)
I climbed.	**bālā raftam** (lit: up went-I)
I stood up.	**boland shodam** (lit: long became-I)

POSSESSION

A possessive relationship between two nouns can be shown in either of two ways:

1. The vowel e, known as *ezafe*, conveys a meaning of possession and ownership. In a sentence the possessor appears before what is possessed, and the two are linked by the vowel e. The linking vowel e takes the form ye when the noun it follows ends in a vowel.

| my book | ketāb e man | (lit: book e I) |
| your house | khāne ye shomā | (lit: house ye you) |

2. Alternatively, a possessive suffix (see box) can be attached to the end of the noun that is possessed.

book	ketāb	(lit: book)
my book	ketābam	(lit: book-my)
your book	ketābat	(lit: book-your)

Possessive Suffixes

my	-am	our	-emān
your	-at	your (pl)	-etān
his/her/its	-ash	their	-eshān

QUESTIONS

Questions in Persian are formed by a rise in intonation at the end of a sentence. Word order doesn't change.

The plane is leaving.	havāpeymā harekat mikonad
	(lit: the-plane move does-it)
Is the plane leaving?	havāpeymā harekat mikonad?
	(lit: the-plane move does-it?)

To form a question in written Persian, the word āyā, 'does', is used at the start of a sentence. The form āyā is never used in spoken Persian.

| Is the plane leaving? | āyā havāpeymā harekat mikonad? |
| | (lit: does the-plane move does-it?) |

GRAMMAR

QUESTION WORDS

where?	kojā?	Where's the bank? bānk kojāst? (lit: bank where-is?)
why?	cherā?	Why is the museum closed? cherā muze baste hast? (lit: why museum closed is?)
when?	key?	When does the festival begin? jashn key shuru' mishe? (lit: festival when start becomes?)
what?	che?	What's he saying? u che miguyad? (lit: he what saying-is?)
how?	chetor?	How do I go there? chetor ānjā beravam? (lit: how there go-I?)
who?	ki?	Who is she? u ki hast? (lit: she who is?)
which?	kodām?	Which is the best? kodām behtar hast? (lit: which better is?)

NEGATIVES

To form the negative, the prefix na- is placed before a verb.

He went to Tehran.	u be tehrān raft (lit: he to Tehran went-he)
He didn't go to Tehran.	u be tehrān naraft (lit: he to Tehran no-went-he)

For the future tense, na- is added to the first verb, as in:

He will go to Tehran.	u be tehrān khāhad raft (he to Tehran want-he went)
He won't go to Tehran.	u be tehrān nakhāhad raft (he to Tehran no-want-he went)

KEY VERBS

Regular verbs

Most Persian verbs are regular, taking the same suffixes.

khāndan (to read)

	Present	Past	Continuous Past	Future
	mikhānam	khāndam	mikhāndam	khāham khānd
you	mikhāni	khāndi	mikhāndi	khāhi khānd
he/she/it	mikhānad	khānd	mikhānd	khāhad khānd
we	mikhānim	khāndim	mikhāndim	khāhim khānd
you (pl)	mikhānid	khāndid	mikhāndid	khāhid khānd
they	mikhānand	khāndand	mikhāndand	khāhand khānd

khordan (to eat)

	Present	Past	Continuous Past	Future
	mikhoram	khordam	mikhordam	khāham khord
you	mikhori	khordi	mikhordi	khāhi khord
he/she/it	mikhorad	khord	mikhord	khāhad khord
we	mikhorim	khordim	mikhordim	khāhim khord
you (pl)	mikhorid	khordid	mikhordid	khāhid khord
they	mikhorand	khordand	mikhordand	khāhand khord

kharidan (to buy)

	Present	Past	Continuous Past	Future
	mikharam	kharidam	mikharidam	khāham kharid
you	mikhari	kharidi	mikharidi	khāhi kharid
he/she/it	mikharad	kharid	mikharid	khāhad kharid
we	mikharim	kharidim	mikharidim	khāhim kharid
you (pl)	mikharid	kharidid	mikharidid	khāhid kharid
they	mikharand	kharidand	mikharidand	khāhand kharid

āvardan (to bring)

	Present	Past	Continuous Past	Future
	miyāvaram	āvardam	miyāvardam	khāham āvard
you	miyāvari	āvardi	miyāvardi	khāhi āvard
he/she/it	miyāvarad	āvard	miyāvarad	khāhad āvard
we	miyāvarim	āvardim	miyāvardim	khāhim āvard
you (pl)	miyāvarid	āvardid	miyāvardid	khāhid āvard
they	miyāvarand	āvardand	miyāvardand	khāhand āvard

GRAMMAR

KEY VERBS

Irregular Verbs

budan (to be)

	Present	Past	Continuous Past	Future
I	hastam	budam	mibudam	khāham bud
you	hasti	budi	mibudi	khāhi bud
he/she/it	hast	bud	mibud	khāhad bud
we	hastim	budim	mibudim	khāhim bud
you (pl)	hastid	budid	mibudid	khāhid bud
they	hastand	budand	mibudand	khāhand bud

raftan (to go)

	Present	Past	Continuous Past	Future
I	miravam	raftam	miraftam	khāham raft
you	miravi	rafti	mirafti	khāhi raft
he/she/it	miravad	raft	miraft	khāhad raft
we	miravim	raftim	miraftim	khāhim raft
you (pl)	miravid	raftid	miraftid	khāhid raft
they	miravand	raftand	miraftand	khāhand raft

dāshtan (to have)

	Present	Past	Continuous Past	Future
I	dāram	dāshtam	midāshtam	khāham dāsht
you	dāri	dāshti	midāshti	khāhi dāsht
he/she/it	dārad	dāsht	midāsht	khāhad dāsht
we	dārim	dāshtim	midāshtim	khāhim dāsht
you (pl)	dārid	dāshtid	midāshtid	khāhid dāsht
they	dārand	dāshtand	midāshtand	khāhand dāsht

tavānestan (to be able to)

	Present	Past	Continuous Past	Future
I	mitavānam	tavānestam	mitavānestam	khāham tavānest
you	mitavāni	tavānesti	mitavānesti	khāhi tavānest
he/she/it	mitavānad	tavānest	mitavānest	khāhad tavānes
we	mitavānim	tavānestim	mitavānestim	khāhim tavānest
you (pl)	mitavānid	tavānestid	mitavānestid	khāhid tavānest
they	mitavānand	tavānestand	mitavānestand	khāhand tavānes

KEY VERBS

dādan (to give)

	Present	Past	Continuous Past	Future
I	midāham	dādam	midādam	khāham dād
you	midāhi	dādi	midādi	khāhi dād
he/she/it	midāhad	dād	midād	khāhad dād
we	midāhim	dādim	midādim	khāhim dād
you (pl)	midāhid	dādid	midādid	khāhid dād
they	midāhand	dādand	midādand	khāhand dād

dānestan (to know)

	Present	Past	Continuous Past	Future
I	midānam	dānestam	midānestam	khāham dānest
you	midāni	dānesti	midānesti	khāhi dānest
he/she/it	midānad	dānest	midānest	khāhad dānest
we	midānim	dānestim	midānestim	khāhim dānest
you (pl)	midānid	dānestid	midānestid	khāhid dānest
they	midānand	dānestand	midānestand	khāhand dānest

kardan (to do)

	Present	Past	Continuous Past	Future
I	mikonam	kardam	mikardam	khāham kard
you	mikoni	kardi	mikardi	khāhi kard
he/she/it	mikonad	kard	mikard	khāhad kard
we	mikonim	kardim	mikardim	khāhim kard
you (pl)	mikonid	kardid	mikardid	khāhid kard
they	mikonand	kardand	mikardand	khāhand kard

khāstan (to want)

	Present	Past	Continuous Past	Future
I	mikhāham	khāstam	mikhāstam	khāham khāst
you	mikhāhi	khāsti	mikhāsti	khāhi khāst
he/she/it	mikhāhad	khāst	mikhāst	khāhad khāst
we	mikhāhim	khāstim	mikhāstim	khāhim khāst
you (pl)	mikhāhid	khāstid	mikhāstid	khāhid khāst
they	mikhāhand	khāstand	mikhāstand	khāhand khāst

GRAMMAR

MISTAKES TO WATCH FOR – PERSIAN SPEAKERS

• Pronunciation of some English words is more difficult for speakers of Persian than others. The sound 'th', as in 'this', is often pronounced 'd', as in 'dis', and 'w', as in 'water', is often pronounced as a 'v' as in 'vater'

• In words beginning with two consonants, Persian speakers often add a vowel at the start:

'estudent' instead of 'student'

• Because nouns in Persian don't pluralise after a number, Persian speakers often leave out the plural 's' in English:

'two book' instead of 'two books'

• In Persian, questions are formed by a rise in intonation at the end of a sentence. Many Persian speakers have a problem using 'do', 'does' and 'did' in forming questions in English:

'Did he came?' instead of 'Did he come?'

• Because Persian words are stressed on the last syllable, Persian speakers often place stress on the last syllable of English words:

'li**brary**' instead of '**li**brary'

MISTAKES TO WATCH FOR – ENGLISH SPEAKERS

• Speakers of English often have trouble pronouncing some sounds in Persian. The sounds kh, gh, ' (glottal stop), ā and h are often mispronounced:

'kune' instead of 'khune'   'motad' instead of 'mo'tād'
'gand' instead of 'ghand'   'momm' instead of 'mohemm'
'salam' instead of 'salām'

• English speakers often forget to add a personal suffix to a verb, or use the wrong one, as in:

'man āmad' instead of 'man āmadam'
(lit: I come)   (lit: I come-I)

• English speakers often place stress on the first syllable of a Persian word instead of the last, for example:

'**sob**-hu-ne' instead of 'sob-hu-**ne**'

GRAMMAR

If an Iranian family invites you to their house, they'll most likely take you to the guestroom – the best place in the room is reserved for the guest. Immediately, the hospitality begins by serving tea and sweets. Iranians are hospitable, especially towards foreigners. Knowing a few formal Persian words for giving thanks and saying goodbye will help show your appreciation.

YOU SHOULD KNOW   شما باید بدانید

Hello.	salām	سلام
Goodbye.	khodā hāfez	خدا حافظ
Yes./No.	bale/na	بله/نه
Excuse me.	bebakhshid	ببخشید
Please.	lotfan	لطفاً
Thank you.	motashakkeram	متشکرم
Many thanks.	kheyli mamnun	خیلی ممنون
OK.	bāshe	باشه
Do you mind?	eshkāl nadāre?	اشکال نداره؟
That's OK.	khāhesh mikonam	خواهش می کنم

FORMALITIES

In Persian, there are both polite and informal forms of the singular pronoun 'you' – the polite form is **shomā** while the informal is **to**.

Only close friends and relatives address each other using **to**. The plural form of 'you', **shomā**, has the same form as the polite singular pronoun.

GREETINGS & GOODBYES   احوالپرسی و خداحافظی

Greetings in Persian are usually accompanied by a handshake and sometimes a kiss on the cheek – but only between people of the same sex. Kissing on the cheek usually takes place between friends and relatives who haven't seen each other for a long time.

People only shake hands with or kiss the opposite sex when they are members of their immediate family, such as a brother or sister. When greeting someone of the opposite sex who isn't a family member, a more formal verbal greeting is used.

Good morning.	sob bekheyr	صبح بخیر
Good day (noon).	ruz bekheyr	روز بخیر
Good afternoon.	asr bekheyr	عصر بخیر
Good evening.	shab bekheyr	شب بخیر
Hello./Hi.	salām	سلام
Goodbye.	khodā hāfez	خدا حافظ

CIVILITIES   احوالپرسی روزانه

The usual form of greeting among friends and relatives is salām, 'hello'.

Hello.	salām	سلام
May I?;/Do you mind?	eshkāl nadāre?	اشکال ندا ره؟
How are you?	hāletun chetor e?	حالتون چطوره؟
Fine!	khubam	خوبم
Not bad!	bad nistam	بد نیستم
Let's go.	befarmāyin berim	بفرمایید برویم
Please sit down.	befarmāyin beshinin	بفرمایید بنشیند
Correct!	doroste!	درسته
That will do.	kāfiye	کافیه
Do you understand?	motavajjeh mishin?	متوجه می شوید؟
Yes, I understand.	bale mifahmam	بله می فهمم
No, I don't understand.	na namifahmam	نه نمی فهمم

Thank you (very much).
   (kheyli) motashakkeram   (خیلی) متشکرم

You're welcome.
   khāhesh mikonam   خواهش می کنم

Excuse me./Sorry. (pol)
   ma'zerat mikhām   معذرت می خواهم

You've gone to a lot of trouble.
   kheyli zahmat keshidin   خیلی زحمت کشیدید

Please wait a while.
   lotfan kami sabr konin   لطفاً کمی صبر کنید

FORMS OF ADDRESS   مخاطب قراردادن

Only close friends and children are addressed by their first name.
If people do call each other by their first name, they generally
add the title 'Mr' or 'Ms' before the name. Most people are
addressed by their surname.

Mr	**āghā**
Ms	**khānom**

The title **dushize**, which was once used to address unmarried
women, is no longer used. The word **khanom** is now used for
all women.

In very formal situations, the following titles are used:

(for men)	**janābe āghā**
(for women)	**sarkār khānom**

Other formal forms of address are still used for the hierarchy,
especially clergymen.

In government offices, especially in Islamic centres, the words
barādar (lit: brother) and **khāhar** (lit: sister) are used instead of
āghā and **khānom**. Co-workers sometimes also address one
another by putting **āghā** or **khānom** before a job title:

Mr engineer	**āghā ye mohandes**
Mrs manager	**khānom e modir**

MEETING PEOPLE

BODY LANGUAGE

زبان اشاره

Persian speakers indicate 'yes' by nodding their head forward and down. In informal situations among close friends and relatives, āre, the informal word for 'yes', is used. 'No' is indicated by nodding the head up and back or by shaking it from side to side. Alternatively, the eyebrows may be raised. (Body language is used in informal situations, and the polite way to indicate 'yes' and 'no' is with bale, 'yes', or na, 'no'.)

HIP TO BE SQUARE

Because the subject of a sentence is indicated in the verb, subject pronouns are optional. In this phrasebook, subject pronouns appear in square brackets.

FIRST ENCOUNTERS

اولین برخورد

Since there are few foreigners in Iran, people will generally be curious about your keshvar, 'country', and may ask a lot of questions about your culture. At the same time, Iranians are very hospitable toward foreigners and, even after a short conversation, may invite you to their home.

How are you?	hāletun chetor e?	حالتون چطوره؟
Fine. And you?	khubam. shomā chetorin?	خوبم. شما چطورید؟
I'd like to introduce you to ...	mikhām shomā ro be ... mo'arefi konam	می خواهم شما را به ... معرفی کنم
I'm pleased to meet you.	az āshnāyitun khoshbakhtam	از آشنایی تان خوشبختم
I'm a friend of (Behzad).	man dust e behzādam	من دوست بهزادم
What's your name?	esmetun chi ye?	اسمتون چیه؟
My name's ...	esmam ... e	اسم ... است
His/her name is ...	esmesh ... e	اسم او ... است

MAKING CONVERSATION

شروع مکالمه

Do you live here?
[shomā] injā zendegi mikonin?
(شما) اینجا زندگی می کنید؟

Where are you going?
[shomā] kojā mirin?
(شما) کجا می روید؟

What are you doing?
[shomā] chikār mikonin?
(شما) چکار می کنید؟

What do you think (about ...)?
[shomā] (dar mored e ...)
chi fekr mikonin?
(شما)(در مورد ...)
چه فکر می کنید؟

Can I take a photo (of you)?
mishe aks (e shomā ro)
begiram?
می شود عکس (شما را)
بگیرم؟

What's this called?
esm e in chi ye?
اسم این چیه؟

Beautiful, isn't it!
ghashang e, mage na!
قشنگه مگه نه

It's very nice here.
injā kheyli khub e
اینجا خیلی خوبه

We love it here.
mā injā ro dust dārim
ما اینجا را دوست داریم

What a cute baby!
che bachche ye ghashangi!
چه بچه ی قشنگی

Are you waiting, too?
[shomā] m montazer in?
شما هم منتظرین؟

Are you here on holiday?
[shomā] barāye ta'tilāt
injā umadin?
(شما) برای تعطیلات
اینجا آمدید؟

| That's strange! | ajib e! | عجیبه |
| That's funny. (amusing) | khandedar e | خنده داره |

I'm here ...	man ... injām	من ... اینجا هستم
for a holiday	barāye ta'tilāt	برای تعطیلات
on business	barāye tejārat	برای تجارت
to study	barāye tahsil	برای تحصیل

How long are you here for?
  cheghadr injā mimunin?
چقدر اینجا می مانید؟

I'm here for ... weeks/days.
  mān ... hafte/ruz injā
  mimunam
من ... هفته/روز اینجا
می مانم

Do you like it here?
  az injā khoshetun miyād?
از اینجا خوشتان می آید؟

We like it here very much.
  mā az injā kheyli
  khoshemun miyād
ما از اینجا خیلی
خوشمان می آید

Where are you staying?
  [shomā] kojā mimunin?
(شما) کجا می مانید؟

How long have you been here?
  [shomā] che moddat e injayin?
(شما) چه مدته اینجایید؟

I've been here (three days).
  man (se ruz e) injā m
من (سه روزه) اینجا هستم

This is my first visit to (Iran).
  in avvalin mosāferat e man
  be (iran) e
این اولین مسافرت من
به (ایران) است

Are you here on your own?
  [shomā] injā tanhā hastin?
(شما)اینجا تنها هستید؟

I'm here with my friend.
  man injā bā dust am hastam
من اینجا با دوستم هستم

Thanks. I don't smoke.
  motashakkeram. man
  sigār nemikesham
متشکرم. من
سیگار نمی کشم

I'll call you later.
  ba'dan be shomā zang mizanam
بعداً به شما زنگ می زنم

Useful Phrases

عبارت های مفید

Sure.	hatman	حتماً
Just a minute.	ye daghighe sabr konin	یک دقیقه صبر کنید
It's OK.	eyb nadāre	عیب ندا ره
It's important.	mohemm e	مهمه
It's not important.	mohemm nist	مهم نیست
It's possible.	emkān dāre	امکان دا ره
It's not possible.	emkān nadāre	امکان ندا ره
Look!	negāh konin	نگاه کنید
Listen (to this)!	(bā in) gush konin	گوش کنید(به این)
I'm ready.	man āmāde am	من آماده ام
Are you ready?	shomā āmāde in?	شما آماده اید؟
Good luck!	mov, affagh bāshin	موفق باشید
Just a second!	ye lahze shabr konin!	یک لحظه صبر کنید

NATIONALITIES

ملیت ها

Most country names in Persian differ from English, and their pronunciation is closer to French.

Where are you from?
[shomā] kojāyi hastin?

(شما) کجایی هستید؟

I'm from ...   man ahl e ... am   من اهل ... هستم

Australia	ostārāliyā	استرالیا
Austria	otrish	اتریش
Canada	kānādā	کانادا
England	ingilis	انگلیس
Europe	urupā	اروپا
Germany	ālmān	آلمان
India	hend	هند
Ireland	irland	ایرلند
Japan	zhāpon	ژاپن
Spain	espāniyā	اسپانیا
Sweden	su'ed	سوئد
the US	āmrikā	آمریکا

MEETING PEOPLE

I come from ...	man az ... miyām	من از ... می آیم
I live in the ...	man dar ... zendegi mikonam	من در... زندگی می کنم
city	shahr	شهر
countryside	rustā	روستا
mountains	kuhestān	کوهستان
seaside	kenāre daryā	کنار دریا
suburbs of ...	home ye ...	حومه ...
a village	ye deh	یک ده

CULTURAL DIFFERENCES

تفاوت های فرهنگی

How do you do this in your country?
[shomā] dar keshvaretun in kār o chetori mikonin?

(شما) در کشورتان این کار را چطوری می کنید؟

Is this a local or national custom?
in ye rasm e mahalli ye yā melli?

این یک رسم محلی است یا ملی؟

I don't want to offend you.
man nemikhām be shomā bi ehterāmi bekonam

من نمی خواهم به شما بی احترامی بکنم

I'm sorry, it's not the custom in my country.
mota'ssefam, in dar keshvar e man rasm nist

متاسفم این درکشور من رسم نیست

I'm not accustomed to this.
man be in kār ādat nadāram

من به این کار عادت ندارم

I don't mind watching, but I'd prefer not to participate.
negāh kardanesh eshkāl nadāre, vali tarjih midam daresh sherkat nakonam

نگاه کردن اش اشکال نداره ولی ترجیح می دهم در آن شرکت نکنم

In my country, we ...
dar keshvar e man, mā ...

در کشور من ما ...

My culture/religion doesn't allow me to ...	farhang/maz-hab e man be man ejāze nemide ...	به فرهنگ/مذهب من من اجازه نمی دهد ...
do this	in kār o bekonam	این کار را بکنم
drink/eat this	in o bekhoram	این را بخورم

AGE سن

How old are you?
[shomā] chand sāletun e?   (شما) چند سالتان است؟

I'm ... years old.
man ... sāl am e   من ... سالم است

How old do you think I am?
fekr mikonin chand sāl am e?   فکر می کنید چند سالم است؟

I think you're ... years old.
fekr mikonam [shomā] ... sāletune   فکر می کنم (شما) ... سالتان است

How old is your son/daughter?
pesar/dokhtar e shomā chand sālesh e?   پسر/دختر شما چند سالش است؟

S/he is ... years old.
un ... sālesh e   او ... سالش است

(See Numbers & Amounts, page 175, for your age.)

DID YOU KNOW ... When meeting someone for the first time, people may ask questions about each other's personal life, such as marital status, number of children, occupation and even salary.

MEETING PEOPLE

OCCUPATIONS

شغل

What (work) do you do?
chi kār mikonin?

چکار می کنید؟

Where do you work?
kojā kār mikonin?

کجا کار می کنید؟

I'm a/an ...	man ... am	من ... هستم
artist	honarmand	هنرمند
businessperson	tājer	تاجر
doctor	doktor	دکتر
engineer	mohandes	مهندس
factory worker	kārgar	کارگر
farmer	keshāvarz	کشاورز
journalist	ruznāme negār	روزنامه نگار
lawyer	vakil	وکیل
mechanic	mekānik	مکانیک
nurse	parastār	پرستار
office worker	kārmand	کارمند
scientist	dāneshmand	دانشمند
secretary	monshi	منشی
student	dāneshju	دانشجو
teacher	mo'allem	معلم
waiter	gārson	گارسن
writer	nevisande	نویسنده

I'm ...	man ... am	من ... هستم
retired	bāzneshaste	بازنشسته
unemployed	bikār	بیکار

I'm self-employed.
man shoghl e āzād dāram

من شغل آزاد دارم

Do you like your job?
shoghletun o dust dārin?

شغل تان را دوست دارید؟

What are you studying?
[shomā] chi mikhunin?

(شما) چه می خوانید؟

I'm studying ...	man ... mikhunam	من ... می خوانم
art	honar	هنر
arts/humanities	ulum e ensāni	علوم انسانی
business	bāzargāni	بازرگانی
engineering	mohandesi	مهندسی
languages	zabān	زبان
law	hughugh	حقوق
medicine	pezeshki	پزشکی
Persian	fārsi	فارسی
science	ulum	علوم
teaching	dabiri	دبیری

RELIGION

دین/مذهب

The overwhelming majority of Iranians follow the Shi'ite sect of Islam. Due to the political and religious climate in the region, most Iranians have a good awareness of different nationalities and religions. Iranians usually won't ask a foreigner about their religion, assuming they belong to a particular religion depending on the country they come from.

It's generally OK to talk about religion, as long as no attempt is made to persuade or influence others. If you don't have a religion, it's better not to mention this.

What's your religion?
maz-hab e shomā chi ye?

مذهب شما چیست؟

I'm (a) ...	man ... am	من ... هستم
Buddhist	budāyi	بودایی
Catholic	kātolik	کاتولیک
Christian	masihi	مسیحی
Hindu	hendu	هندو
Jewish	yahudi	یهودی
Muslim	mosalmun	مسلمان

I believe in God.
[man] be khodā e'teghād dāram

من به خدا اعتقاد دارم

FEELINGS

احساسات

I'm ...	man ... am	من ... هستم
angry	asabāni	عصبانی
happy	khoshhāl	خوشحال
hungry	gorosne	گرسنه
thirsty	teshne	تشنه
tired	khaste	خسته

Are you ...?	[shomā] ... hastin?	(شما) ... هستید؟
happy	khoshhāl	خوشحال
sad	nārāhat	ناراحت
sleepy	khābālud	خواب آ لود
sorry (condolence)	mota'assef	متاسف
sorry (regret)	pashimun	پشیمان
worried	negarān	نگران

| Are you hot? | [shomā] garm etun e? | (شما) گرمتان هست؟ |
| Are you in a hurry? | [shomā] ajale dārin? | (شما) عجله دا رید؟ |

LANGUAGE DIFFICULTIES

مشکل زبان

Do you speak English?
[shomā] ingilisi baladin?

(شما) انگلیسی بلدید؟

Yes, I do.
bale, baladam

بله بلد هستم

No, I don't.
na, balad nistam

نه بلد نیستم

Does anyone here speak English?
injā kesi ingilisi balad e?

اینجا کسی انگلیسی بلد هست؟

I speak a little.
[man] ye kami balad am

من یک کمی بلد هستم

Do you understand?
motavajjeh mishin?

متوجه می شوید؟

I (don't) understand.
(na) mifahman

(نه) می فهمم

Could you speak more slowly?
mitunin yavāsh tar sohbat konin?

می توانید یواش تر صحبت کنید؟

Could you repeat that?
mishe un o tekrār konin?

می شود آنرا تکرار کنید؟

Please write it down.
lotfan un o benevisin

لطفاً آنرا بنویسید

How do you say ...?
... ro chetori migin?

... را چطوری می گویید؟

MEETING PEOPLE

What does ... mean?
ma'ni ye ... chi ye?

معنی ... چیست؟

What languages do you speak?
che zabānhāyi baladin?

چه زبانهایی بلد هستید؟

I speak (English) and (German).
man (ingilisi) va
(ālmāni) baladam

من (انگلیسی) و
(آلمانی) بلد هستم

I don't speak Persian.
man fārsi balad nistam

من فارسی بلد نیستم

Do you have an interpreter?
[shomā] motarjem dārin?

(شما) مترجم دارید؟

Please point to it in this book.
lotfan uno tu ye in ketāb
neshun bedin

لطفاً آنرا توی این
کتاب نشان بدهید

> **DID YOU KNOW ...** In Middle Persian, especially in the written style, there were different ways of addressing different classes of people. In Modern Persian, these have been reduced to a few words used for all kinds of people.

MEETING PEOPLE

جابجاشدن GETTING AROUND

Since flights only land in large cities, you'll need to travel by coach to get around Iran. Bus and minibus are the main form of public transport in cities. Bus terminals are busy, so you'll need to reserve a ticket several days in advance for intercity travel.

FINDING YOUR WAY

پیدا کردن راه

Where's the ...?	... kojā st?	... کجاست؟
bus station	termināl	ترمینال
bus stop	istgāh e utubus	ایستگاه اتوبوس
city centre	markaz e shahr	مرکز شهر
train station	istgāh e ghatār	ایستگاه قطار

Excuse me, can you help me, please?
bebakhshin, mishe lotfan
be man komak konin?

ببخشید می شود لطفا
به من کمک کنید؟

I'm looking for ...
man donbāl e ... migardam

من دنبال ... می گردم

How do I get to ...?
chetor mitunam be ... beram?

چطور می توانم به ... بروم؟

Is it far from here?
un az injā dur e?

آن از اینجا دور است؟

Where are we now?
mā hālā kojā im?

ما حالا کجا هستیم؟

What's the best way to get there?
behtarin rāh e raftan be
unjā kodum e?

بهترین راه رفتن به
آنجا کدام است؟

Can I walk there?
[man] mitunam piyāde
be unjā beram?

(من) می توانم پیاده
به آنجا بروم؟

Can you show me (on the map)?
mishe (tu naghshe) be?
man neshun bedin?

می شود (توی نقشه) به
من نشان بدهید؟

GETTING AROUND

What time does the ... leave/arrive?	... che sā'ati harekat mikone/mirese?	... چه ساعتی حرکت می کند/میرسد؟
aeroplane	havāpeymā	هواپیما
boat	ghāyegh	قایق
bus	utubus	اتوبوس
train	ghatār	قطار
What ... is this?	in kodum ... e?	این کدام ... است؟
city	shahr	شهر
street	khiyābun	خیابان
village	deh	ده

Directions
جهات

Turn at the ...	... bepichin	... بپیچید
next corner	dar taghāto' e ba'di	در تقاطع بعدی
roundabout	tu ye meydun	توی میدان
traffic lights	sar e cherāgh	سر چراغ
To the right/left.	samt e rāst/chap	سمت راست/چپ
Go straight ahead.	mostaghim berin	مستقیم بروید

It's two streets down.
do kiyābun pāyintar e
دو خیابان پایین تر است

You can go on foot.
mitunin piyāde berin
می توانید پیاده بروید

behind	aghab	عقب
in front of	jelo ye	جلوی
far	dur	دور
near	nazdik	نزدیک
opposite	moghābel	مقابل
here	injā	اینجا
there	unjā	آنجا
north	shomāl	شمال
south	junub	جنوب
east	shargh	شرق
west	gharb	غرب

ADDRESSES

نشانی ها

Unlike in English, Persian addresses are given with city name first, followed by the street, then the alley, and then the number. The name of the addressee is given last:

Tehran	تهران
Jomhuri Street	خیابان جمهوری
Sa'ādat Alley	کوچه سعادت
No. 32	شماره ۳۲
Third floor	طبقه سوم
Mr Ali Ahmadi	آقای علی احمدی

This order is followed when giving an address, and you usually won't have a problem finding an address, if you ask for it.

BUYING TICKETS

خریدن بلیط

Where can I buy a ticket?
    [man] kojā mitunam
    belit bekharam?

(من) کجا می توانم
بلیط بخرم؟

We want to go to ...
    mā mikhāyim be ... berim

ما می خواهیم به ... برویم

Do I need to book?
    lāzem e ke rezerv konam?

لازم است که رزرو کنم؟

I'd like to book a seat to ...
    [man] ye jā barāye ... mikhām

(من) یک جا برای ... می خواهم

Can I get a stand-by ticket?
    [man] mitunam ye belit e
    list e entezār begiram?

(من) می توانم یک بلیط
لیست انتظار بگیرم؟

GETTING AROUND

I'd like ...	[man] ... mikhām	(من) می ... خواهم
a one-way ticket	ye belit e ye sare	یک بلیط یک سره
a return ticket	ye belit e do sare	یک بلیط دوسره
two tickets	do tā belit	دو تا بلیط
a student's fare	ye belit e dāneshjuyi	یک بلیط دانشجویی
a child's fare	ye belit barāye bachche	یک بلیط برای بچه

1st class
daraje yek   درجه یک

2nd class
daraje do   درجه دو

THEY MAY SAY ...

por e   It's full.

How long does this trip take?
in mosāferat cheghadr
tul mikeshe?

این مسافرت چقدر
طول می کشد؟

I'd like a window seat, please.
lotfan, [man] ye sandali
kenār e panjare mikham

لطفاً (من) یک صندلی کنار
پنجره می خواهم

I'd like a hot meal.
[man] ghazā ye garm mikham

(من) غذای گرم می خواهم

I'd like a meal with meat.
[man] ghazā ye gushti mikham

(من) غذای گوشتی می خواهم

I'd like to ...	mikhām belit am	می خواهم بلیط
my ticket.	o ... bekonam	ام را ... بکنم
cancel	kansel	کنسل
change	avaz	عوض
confirm	kānfirm	کانفیرم

AIR   مسیر هوایی

Be prepared for long queues at customs. It may take hours, and
could be a good opportunity to try out a few Persian phrases.

Is there a flight to Esfahān tonight?
emshab be esfahān parvāzi
dārin?

امشب به اصفهان
پروازی دارید؟

Is this a nonstop flight?
in parvāz bedun e tavaghghof e?

این پرواز بدون توقف است؟

What's the flight number?
شماره پرواز چند است؟

    shomāre ye parvāz chand e?

Can I go to the airport by bus?
(من) می توانم با اتوبوس
به فرودگاه بروم؟

    [man] mitunam bā utubus
    be furudgāh beram?

Is there a departure tax here?
اینجا عوارض خروجی دارد؟

    injā avārez e khuruji dāre?

When's the next flight to Shiraz?
پرواز بعدی به شیراز کی
هست؟

    parvāz e ba'di be shirāz
    key hast?

How long does this flight take?
این پرواز چقدر طول
می کشد؟

    in parvāz cheghadr
    tul mikeshe?

What time do I have to be at
the airport?
چه ساعتی باید
در فرودگاه باشم؟

    che sā'ati bāyad dar
    furudgāh bāsham?

Where's the baggage claim?
قسمت تحویل وسایل کجاست؟

    ghesmat e tahvil e vasāyel kojā st?

I'd like to check in my luggage.
می خواهم بارم را تحویل بدهم

    mikhām bār am o tahvil bedam

What's the charge for each excess kilo?
هر کیلو اضافه بار چند است؟

    har kilo ezāfe bār chand e?

My luggage hasn't arrived.
بار من نرسیده

    bār e man nareside

airport tax	avārez e furudgāh	عوارض فرودگاه
arrivals	vurud	ورود
departure	harekat	حرکت
domestic	dākheli	داخلی
exchange	ta'viz	تعویض
flight	parvāz	پرواز
gate	dar e khuruji	در خروجی
international	beynolmelali	بین المللی
passport	gozarnāme/pāsport	گذرنامه/پاسپورت
plane	havāpeymā	هواپیما
transit lounge	sālon e terānsit	سالن ترانزیت

AT CUSTOMS

در گمرک

I have nothing to declare.
  [man] chiz e khāssi
  nadāram ke ettelā' bedam

(من) چیز خاصی
ندارم که اطلاع بدهم

I have something to declare.
  [man] chizi barāye ettelā'
  dādan dāram

(من) چیزی برای اطلاع
دادن دارم

Do I have to declare this?
  [man] bāyad in o ettelā' bedam?

(من) باید این را اطلاع بدهم؟

This is all my luggage.
  koll e bār e man in e

کل بار من این است

Can I go through?
  mishe rad besham?

می شود رد بشوم؟

I didn't know I had to declare it.
  [man] nemidunestam ke
  bāyad in o ettelā' bedam

(من) نمی دانستم که
باید این را اطلاع بدهم

Can I call my embassy/consulate?
  mishe be sefārat/
  konsulgari am telefon konam?

می شود به سفارت/
کنسولگری ام تلفن کنم؟

BUS & COACH

اتوبوس شهری و بین شهری

Where's the bus stop?
  istgāh e utubus kojā st?

ایستگاه اتوبوس کجاست؟

Which bus goes to ...?
  kodum utubus be ... mire?

کدام اتوبوس به ... می رود؟

Do you stop at ...?
  [shomā] dar ... tavaghghof dārin?

(شما) در ... توقف دارید؟

(Two) tickets, please.
  lotfan, (do tā) belit

لطفاً (دوتا) بلیط

Can we smoke on this bus?
  mishe tuye in utubus
  sigār bekeshim?

می شود توی این اتوبوس
سیگار بکشیم؟

Does this bus go to ...?
  in utubus be ... mire?

این اتوبوس به ... می رود؟

How often do buses come?
  utubusā key be key miyān?

اتوبوس ها کی به کی می آیند؟

What time's the ... bus?	utubus e ... key miyād?	اتوبوس ... کی می آید؟
first	avval	اول
last	ākhar	آخر
next	ba'di	بعدی

| Could you let me know when we get to ...? | | |
| mishe vaghti be ... residim
be man begin? | | می شود وقتی به ...
رسیدیم به من بگویید؟ |

| Where do I get the bus for ...? | | |
| [man] kojā mitunam utubus e
... ro savār sham? | | (من) کجا می توانم اتوبوس
... را سوار بشوم؟ |

| I want to get off! | | |
| [man] mikhām piyāde sham | | (من) می خواهم پیاده بشوم |

TRAIN   قطار

Train travel is cheaper than airfares, but more expensive than buses. All trains are operated by state railways.

| Where's the train station? | |
| istgāh e ghatār kojā st? | ایستگاه قطار کجاست؟ |

| What's the next station? | |
| istgāh e ba'di kodum e? | ایستگاه بعدی کدام است؟ |

| Does this train stop at Maraghe? | |
| in ghatār dar marāghe
tavaghghof dāre? | این قطار در مراغه
توقف دارد؟ |

| How long will it be delayed? | |
| che ghadr ta'khir dāre? | چقدر تاخیر دارد؟ |

| How long does the trip take? | |
| mosāferat che ghadr tul mikeshe? | مسافرت چقدر طول می کشد؟ |

| Is this seat taken? | |
| in jā ye kesi ye? | این جای کسی است؟ |

| Is this the platform for ...? | |
| in sakko ye ... e? | این سکوی ... است؟ |

| Do I have to change trains? | |
| [man] bāyad ghatār o
avaz konam? | (من) باید قطار را
عوض کنم؟ |

GETTING AROUND

I can't find my ...	[man] nemitunam ... am o peydā konam	... (من) نمی توانم ام را پیدا کنم
platform	sakko	سکو
ticket	belit	بلیط
train	ghatār	قطار

Do you mind if I smoke?
[man] eyb nadāre sigār
bekesham?

(من) عیب نداره سیگار
بکشم؟

I want to get off at ...
[man] mikhām dar ...
piyāde sham

(من) می خواهم در ... پیاده بشوم

platform number	shomāre ye sakko	شماره سکو
railway	rāh āhan	راه آهن
ticket collector	bāzras e belit	بازرس بلیط

THEY MAY SAY ...

ghatār ta'khir dāre	The train is delayed.
harekat e ghatār laghv shod	The train is cancelled.

TAXI تاکس

Taxis usually take more than one, and up to five passengers.
Obviously, it's more expensive to hire a taxi just for yourself.

Private cars also pick up passengers, but to be on the safe
side, it's better to use a taxi.

Is this taxi free?	in tāksi khāliy e?	این تاکسی خالی است؟
Please take me to ...	lotfan man o bebarin be ...	... لطفاً مرا ببرید به
this address	in ādres	این آدرس
the airport	furudgāh	فرودگاه
the city centre	markaz e shahr	مرکز شهر
the railway station	istghāh e rāh āhan	ایستگاه راه آهن

How much is the fare?
    keräye che ghadr e? کرایه چقدر می شود؟

Do you get extra for luggage?
    baräye bär keräye ye برای بار کرایه اضافی
    ezäfi migirin? می گیرید؟

Are you going to ...?
    [shomä] be ... mirin? (شما) به ... می روید؟

Do you have change of 100 Toman?
    [shomä] sad toman khurd därin? (شما) صد تومان خرد دارید؟

Please don't pick up any other
passengers.
    lotfan mosäfer e dige savär nakonin لطفاً مسافر دیگر سوار نکنید

How much do I owe you?
    che ghadr bäyad be shomä bedam? چقدر باید به شما بدهم؟

Instructions راهنمائی

The next street to the left/right.
    khiyäbun e ba'di bepichin خیابان بعدی بپیچید
    samt e chap/räst سمت چپ/راست

Please wait here.
    lotfan injä montazer bäshin لطفاً اینجا منتظر باشید

Continue!	edäme bedin!	ادامه بدهید
Please slow down.	loftan yaväsh berin	لطفاً یواش بروید
Stop here!	injä negah därin!	اینجا نگه دارید
Stop at the corner.	in kenär negah därin	این کنار نگه دارید

THEY MAY SAY ...

If a taxi driver asks you:

darbast mikhäyin?

they want to know whether you'd like the taxi just
for yourself, or whether you want to pick up other
passengers along the way. If you say **bale**, 'yes', you'll
pay the difference for missed passengers.

GETTING AROUND

CAR

ماشین

Road rules in Iran are unofficially flexible, but the general idea is to drive on the right. Petrol is cheap, and so many Iranians drive a vehicle that there's usually a repair shop in even the tiniest villages. Car hire is only available in larger cities.

Where can I rent a car?

(من) از کجا می توانم
یک ماشین کرایه کنم؟

    [man] az kojā mitunam ye
    māshin kerāye konam?

How much is it daily/weekly?

هفته ای/ما هی چقدر می شود؟

    hafteyi/māh i che ghadr mishe?

Does that include insurance?

آن شامل بیمه هم می شود؟

    un shāmel e bime ham mishe?

Where's the next petrol station?

پمپ بنزین بعدی کجاست؟

    pomp e benzin e ba'di kojā st?

Please fill the tank.

لطفاً باک را پر کنید

    lotfan bāk o por konin

I'd like ... litres of petrol (gas).

(من) ... لیتر بنزین می خواهم

    [man] ... litr benzin mikhām

Please check the ...	lotfan ... ro chek konin	لطفاً ... را چک کنید
oil	roghan	روغن
tyre pressure	bād e tāyer	باد تایر
water	āb	آب

Can I park here?
  [man] mitunam injā pārk konam? (من) می توانم اینجا پارک کنم؟
How long can we park here?
  che ghadr mishe injā pārk kard? چقدر می شود اینجا پارک کرد؟
Does this road lead to ...?
  in jādde be ... mire? این جاده به ... می رود؟

air	bād	باد
battery	bātri	باطری
brakes	tormoz	ترمز
clutch	kelāj	کلاج
driving licence	gavāhināme ye rānandegi	گواهینامه رانندگی
engine	motor	موتور
garage	mekāniki	مکانیکی
indicator	rāhnamā	راهنما
leaded (regular)	ma'muli	معمولی
lights	cherāgh	چراغ
main road	jādde ye asli	جاده اصلی
puncture	panchari	پنچری
radiator	rādiyātor	رادیاتور
ring road	jādde ye kamarbandi	جاده کمربندی
road map	naghshe ye jādde	نقشه جاده
seat belt	kamarband	کمربند
self-service	selfservis	سلف سرویس
speed limit	hadd e aksar e sor'at	حد اکثر سرعت
tollway	utubān	اتوبان
tyres	tāyer	تایر
unleaded	bedun e sorb	بدون سرب
windscreen	shishe ye jelo	شیشه جلو

DRIVE YOURSELF CRAZY

In larger cities, road rage is rife. Expect to encounter
hornblasts and insults, and drivers who follow their own rules.

Car Problems

خرابی ماشین

We need a mechanic.
mā ye mekānik mikhāyim

ما یک مکانیک می خواهیم

What make is it?
modelesh chi ye?

مدل اش چیست؟

The car broke down at ...
māshin dar ... kharāb shode

ماشین در ... خراب شده

The battery's flat.
bātri khāliy e

باطری خالی است

The radiator's leaking.
rādiyātor surākh shode

رادیاتور سوراخ شده

I have a flat tyre.
[man] ye charkh am
panchar shode

(من) یک چرخ ام
پنچر شده

I've lost my car keys.
[man] suvich e māshin am
o gom kardam

(من) سویچ ماشین ام
را گم کردم

I've run out of petrol.
[man] benzin am tamum shode

(من) بنزین ام تمام شده

It's overheating.   jush āvorde

جوش آورده

It's not working.   kār nemikone

کار نمی کند

SIGNS	
احتیاط	CAUTION
خطر	DANGER
سبقت ممنوع	DO NOT OVERTAKE
ورود	ENTRY
خروج	EXIT
حق تقدم	GIVE WAY
ورود ممنوع	NO ENTRY
پارک ممنوع	NO PARKING
یکطرفه	ONE WAY
محل عبور عابرپیاده	PEDESTRIANS
جاده دردست تعمیر	ROAD WORKS
ایست	STOP

BICYCLE

دوچرخه

Is it within cycling distance?
mishe bā docharkhe be
unjā raft?

می شود با دوچرخه به
آنجا رفت؟

Where can I hire a bicycle?
[man] kojā mitunam ye
docharkhe kerāye konam?

(من) کجا می توانم یک
دوچرخه کرایه کنم؟

Where can I find second-hand bikes for sale?
[man] kojā mitunam ye
docharkhe ye dast e dovvom
bekharam?

(من) کجا می توانم یک
دوچرخه دست دوم بخرم؟

Can you recommend a good place
for a bike ride?
[shomā] mitunin ye jā ye khub
barāye docharkhe savāri
pishnehād konin?

(شما) می توانید یک جای
خوب برای دوچرخه سواری
پیشنهاد کنید؟

Is it safe to cycle around here?
injā barāye docharkhe
savāri amne?

اینجا برای دوچرخه سواری
امن است؟

How much is it for ...?	kerāye ye ... che ghadr mishe?	کرایه ... چقدر می شود؟
an hour	ye sā'at	یک ساعت
the morning	sob	صبح
the afternoon	ba'd az zohr	بعد از ظهر
the day	ye ruz	یک روز

Can you raise/lower the seat?
mitunin zin o bālā/pāyin
biyārin?

می توانید زین را بالا/پایین
بیاورید؟

Is it compulsory to wear a helmet?
gozāshtan e kolāh e imani
ejbāriy e?

گذاشتن کلاه ایمنی
اجباری است؟

Where can I leave the bicycle?
[man] kojā mitunam
docharkhe ro bezāram?

(من) کجا می توانم
دوچرخه را بگذارم؟

GETTING AROUND

Can I leave the bicycle here?
  [man] mitunam docharkhe
  ro injā bezāram?

(من) می توانم دوچرخه
را اینجا بگذارم؟

Where are bike repairs done?
  kojā docharkhe ta'mir mikonan?

کجا دوچرخه تعمیر می کنند؟

bike	docharkhe	دوچرخه
brakes	tormoz	ترمز
to cycle	docharkhe savāri kardan	دوچرخه سواری کردن
gear stick	pedāl	پدال
handlebars	farmun	فرمان
helmet	kolāh e imani	کلاه ایمنی
inner tube	tuyub	تیوب
lights	cherāgh	چراغ
padlock	ghofl e zanjir	قفل زنجیر
pump	tolombe	تلمبه
puncture	panchari	پنچری
racing bike	docharkhe ye kursi	دوچرخه کورسی
saddle	zin	زین
wheel	charkh	چرخ

Accommodation in Iran ranges from private rental flats to international luxury hotels, depending on your budget.

FINDING ACCOMMODATION پیدا کردن محل سکونت

I'm looking	[man] donbāl e ye	(من) دنبال یک
for a ... hotel.	hotel e ... migardam	... هتل می گردم
cheap	arzun	ارزان
clean	tamiz	تمیز
nearby	nazdik	نزدیک

Where's the ... hotel?	... hotel kojā st?	... هتل کجاست؟
best	behtarin	بهترین
cheapest	arzuntarin	ارزان ترین

What's the address?
ādresesh kojā st?   آدرس اش کجاست؟
Could you write down
the address, please?
mishe lotfan ādres o benevisin?   می شود لطفا آدرس را بنویسید؟

BOOKING AHEAD از قبل رزرو کردن

I'd like to book a room, please.
lotfan mikhām ye otāgh   لطفاً می خواهم یک اتاق
rezerv konam   رزرو کنم
Do you have any rooms available?
otāgh khāli dārin?   اتاق خالی دارید؟
For (three) nights.
barāye (se) shab   برای (سه) شب

How much for ...?	barāye ...	برای ...
	cheghadr mishe?	چقدر می شود؟
one night	ye shab	یک شب
a week	ye hafte	یک هفته
two people	do nafar	دو نفر

We'll be arriving at ...	mā ... miresim	ما ... می رسیم
My name's ...	esm e man ... e	اسم من ... است

Is there hot water all day?
  āb e garm hamishe hast?   آب گرم همیشه هست؟

I'm not sure how long I'm staying.
  [man] motma'n nistam
  chghadr mimunam   (من) مطمئن نیستم
  چقدر می مانم

We'll be staying for (two weeks).
  mā (do hafte) mimunim   ما (دو هفته) می مانیم

CHECKING IN   جا رزرو کردن

In international hotels you won't have a problem finding
people who can speak English, but you might not be so lucky
in smaller hotels.

Do you have any rooms available?
  otāgh khāli dārin?   اتاق خالی دارید؟

Do you have a room with two beds?
  otāgh e dokhābe dārin?   اتاق دوخوابه دارید؟

Do you have a room with a double bed?
  otāgh e dotakhte dārin?   اتاق دوتخته دارید؟

I'd like a ... room.	[man] ye otāgh e ... mikhām	(من) یک اتاق ... می خواهم
shared	moshtarak	مشترک
single	taki	یک اتاق تکی

We want a room with a ...	mā ye otāgh bā ye ... mikhāyim	ما یک اتاق با یک ... می خواهیم
bathroom	dastshuyi	دستشویی
shower	dush	دوش
TV	televiziyon	تلویزیون
window	panjere	پنجره

Can I see it?
  [man] mitunam un o bebinam?   (من) می توانم آن را ببینم؟

Are there any others?
otāghā ye dige ham hast?   اتاق های دیگر هم هست؟

Are there any cheaper rooms?
otāghā ye arzuntari ham hast?   اتاق های ارزان تری هم هست؟

Do you charge for the baby?
barāye nozād ham kerāye migirin?   برای نوزاد هم کرایه می گیرید؟

Can I pay by credit card?
[man] mitunam bā kārt
e e'tebāri bepardāzam?   من میتوانم با کارت اعتباری بپردازم؟

Do you need a deposit?
bey'āne ham mikhāyin?   بیعانه هم می خواهید؟

How many Tomans?
chand toman?   چند تومان؟

Where's the manager?
modir kojā st?   مدیر کجاست؟

Where's the bathroom?
dastshuyi kojā st?   دستشویی کجاست؟

Is there hot water all day?
āb e garm hamishe hast?   آب گرم همیشه هست؟

How much for ...?	barāye ... cheghadr mishe?	برای ... چقدر می شود؟
one night	ye shab	یک شب
a week	ye hafte	یک هفته
two people	do nafar	دو نفر

Is there a discount for children/students?
barāye bachchehā/dāshjuhā
takhfifi hast?   برای بچه ها/دانشجوها تخفیفی هست؟

It's fine. I'll take it.
khub e [man] un o mikhām   خوب است. من آن را می خواهم

DID YOU KNOW ...   It's costumary to remove your shoes in most homes and in public places such as mosques.

ACCOMMODATION

REQUESTS & COMPLAINTS

درخواست ها و
شکایت ها

In Iran, most toilets are the squat type. Iranians normally use water instead of toilet paper. If you want toilet paper, you'll probably need to ask at your hotel.

I need a(nother) ...
[man] ye ... (dige) lāzem dāram

(من) یک ... (دیگر) لازم دارم

Can I use the kitchen?
[man] mitunam az
āshpazkhune estefāde konam?

(من) می توانم از آشپز
خانه استفاده کنم؟

Is there a lift?
āsānsor hast?

آسانسور هست؟

I've locked myself out of my room.
dar e otāgham ghofl shode

در اتاق ام قفل شده

Do you change money here?
[shomā] injā arz migirin?

(شما) اینجا ارز می گیرد؟

Should I leave my key at reception?
bāyad kelid am o dar
paziresh bezāram?

باید کلید ام را در
پذیرش بگذارم؟

Is there a message for me?
peyghāmi barāye man hast?

پیغامی برای من هست؟

Can I send my letters from here?
[man] mitunam nāmehā m
o az injā beferestam?

(من) می توانم نامه هایم
را از اینجا بفرستم؟

The key for room (12), please.
lotfan kelid e otāgh e
(shomāre ye davāzdah)

لطفاً کلید اتاق
(شماره دوازده)

Please wake me up at (six) o'clock.
lotfan man o (sā't e shish)
bidār konin

لطفاً مرا (ساعت شش)
بیدار کنید

The room needs to be cleaned.
otāgh niyāz be tamiz kardan dāre

اتاق نیاز به تمیز کردن دارد

Please change the sheets.
lotfan malāfehā ro avaz konin

لطفاً ملافه ها را عوض کنید

Can you give me an extra blanket, please?
    lotfan mishe be man ye
    patu ye ezāfe bedin?

لطفاً می شود به من یک
پتوی اضافه بدهید؟

Do you have a safe where I
can leave my valuables?
    [shomā] sandughi dārin ke
    [man] vasāyel e gheymati
    m o bezāram?

(شما) صندوقی دارید که (من)
وسایل قیمتی ام را بگذارم؟

Could I have a receipt for them?
    mishe barāye unā be man
    resid bedin?

می شود برای آنها به من
رسید بدهید؟

Is there somewhere to wash clothes?
    jāyi barāye shostan
    e lebāsā hast?

جایی برای شستن
لباس ها هست؟

Can we use the telephone?
    [mā] mitunim az telefon
    estefāde konim?

(ما) می توانیم از تلفن
استفاده کنیم؟

My room's too dark
    utāgh e man kheyli tārik e

اتاق من خیلی تاریک است

It's too cold/hot.
    un kheyli sard/garm e

آن خیلی سرد/گرم است

It's too noisy.
    un kheyli por sarosedā st

آن خیلی پر سر و صدا است

I can't open/close the window.
    [man] nemitunam panjere
    ro bāz konam/bebandam

(من) نمی توانم پنجره
را باز کنم/ببندم

ACCOMMODATION

SIGNS

سالن غذا خوری	DINING ROOM
پذیرش	RECEPTION
توالت	TOILET
زنانه	FEMALE
مردانه	MALE

ACCOMMODATION

This ... isn't clean.	in ... tamiz nist	این ... تمیز نیست
blanket	patu	پتو
pillow	bālesh	بالش
pillow case	rubāleshi	روبالشی
sheet	malāfe	ملافه

Please change it/them.
lotfan unā/un ro avaz konin

لطفاً آنها/آن را عوض کنید

I don't like this room.
[man] in otāgh o nemikhām

(من) این اتاق را نمی خواهم

The toilet doesn't flush.
sifun e tuvālet kharāb e

سیفون توالت خراب است

CHECKING OUT

تحویل دادن اتاق

Can I pay by travellers cheque?
[man] mitunam bā chek e
mosāferati bepardāzam?

(من) می توانم با چک
مسافرتی بپردازم؟

Could I have the bill, please?
lotfan mishe surat hesāb
o bedin?

لطفاً می شود صورت حساب
را بدهید؟

There's a mistake in the bill.
ye eshtebāhi dar surat
hesāb shode

یک اشتباهی در صورت حساب شده

When do we have to check out?
key bāyad otāgh o takhliye konim?

کی باید اتاق را تخلیه کنم؟

I'm leaving now.
[man] al'ān mikhām beram

(من) الان می خواهم بروم

Can I leave my luggage with you until (2) o'clock?

[man] mitunam vasāyel am
o tā sāa't e (do) pish e shomā
bezāram?

(من) می توانم وسایل ام را
تا ساعت (دو) پیش شما
بگذارم؟

Please call a taxi for me.

lotfan ye tāksi barāye man
khabar konin

لطفاً یک تاکسی برای من خبر کنید

PAPERWORK

ACCOMMODATION

address	آدرس
age	سن
date of birth	تاریخ تولد
name	اسم
nationality	ملیت
place of birth	محل تولد
profession/work	شغل
reason for travel	علت مسافرت
religion	دین/مذهب
sex	جنس
marital status	وضعیت تاهل
divorced	طلاق گرفته
married	متاهل
single	مجرد
widowed	بیوه
customs	گمرک
driver's licence	گواهینامه رانندگی
identification	کارت شناسایی
immigration	مهاجرت
passport number	شماره پاسپورت/گذرنامه
visa	ویزا/روادید
purpose of visit	هدف از دیدار
business	تجارت
holiday	تعطیلات
visiting relatives	دیدار بستگان
visiting the homeland	دیدار وطن

ACCOMMODATION

USEFUL WORDS
کلمه های مفید

air-conditioning	tahviye ye matbu'	تهویه مطبوع
clean	tamiz	تمیز
key	kelid	کلید
face cloth	dastmāl	دستمال
bottle of water	botri ye āb	بطری آب
lamp	lāmp	لامپ
lock	ghofl	قفل
mosquito coil	magas kosh	مگس کش
soap	sābun	صابون
toilet (paper)	(kāghaz) tuvālet	(کاغذ) توالت
towel	hole	حوله
(cold/hot) water	āb (sard/garm)	آب (سرد/گرم)

RENTING
کرایه/اجاره

Do you have any rooms to rent?
otāghi barāye kerāye dārin? — اتاقی برای کرایه دارید؟

I'm here about your ad for a room to rent.
[man] dar mored e āgahi tun barāye kerāye ye otāgh umadam — (من) در مورد آگهی تان برای کرایه اتاق آمدم

Is there anything cheaper?
chiz e arzuntari ham hast? — چیز ارزان تری هم هست؟

Can I see it?
mishe un o bebinam? — می شود آن را ببینم؟

I'm looking for something close to the ...
[man] donbāl e jāyi nazdik be ... migardam — (من) دنبال جایی نزدیک به ... می گردم

beach	sāhel	ساحل
city centre	markaz e shahr	مرکز شهر

LOOKING FOR ...

گشتن برای ...

Where's the ...?	... kojā st?	... کجاست؟
bank	bānk	بانک
cinema	sinemā	سینما
consulate	konsulgari	کنسول گری
embassy	sefārat	سفارت
hotel	hotel	هتل
market	bāzār	بازار
museum	muze	موزه
police	polis	پلیس
post office	edāre ye post	اداره پست
public telephone	telefon e umumi	تلفن عمومی
public toilet	tuvālet e umumi	توالت عمومی
tourist information office	edāre ye jahāngardi	اداره جهانگردی
town square	meydun e shahr	میدان شهر

AT THE BANK

در بانک

Money can be exchanged at the main branches of most banks, but you might have to wait in a long queue.

Can I use my credit card to withdraw money?
[man] mitunam az kārt e
e'tebāri yam barāye bardāsht
e pul estefāde konam?

(من) می توانم از
کارت اعتبار ی ام برای برداشت
پول استفاده کنم؟

Can I exchange money here?
[man] mitunam pul am o
injā tabdil konam?

(من) می توانم پولم
راینجا تبدیل کنم؟

Can I have smaller notes?
mishe eskenās e kuchik tar
be man bedin?

می شود اسکناس کوچکتر
به من بدهید؟

The automatic teller machine (ATM)
swallowed my card.
āber bānk kārt e man o khord

عابر بانک کارت مرا خورد

I want to	[man] mikhām ...	(من) می خواهم ...
change ...	tabdil konam	... تبدیل کنم
cash	pul	پول
a cheque	ye chek	یک چک
a travellers cheque	ye chek e mosāferati	یک چک مسافرتی

What time does the bank open?
bānk key bāz mishe?
بانک کی باز می شود؟

Where can I cash a travellers cheque?
[man] kojā mitunam ye chek e
mosāferati naghd konam?
(من) کجا می توانم یک
چک مسافرتی نقد کنم؟

What's the exchange rate?
nerkh e arz chand e?
نرخ ارز چند است؟

How many Tomans per (dollar)?
chand toman barāye
har (dolār)?
چند تومان برای
هر (دلار)؟

What's your commission?
komisiyon e shomā cheghadr e?
کمیسیون شما چقدر است؟

Please write it down.
lotfan un o benevisin
لطفاً آن را بنویسید

Can I transfer money here
from my bank?
[man] mitunam az bānk e
khod am be injā pul
enteghāl bedam?
(من) می توانم از بانک
خودم به اینجا پول
انتقال بدهم؟

Can I transfer money from overseas?
[man] mitunam be khārej
pul enteghāl bedam?
(من) می توانم به خارج
پول انتقال بدهم؟

How long will it take to arrive?
cheghadr tul mikeshe
tā berese?
چقدر طول می کشد
تا برسد؟

Has my money arrived yet?
pul e man hanuz nareside?
پول من هنوز نرسیده ؟

Where do I sign?
[man] kojā ro emzā konam?
(من) کجا را امضا کنم؟

cash	naghd	نقد
cashier	sandugh	صندوق
cheque	chek	چک
coins	sekke	سکه
credit card	kārt e e'tebāri	کارت اعتباری
exchange rate	nerkh e arz	نرخ ارز
identification	kārt e shenāsāyi	کارت شناسایی
foreign currency	arz e khāreji	ارز خارجی
money	pul	پول
purchase	kharid	خرید
sale	furush	فروش
signature	emzā	امضا
tax	māliyāt	مالیات

AROUND TOWN

SIGNS

ورود	ENTRANCE
خروج	EXIT
سرد	COLD
گرم	HOT
ورود ممنوع	NO ENTRY
دخانیات ممنوع	NO SMOKING
بسته	CLOSED
باز	OPEN
ممنوع	PROHIBITED
توالت	TOILET

AT THE POST OFFICE

در اداره پست

Expect a delay in sending or receiving mail or parcels sent by ordinary mail. The safest option is to send mail – especially documents – by registered, express mail.

I want to buy (a) ...	[man] mikhām ... bekharam	(من) می خواهم ... بخرم
postcard	kārt e postāl	کارت پستال
stamp	tambr	تمبر

I want to send a ...	[man] mikhām ye ... beferestam	(من) می خواهم یک ... بفرستم
letter	nāme	نامه
parcel	baste	بسته
telegram	telgerāf	تلگراف

PEOPLE YOU SEE		
beggar	gedā	گدا
flower seller	gol furush	گل فروش
fortune teller	fālbin	فال بین
street seller	furushande ye doregard	فروشنده دوره گرد

AROUND TOWN

Please send it by ...	lotfan un o bā ... beferestin	لطفاً آن را با ... بفرستید
express mail	post e ekspres	پست اکسپرس
registered mail	post e sefāreshi	پست سفارشی
surface mail	pot e zamini	پست زمینی

How much does it cost to send this to ...?
hazine ye ferestādan e in be ... cheghadr mishe?
هزینه فرستادن این به ... چقدر می شود؟

I'd like an air mail stamp to (the US).
[man] ye tambr e havāyi barāye (āmrikā) mikhām
(من) یک تمبر هوایی برای (آمریکا) می خواهم

How many Tomans to send
this to (Australia)?

    chand toman barāye ferestādan
    e in be (ostārāliyā)?

چند تومان برای فرستادن
این به (استرالیا)؟

air mail	post e havāyi	پست هوایی
envelope	pākat	پاکت
mail box	sandogh e post	صندوق پست
parcel	baste	بسته
pen	khodkār	خودکار
postcode	kod e posti	کد پستی

TELECOMMUNICATIONS   مخابرات

You won't be able to use a public telephone to call overseas
from Iran. Either use a telephone at your hotel or go to a
telephone centre.

Could I please use the telephone?

    lotfan mishe az telefon
    estefāde konam?

لطفاً می شود از تلفن
استفاده کنم؟

I want to call ...

    [man] mikhām be ...
    zang bezanam

(من) می خواهم به ...
زنگ بزنم

The number is ...

    shomāre ... hast

شماره ... است

How much does a (three)-minute call cost?

    (se) daghighe telefon
    cheghadr mishe?

(سه) دقیقه تلفن
چقدر می شود؟

I want to make a long-distance
call to (Australia).

    [man] mikhām be (ostārāliyā)
    telefon bekonam

(من) می خواهم به
(استرالیا) تلفن کنم

I'd like to make a reverse-charge
(collect) call to ...

    [man] mikhām ye telefon
    bekonam ke hazine ash dar
    maghsad pardākht beshe

(من) میخواهم یک تلفن
بکنم که هزینه اش در مقصد
پرداخت شود

AROUND TOWN

What's the area code for ...?

   kod e telefon e ... chand e?   کد تلفن ... چند است؟

It's engaged.

   mashghul e   مشغول است

I've been cut off.

   telefon e man ghat shod   تلفن من قطع شد

answering machine	payām gir	پیام گیر
dial tone	zang	زنگ
operator	operātor	اوپراتور
phone book	daftar e telefon	دفتر تلفن
phone box	bāje ye telefon	باجه تلفن
phonecard	kart e telefon	کارت تلفن
telephone	telefon	تلفن
urgent	zaruri	ضروری

Making a Call   تلفن زدن

Hello, is ... there?   alo, ... unjast?   الو، ... آنجاست؟

Hello. (answering a call)   alo   الو

Can I speak to ...?

   mishe bā ... sohbat konam?   می شود با ... صحبت کنم؟

Who's calling?

   [shomā] ki hastin?   (شما) کی هستید؟

It's ...

   [man] ... am   (من) ... هستم

Yes, s/he's here.

   bale un injāst   بله، او اینجاست

One moment, please.

   ye daghighe lotfan   یک دقیقه لطفاً

I'm sorry, he's not here.

   mota'ssefam, un injā nist   متاسفم، او اینجا نیست

What time will she be back?

   un key barmigarde?   او کی بر می گردد؟

Can I leave a message?

   mishe ye peyghām bezāram?   می شود یک پیغام بگذارم؟

Please tell her I called.
   lotfan behesh begin man
   zang zadam

لطفاً به او بگویید من
زنگ زدم

I'll call back later.
   ba'dan zang mizanam

بعداً زنگ می زنم

Internet

اینترنت

Where can I get Internet access?
   kojā mitunam be internet
   dastrasi dāshte bāsham?

کجا میتوانم به اینترنت
دسترسی داشته باشم؟

I want to access the Internet.
   [man] internet lāzem dāram

(من) اینترنت لازم دارم

I want to check my email.
   mikhām imeyl amo chek
   konam

می خواهم ایمیل ام
را چک کنم

SIGHTSEEING

تماشا

Where's the tourist information office?
edāre ye jahāngardi kojā st?

اداره جهانگردی کجاست؟

Do you have a local map?
[shomā] naghshe ye mahalli dārin?

(شما) نقشه محلی دارید؟

What are the main attractions?
jāhā ye didani kojāhā hastan?

جا های دیدنی کجاها هستند؟

I'd like to see the bazaar of Tehran.
[man] mikhām bāzār e
tehrān o bebinam

(من) می خواهم بازار
تهران را ببینم

What time does
(Takht Jamshid) open?
(takht e jamshid)
key bāz mishe?

(تخت جمشید)
کی باز می شود؟

What time does the (mosque) close?
(masjed) key baste mishe?

(مسجد) کی بسته می شود؟

What's that building?
un sākhtemun chiy e?

آن ساختمان چیست؟

What's this monument?
in banā chi ye?

این بنا چیست؟

How old is (Ali Ghapu Square)?
meydun e (āli ghāpu)
cheghadr ghedmat dāre?

میدان (عالی قاپو)
چقدر قدمت دارد؟

Can we take photographs from
the shrine?
mishe az ārāmgāh aks begirim?

می شود از آرامگاه عکس بگیریم؟

I'll send you the photograph.
[man] barāye shomā aks
khāham ferestād

(من) برای شما عکس
خواهم فرستاد

Could you take a photograph
of me?
mishe ye aks az man begirin?

می شود یک عکس از من بگیرید؟

Can we come inside?
mishe [mā] biyāyim tu?

می شود (ما) بیاییم تو؟

Is there an admission charge?
[shomā] vurudi ham migirin?

(شما) ورودی هم میگیرید؟

AROUND TOWN

Is there a discount for ...?	takhfifi barāye ... hast?	تخفیفی برای ... هست؟
children	bachchehā	بچه ها
students	dāneshjuhā	دانشجو ها

ancient	bāstāni	باستانی
castle	ghal'e	قلعه
cathedral/church	kelisā	کلیسا
concert	konsert	کنسرت
fortress	ghal'e	قلعه
market	bāzār	بازار
mosque	masjed	مسجد
museum	muze	موزه
park	pārk	پارک
ruin	kharābe	خرابه
shrine	maghbare	مقبره
statue	mojassame	مجسمه
university	dāneshgāh	دانشگاه

ON THE STREET

What's this?	in chi ye?	این چیه؟
What's happening?	che khabar e?	چه خبره؟
What's s/he doing?	un chikār mikone?	او چکار می کند؟
How much is it?	cheghdr mishe?	چقدر می شود؟

What do you charge?		
[shomā] cheghadr migirin?		(شما) چقدر می گیرید؟
Can I have one, please?		
mishe ye dune be man bedin?		می شود یک دانه به من بدهید؟

festival	eyd	عید
newspaper kiosk	dakke ye ruznāme furushi	دکه روزنامه فروشی
street	khiyābun	خیابان
street	rāhpeymāyi/ tazāhorāt	راهپیمایی/ تظاهرات
demonstration		
suburb	home	حومه
tobacco kiosk	dakke ye sigār furushi	دکه سیگار فروشی

GUIDED TOURS

تور های راهنما دار

Do you organise group tours?
[shomā] turhā ye dastejam'i
tartib midin?

(شما) تور های دسته
جمعی ترتیب می دهید؟

What sort of people go
on your tours?
che afrādi dar un sherkat
mikonan?

چه افرادی در آن شرکت
می کنند؟

Will we have any free time in the tour?
dar tur [mā] vaght e āzād dārim?

در تور (ما) وقت آزاد داریم؟

Do you have to join in all
group activities?
[man] bāyad dar hame ye
fa'āliyathā ye guruhi
sherkat konam?

(من) باید در همه فعالیت
های گروهی شرکت کنم؟

How long will we stop there?
[mā] cheghadr unjā
khāhim mund?

(ما) چقدر آنجا
خواهیم ماند؟

What time do I have to be back?
[man] che sā'ati bāyad
bargardam?

(من) چه ساعتی
باید بر گردم؟

The guide has paid/will pay.
rāhnamā pul dāde/khāhad dād

راهنما پول داده/خواهد داد

I'm with them.
[man] bā unā hastam

(من) با آنها هستم

I've lost my group.
[man] guruh am o gom kardam

(من) گروه ام را کم کردم

Have you seen a group of (Australians)?
[shomā] ye guruh e
(ostārāliyāyi) nadidin?

(شما) یک گروه
(استرالیایی) ندیدید؟

GOING OUT

بیرون رفتن

Because of Islamic rules, most Western-style entertainment such as nightclubs, bars, casinos, concerts and operas aren't available in Iran. An alternative is concert halls where traditional Persian music is played and sung.

Ghahve khune, 'tea houses', where men are able to meet and chat, are popular. Recently, some modern tea houses accept both male and female costumers. Cinema and theatre also have their fans.

Where to go

کجا باید رفت

Do you want to go ...?

[shomā] mikhāhin be ... berin?   (شما) می خواهید به ... بروید؟

What's on today?

emruz che barnāmeyi hast?   امروز چه برنامه ای هست؟

How much does it cost to get in?

vurudi ye un cheghadr e?   ورودی آن چقدر است؟

I'd like to go	[man] dust dāram	(من) دوست دارم
to a/the ...	be ... beram	به ... بروم
cafe	ye ghahve khune	یک قهوه خانه
cinema	sinemā	سینما
restaurant	ye resturān	یک رستوران
theatre	te'ātr	تئاتر

THEY MAY SAY ...

[un] majjāniye   It's free of charge.

It's beautiful here.

    injā ghashang e   اینجا قشنگ است

I had a good time.

    be man kheyli khosh gozasht   به من خیلی خوش گذشت

Do you want to go some place else?

    mishe berim ye jā ye dige?   می شود برویم یک جای دیگر؟

Invites   دعوت

What are you doing this evening/weekend?

    [shomā] emshab/ākher   (شما) امشب/آخر هفته

    e hafte chikār mikonin?   چکار می کنید؟

Would you like to go out somewhere?

    [shomā] dust dārin jāyi berim? (شما) دوست دارید جایی برویم؟

Do you know a good restaurant?

    [shomā] resturān e khub   (شما) رستوران خوب می

    mishenāsin?   شناسید؟

Would you like to go for a meal?

    [shomā] dust dārin berim   (شما) دوست دارید

    ghazā bekhorim?   برویم غذا بخوریم؟

My shout. (I'll buy.)

    [man] hesāb mikonam   (من) حساب می کنم

We're having a party.

    [mā] ye mehmuni dārim   (ما) یک مهمانی داریم

Come along.

    shomā ham biyāyin   شما هم بیایید

THEY MAY SAY ...

[man] movāfegh am	I agree.
hatman!	Sure!
kāmelan dorost e!	Very true!
albatte	Of course.
be hich vajh!	No way!
[man] mokhālef am	I don't agree.
(un) dorost nist	That's not true.
pas injur!	Is that so!
bale, ammā ...	Yes, but ...

Responding to Invites

جواب دادن به دعوت ها

Yes, I'd love to come.
bale, dust dāram biyām

بله، دوست دارم بیایم

That's very kind of you.
[shomā] kheyli lotf dārin?

(شما) خیلی لطف دارید

Yes, let's. Where shall we go?
bale, berim. kojā berim?

بله برویم. کجا برویم؟

No, I'm afraid I can't.
na, mota'assefāne nemitunam

نه، متاسفانه نمی توانم

Sure!   **hatman!**

حتماً

ARRANGING TO MEET

ترتیب دادن ملاقات

Because extramarital relationships are taboo in Iran, it isn't considered acceptable to date an Iranian.

Where shall we meet?

[mā] kojā hamdige ro bebinim?
(ما) کجا همدیگر را ببینیم؟

What time shall we meet?

[mā] key hamdige ro bebinim?
(ما) کی همدیگر را ببینیم؟

Let's meet at (eight) o'clock.

sā'at e hasht hamdige ro bebinim
ساعت هشت همدیگر را ببینیم

OK. See you then.

bāshe. pas ba'dan shomā
ro mibinam
باشه. پس بعداً شما را می بینم

Sorry I'm late.

bebakhshin. [man] dir kardam
ببخشین. (من) دیر کردم

Never mind!   eyb nadāre!
عیب نداره

POLITENESS

Persian is rich in formal and polite ways of giving and responding to invitations, but as a foreigner, you won't be expected to learn and use all of them.

mahabbat dārin
    (lit: kindness have-you)

You're very kind.

kheyli mamnun
    (lit: very thanks)

Thank you so much.

khāhesh mikonam
    (lit: request do-I)

Don't mention it.

GOING OUT

Iranian families are very stable, and children usually live with parents until they marry. On the surface, relationships may not seem as complicated as in the West. As extramarital relationships aren't accepted in society, terms like 'de facto', 'boyfriend', 'girlfriend', 'living together', 'gay couples' and so on, aren't familiar.

The family structure is extended, although it's been changing in cities toward the nuclear model.

QUESTIONS

پرسش ها

Are you married?
    [shomā] mota'ahhel in?

(شما) متاهل هستید؟

Are you engaged?
    [shomā] nāmzad dārin?

(شما) نامزد دارید؟

How many children do you have?
    [shomā] chand tā bachche dārin?

(شما) چند تا بچه دارید؟

How many brothers/sisters do you have?
    [shomā] chand tā khāhar/
    barādar dārin?

(شما) چند تا خواهر/
برادر دارید؟

Do you live with your family?
    [shomā] bā khānavāde
    tun zendegi mikonin?

(شما) با خانواده تان زندگی
می کنید؟

Is your (husband) here?
    (shohar) e shomā injāst?

(شوهر) شما اینجاست؟

FAMILY

REPLIES

پاسخ ها

I'm ...

[man] ... am

(من) ... هستم

engaged	nāmzad	نامزد
married	mota'ahhel	متاهل
single	mojarrad	مجرد
widowed	bive	بیوه
divorced	talāgh gerefte	طلاق گرفته

I live with my family.

[man] bā khānevāde am
zendegi mikonam

(من) با خانواده ام
زندگی می کنم

MIND YOUR MANNERS

Never turn your back on anyone; point the sole of your
shoe or foot at anyone; or walk in front of someone
praying. If you do so inadvertently or unavoidably, excuse yourself by saying bebakhshid

Never sit next to a member of the opposite sex who
is not your spouse or a close relative, unless specifically
invited to do so, even if there is no other spare seat
(except in a shared taxi or on an aeroplane).

TALKING WITH PARENTS

صحبت با والدین

When's your baby due?

bachche ye shomā key be
donyā miyād?

بچه شما کی به
دنیا می آید؟

What are you going to call the baby?

esm e bachche ro chi
mikhāyin bezārin?

اسم بچه را چه
می خواهید بگذارید؟

Is this your first child?

in bachche ye avval e shomā st?

این بچه اول شماست؟

How many children do you have?

[shomā] chand tā bachche dārin?

(شما) چند تا بچه دارید؟

FAMILY

How old is your child?
  bachche tun chand sāl esh e?

بچه تان چند سالش است؟

Does s/he attend school?
  [un] madrese mire?

(او) مدرسه می رود؟

I don't have any children.
  [man] bachche nadāram

(من) بچه ندارم

I have a daughter/son.
  [man] ye dokhtar/pesar dāram

(من) دختر/یک پسر دارم

Is it a private or state school?
  madrese khosusi
  ye yā dolati?

مدرسه خصوصی است
یا دولتی؟

Who looks after the children?
  ki az bachchehā morāghebat
  mikone?

کی از بچه ها مراقبت
می کند؟

Do you have grandchildren?
  [shomā] nave dārin?

(شما) نوه دارید؟

What's your baby's name?
  esm e nozād e shomā chi ye?

اسم نوزاد شما چیست؟

Is the baby a boy or a girl?
  nozād pesar e yā dokhtar?

نوزاد پسر است یا دختر؟

Does s/he let you sleep at night?
  [un] mizāre [shomā] shabā
  bekhābin?

(او) می گذارد (شما) شب ها
بخوابید؟

S/he is very big for her/his age.
  [un] nesbat be senn esh
  kheyli bozorg e

(او) نسبت به سن اش
خیلی بزرگ است

What a beautiful child!
  che bachche ye khoshgeli!

چه بچه خوشگلی

S/he looks like you.
  [un] shabih e shomā st

(او) شبیه شماست

FAMILY

FAMILY MEMBERS

اعضای خانواده

baby	nozād	نوزاد
boy	pesar	پسر
child	bachche	بچه
dad	bābā	بابا
daughter	dokhtar	دختر
father	pedar	پدر
father-in-law (husband's father)	pedar shohar	پدر شوهر
father-in-law (wife's father)	pedar zan	پدر زن
girl	dokhtar	دختر
grandfather	pedarbozorg	پدر بزرگ
grandmother	mādarbozorg	مادر بزرگ
husband	shohar	شوهر
mother	mādar	مادر
mother-in-law (husband's mother)	mādar shohar	مادر شوهر
mother-in-law (wife's mother)	mādar zan	مادر زن
mum	māmān	مامان
sister	khāhar	خواهر
son	pesar	پسر
wife	zan	زن

DID YOU KNOW ... Keeping a pet is unusual in Iran. For those who do, the most popular pets are birds and cats. Because of religious rules, dogs aren't allowed inside homes, but are kept as guard dogs in some houses.

TALKING WITH CHILDREN

صحبت با بچه ها

What's your name?
esm e shomā chi ye?

اسم شما چیست؟

How old are you?
chand sāl et e?

چند سالت است؟

FAMILY

When's your birthday?
ruz e tavallod et key e?

روز تولدت کی است؟

Have you got brothers and sisters?
barādar o khāhar dāri?

برادر و خواهر داری؟

Do you have a cat at your home?
dar khune tun gorbe dāri?

در خانه تان گربه داری؟

Do you go to school or kindergarten?
[shomā] be madrese miri
yā kudakestān?

(شما) به مدرسه می
روی یا کودکستان؟

Is your teacher nice?
mo'allem etun khub e?

معلم تان خوب است؟

Do you like school?
[shomā] madrese ro dust dāri?

(شما) مدرسه را دوست داری؟

Do you play sport?
[shomā] varzesh mikoni?

(شما) ورزش می کنی؟

What sport do you play?
[shomā] che varzeshi mikoni?

(شما) چه ورزشی می کنی؟

What do you do after school?
[shomā] ba'd az madrese
chikār mikoni?

(شما) بعد از مدرسه
چکار می کنی؟

FAMILY

Do you learn English?
[shomā] ingilisi yād migiri?

(شما) انگلیسی یاد می گیری؟

We speak a different language
in my country.
mā dar keshvar emun be
zabun e digeyi harf mizanim

ما در کشور مان به زبان
دیگری حرف می زنیم

I don't understand you very well.
[man] harfā ye shomā ro
khub nemifahmam

(من) حرف های شما را
خوب نمی فهمم

I come from very far away.
[man] az jā ye kheyli
duri miyām

(من) از جای خیلی
دوری می آیم

Do you want to play?
mikhāy bāzi konim?

می خواهی بازی کنیم؟

What shall we play?
che bāzi yi bekonim?

چه بازی ای بکنیم؟

کارهای مورد علاقه

COMMON INTERESTS

علاقه مشترک

What do you do in your spare time?
[shomā] dar oghāt e farāght
e tun chikār mikonin?

(شما) در اوقات فراغت
تان چکار می کنید؟

I like ...	[man] az ... khosh am miyād	(من) از ... خوشم می آید
I don't like ...	[man] az ... khosh am nemiyād	(من) از ... خوشم نمی آید
Do you like ...?	[shomā] az ... khosh etun miyād?	(شما) از ... خوشتان می آید؟
art	honar	هنر
cooking	āshpazi	آشپزی
dancing	raghs	رقص
film	film	فیلم
going out	gardesh	گردش
music	musighi	موسیقی
photography	akkāsi	عکاسی
playing games	bāzi	بازی
playing soccer	bāzi ye futbāl	بازی فوتبال
playing sport	varzesh	ورزش
reading books	khundan e ketāb	خواندن کتاب
shopping	kharid	خرید
the theatre	te'ātr	تئاتر
travelling	mosāferat	مسافرت
watching TV	tamāshā ye televiziyon	تماشای تلویزیون
writing	neveshtan	نوشتن

INTERESTS

STAYING IN TOUCH

تماس داشتن

Tomorrow's my last day here.

    fardā ākherin ruz e man
    dar injā st

فردا آخرین روز من
در اینجاست

Let's swap addresses.

    biyāyin ādresā mun o be
    hamdige bedim

بیایید آدرس هایمان را به
همدیگر بدهیم

Do you have a pen and paper?

    [shomā] ghalam o kāghaz dārin?

(شما) قلم و کاغذ دارین؟

What's your address?

    ādres e [shomā] chi ye?

آدرس (شما) چیست؟

Here's my address.

    in ādres e man e

این آدرس من است

If you ever visit (Scotland) you
must come and visit us.

    agar ruzi be (eskātland)
    umadin, bāyad pish e mā biyāyin

اگر روزی به (اسکاتلند)
آ مدید باید پیش ما بیایید

If you come to (Melbourne)
you've got a place to stay.

    agar be (melborn) umadin
    jā yi barāye eghāmat dārin

اگر به (ملبورن) آمدید،
جایی برای اقامت دارید

Do you have an email address?

    [shomā] ādres e imeyl dārin?

(شما) آدرس ای میل دارید؟

Do you have access to a fax machine?

    [shomā] dastrasi be faks dārin?

(شما) دسترسی به فکس دارید؟

I'll send you copies of my photos.

    az aksā barāye [shomā]
    miferestam

از عکس ها برای (شما)
می فرستم

Don't forget to write.

    farāmush nakonin ke nāme
    benevisin

فراموش نکنید که نامه
بنویسید

WRITING LETTERS

نامه نوشتن

Once you get back home, you may want to drop a line to people you met. If you feel like tackling Persian script, here are a few suggestions to help you.

Dear ...	... عزیز
I'm sorry it's taken so long to write.	معذرت می خواهم که خیلی طول کشید تا نامه بنویسم
It was great to meet you.	از دیدن شما خیلی خوشبخت شدم
Thank you so much for your hospitality.	از مهمان نوازی شما خیلی متشکرم
I had a fantastic time in ...	در ... به من خیلی خوش گذشت
My favourite place was ...	جای مورد علاقه من ... بود
I hope to visit ... again.	(من) امیدوارم که ... را دوباره ببینم
Say 'hi' to ... for me.	به ... از طرف من سلام برسانید
I miss you.	دلم برایتان تنگ شده
I'd love to see you again.	(من) دوست دارم شما را دوباره ببینم

CINEMA & THEATRE

سینما و تئاتر

Many Iranian films have won international awards, including *Gabe* and *Salam Cinema* by Mohsen Makhmalbaf, along with *Where is the Friend's Home?* and *The Taste of Cherry* by Abbas Kiyarostami. The film *Children of Heaven* by Majid Majidi was nominated for an Academy Award in 1999.

Sex, violence, coarse language, singing, dancing and alcohol aren't permitted in Iranian films. Most are simple and realistic, and sometimes use amateur actors.

Foreign movies in Iran are dubbed and censored for material considered offensive. A couple of cinemas in Tehran show movies in English or with English subtitles.

documentary	mostanad	مستند
drama	derāmā	دراما
horror film	film e vahshatnāk	فیلم وحشتناک
science fiction film	film e elmi-takhayyoli	فیلم علمی تخیلی
short film	film e kutāh	فیلم کوتاه
war film	film e jangi	فیلم جنگی

What's on at the cinema tonight?
 emshab che filmi
 tu sinemā hast?

امشب چه فیلمی
تو سینما هست؟

Where can I find a cinema guide?
 [man] az kojā mitunam
 barnāme ye sinemāhā ro
 peydā konam?

(من) از کجا می توانم برنامه
سینماها را پیدا کنم؟

Are there any tickets for ...?
 barāye ... belit dārin?

برای ... بلیط دارید؟

Is this film in English?
 in film be zabān e ingilisi ye?

این فیلم به زبان انگلیسی است؟

Does this movie have
English subtitles?
 in film zirnevis e ingilisi dāre?

این فیلم زیرنویس انگلیسی دارد؟

Is there a short before the film?
 ghabl az film pishparde hast?

قبل از فیلم پیش پرده هست؟

Is this seat taken?
 injā jā ye kesi ye?

اینجا جای کسی است؟

Have you seen ...?
 [shomā] ... ro didin?

(شما) ... را دیده اید؟

Have you seen the latest film
by (Kiarostami)?
 [shomā] ākherin film e
 (kiyārostami) ro didin?

(شما) آخرین فیلم
(کیارستمی) را دیدید؟

Who's in it?
 ki dar un bāzi mikone?

کی در آن بازی می کند؟

It stars ...
 bāzigarān e un ... and

بازیگران آن ... هستند

Who's it by?
 kārgardān e un ki ye?

کارگردان آن کی هست؟

It's directed by ...
 un o ... kārgardāni karde

آنرا ... کارگردانی کرده

THEY MAY SAY ...
mota'assefāne, belit tamum shode
Sorry, we've sold out.

Opinions

نظرها

Did you like the film?
[shomā] az film khosh etun umad?

(شما) از فیلم خوشتان آمد؟

I liked it a lot.
[man] kheyli az un
khosh am umad

(من) خیلی از آن
خوشم آمد

I didn't like it very much.
[man] az un ziyād
khosh am nayumad

(من) از آن خیلی
خوشم نیامد

I thought it was excellent.
[man] fekr mikonam ke āli bud

(من) فکر می کنم که عالی بود

I had some problems with the
language.
dar mored e zabān kami
moshkel dāshtam

در مورد زبان کمی
مشکل داشتم

MUSIC

موسیقی

Different ethnic groups such as Azerbaijani, Gilaki, Lori and
Kurdish have different styles of music. Traditional music in Iran
has a lot of fans. Western-style music like pop and rock are
banned, and women aren't allowed to sing in Iran.

Do you like to listen to music?
[shomā] dust dārin musighi
gush konin?

(شما) دوست دارید موسیقی
گوش کنید؟

What kind of music do you like?
[shomā] che nu' musighi
dust dārin?

(شما) چه نوع موسیقی
دوست دارید؟

Do you sing?
[shomā] āvāz mikhunin?

(شما) آواز می خوانید؟

Have you heard (Shajariyan)'s
latest cassette?
[shomā] navār e jadid e
(shajariyān) o shenidin?

(شما) نوار جدید
(شجریان) را شنیدید؟

Where can we hear some traditional music?
[mā] kojā mitunim musighi
ye asil ghush konim?

(ما) کجا می توانیم
موسیقی اصیل گوش کنیم؟

band	guruh e āvāz	گروه آواز
concert	konsert	کنسرت
concert hall	tālār e musighi	تالار موسیقی
drums	tunbak	تنبک
famous	mashhur	مشهور
guitar	gitār	گیتار
musician	musighidān	موسیقی دان
orchestra	orkestr	ارکستر
performance	ejrā	اجرا
song	āvāz	آواز
singer	khānande	خواننده
songwriter	āhangsāz	آهنگساز
stage	sahne	صحنه
ticket	belit	بلیط
voice	sedā	صدا

INTERESTS

SPORT
ورزش

Do you like sport?
[shomā] az varzesh
khosh etun miyād?

(شما) از ورزش
خوشتان می آید؟

I like playing sport.
[man] az varzesh kardan
khosh am miyād

(من) از ورزش کردن
خوشم می آید

I prefer to watch rather than play sport.
[man] tarjih midam tamāshā
konam tā varzesh

(من) ترجیح می دهم
تماشا کنم تا ورزش

DID YOU KNOW ...   In everyday conversation, swearing isn't as common as it is in English. It's mainly reserved for fighting and serious quarrels.

Do you (play/go/do) ...?	[shomā] ... bāzi mikonin?	(شما) ... بازی می کنید؟
Would you like to (play/go/do) ...?	[shomā] mikhāyin ... bāzi konin?	(شما) می خواهید ... بازی کنید؟
basketball	basketbāl	بسکتبال
boxing	moshtzani/boks	مشت زنی/بوکس
diving	ghavvāsi	غواصی
gymnastics	zhimnāstik	ژیمناستیک
hockey	hāki	هاکی
keep fit	badan sāzi	بدن سازی
martial arts	honarhā ye razmi	هنرهای رزمی
skiing	eski	اسکی
soccer	futbāl	فوتبال
swimming	shena	شنا
tennis	tenis	تنیس
wrestling	koshti	کشتی

INTERESTS

Soccer فوتبال

The most popular sport in Iran is soccer, and the most popular teams are Esteghlal and Piruzi. Up to 100,000 fans pack into the Azadi stadium in Tehran to see a match.

Do you like soccer?	[shomā] az futbāl khosh etun miyād?	(شما) از فوتبال خوشتان می آ ید؟
Which team do you support?	[shomā] tarafdār e che timi hastin?	(شما) طرفدار چه تیمی هستید؟
I support (Piruzi).	[man] tarafdār e (piruzi) am	(من) طرفدار (پیروزی) هستم
(Esteghlal) is better than the other team.	(esteghlāl) behtar az tim e dige ast	(استقلال) بهتر از تیم دیگر است
What a team!	ajab timi!	عجب تیمی
seat	sandali	صندلی
ticket	belit barāye mosābeghe	بلیط برای مسابقه

Omar Khayyam (1047-1123) was born in Naishapur. He was a scientist, astronomer, mathematician and poet. He wrote The Rubaiyat, a collection of around 150 quatrain poems that celebrate pleasure and destiny, and are high in allegorical references, humour and satire. He is probably the best-known Iranian poet in the West because many of his poems were translated into English. These poems were translated by Edward FitzGerald.

And strange to tell, among that Earthen Lot
Some could articulate, while others not:
And suddenly one more impatient cried —
'Who is the Potter, pray, and who the Pot?'

dar kārgah e kuzegari raftam dush
didam dohezār kuze guyā vo khamush
nāgāh yeki kuze bar āvard khurush
ku kuzegar o kuzekhar o kuzefurush

در کارگه کوزه گری رفتم دوش
دیدم دو هذار کوزه گویا وخموش
ناگه یکی کوزه برآورد خروش
کو کوزه گروکوزه خر وکوزه فروش

INTERESTS

Oh, come with old Khayyam, and leave the Wise
To talk, one thing is certain, that life flies;
One thing is certain and the rest is lies;
The Flower that once has blown for ever dies

mey bar kaf e man neh ke delam dar tāb ast
vin omr e gorizpāy chon simāb ast
daryāb ke ātash e javāni āb ast
hoshdār ke bidāri ye dolat khāb ast

می یکف من نه که دلم درتاب است
وین عمر گریزپای چون سیماب است
دریاب که آتش جوانی آب است
هشدارکه بیداری دولت خواب است

The Moving Finger writes; and having writ,
Moves on: nor all your Piety nor Wit
Shall lure it back to cancel half a Line
Nor all your Tears wash out a Word of it

bar loh e neshān budanihā budast
peyvaste ghalam ze nik o bad farsudast
dar ruz e azal har ānche bāyest bedād
gham khordan o kushidan e mā bihudast

برلوح نشان بودنیها بوده است
پیوسته قلم ز نیک وبد فرسوده است
در روز ازل هرآ نچه بایست بداد
غم خوردن وکوشیدن مابیهوده است

LITERATURE

ادبیات

Who's your favourite author?
  nevisande ye mored e alāghe
  ye shomā ki ye?

نویسنده مورد علاقه
شما کی هست؟

I read ...
  [man] ketābā ye ...
  ro mikhunam

(من) کتابهای ...
را می خوانم

I've read everything by ...
  [man] hame ye ketābā ye
  ... ro khundam

(من) همه کتابهای
... را خوانده ام

I prefer the works of ...
  [man] neveshtehā ye ...
  ro tarjih midam

(من) نوشته های ...
را ترجیح می دهم

What kind of books do you read?
  [shomā] che no' ketābāyi
  mikhunin?

(شما) چه نوع کتابهایی
می خوانید؟

I (don't) like ...	[man] az ... khosh am (ne) miyād	(من) از ... خوشم (نه) می آید
biography	sharhe hāl	شرح حال
comics	tanz	طنز
contemporary literature	adabiyyāt e mo'āser	ادبیات معاصر
crime/detective novels	romānhā ye polisi jenāyi	رمانهای پلیسی جنایی
fiction	dāstān e takhayyoli	داستان تخیلی
non-fiction	dāstān e gheyr e takhayyloi	داستان غیر تخیلی
novels	roman	رمان
poetry	she'r	شعر
romance	dāstān e eshghi	داستان عشقی
short stories	dāstānhā ye kutāh	داستانهای کوتاه
travel writing	safarnāme	سفرنامه

Have you read ...?
[shomā] ... ro khundin
(شما) ... را خوانده اید؟

What did you think of ...?
[shomā] nazar etun dar
mored e ... chi bud?
(شما) نظرتان در
مورد ... چه بود؟

Can you recommend a book for me?
[shomā] mitunin ye ketāb
be man pishnahād konin?
(شما) می توانید یک کتاب
به من پیشنهاد کنید؟

I thought	[man] fekr mikonam	(من) فکر می
it was ...	un ... bud	کنم آن ... بود
badly-written	bad neveshte shode	بد نوشته شده
better/worse than	behtar/badtar az	بهتر/بدتر از
their previous book	ketāb e ghabli	کتاب قبلی
boring	khaste konande	خسته کننده
entertaining	sargarm konande	سرگرم کننده
well-written	khub neveshte shode	خوب نوشته شده

HOBBIES   سرگرمی ها

Do you have any hobbies?
[shomā] hich gune sargarmi
dārin?
(شما) هیچ گونه سرگرمی
دارید؟

I like ...	[man] az ... khosh am miyād	(من) از ... خوشم می آید
cooking	āshpazi	آشپزی
drawing	naghghāshi	نقاشی
gardening	bāghbuni	باغبانی
sewing	khayyāti	خیاطی
taking photographs	akkāsi	عکاسی
travelling	mosāferat	مسافرت

I collect ...	[man] ... jam mikonam	(من) ... جمع می کنم
books	ketāb	کتاب
coins	sekke	سکه
dolls	arusak	عروسک
stamps	tambr	تمبر

INTERESTS

TALKING ABOUT TRAVELLING

صحبت در مورد
مسافرت

Have you travelled much?
[shomā] ziyād mosāferat kardin?

(شما) زیاد مسافرت کردید؟

How long have you been travelling?
[shomā] che moddat e ke
mosāferat mikonin?

(شما) چه مدت است که
مسافرت می کنید؟

I've been travelling for (two months).
[man] (do māh) e ke
mosāferat mikonam

(من) (دو ماه) ا است
که مسافرت می کنم

Where have you been?
[shomā] kojāhā budin?

(شما) کجاها بودید؟

I've been to ...
[man] dar ... budam

(من) در ... بودم

What do you think of (London)?
[shomā] nazar etun dar
mored e (landan) chi ye?

(شما) نظرتان در
مورد (لندن) چیست؟

I think it's ...	[man] fekr	(من) فکر
	mikonam ... e	می کنم ... است
great	jāleb	جالب
horrible	vahshatnāk	وحشتناک
OK	khub	خوب
too expensive	kheyli gerun	خیلی گران

There are too many tourists there.
turistā ye ziyādi unjā hastan

توریست های زیادی آنجا هستند

People are really friendly there.
mardom unjā vāghe'an
mehrabun hastan

مردم آنجا واقعاً مهربان هستند

What's there to do in (Athens)?
dar (āten) che kārāyi mishe
kard?

در (آتن) چه کارهایی می
شود کرد؟

There's a good restaurant/hotel there.
unjā ye resturān/
hotel e khub hast

آنجا رستوران/
هتل خوبی هست

INTERESTS

I'll write down the details for you.
[man] jozi'yāt esh ro
barāye shomā minevisam

(من) جزئیات اش را برای
شما می نویسم

The best time to go is in (December).
behtarin moghe' barāye
raftan be unjā (desāmr) e

بهترین موقع برای رفتن
به آنجا (دسامبر) است

Is it expensive there?
dar unjā geroni ye?

در آنجا گرانی است؟

Is it safe for women travellers to go alone?
unjā barāye zanāyi ke tanhā
safar mikonan, amn e?

آنجا برای زنهایی که تنها
سفر می کنند، امن است؟

STARS
Astrology

ستاره ها
فال بینی

When's your birthday?
[shomā] ruz e tavallod etun key e?

(شما) روز تولد تان کی ه؟

What star sign are you?
[shomā] neshune ye borj
e falaki tun chi ye?

(شما) نشانه برج فلکی
تان چیست؟

I don't believe in astrology.
[man] be fālbini e'teghād
nadāram

(من) به فال بینی اعتقاد
ندارم

I'm a(n) ...	[man] motavvaled e borj e ... am	(من) متولد برج ... هستم
Aries	hamal	حمل
Taurus	sor	صور
Gemini	jozā	جوزا
Cancer	saratān	سرطان
Leo	asad	اسد
Virgo	sonbol	سنبل
Libra	mizān	میزان
Scorpion	aghrab	عقرب
Sagittarius	ghos	قوس
Capricorn	joday	جدی
Aquarius	dalv	دلو
Pisces	hut	حوت

Ah, that explains it!	āhā, dalil esh in e!	آهان ، دلیل اش این است
(Leos) are very ...	motavalledin e (borj e asad) kheyli ... and	متولدین (برج اسد) خیلی ... هستند
aggressive	parkhāshgar	پرخاشگر
caring	delsuz	دلسوز
charming	delrobā	دلربا
crafty	māher	ماهر
creative	khallāgh	خلاق
emotional	ehsāsāti	احساساتی
indecisive	dodel	دودل
intense	ghavi	قوی
interesting	jāleb	جالب
jealous	hasud	حسود
loyal	vafādār	وفادار
outgoing	mo'āsherati	معاشرتی
passive	monfa'el	منفعل
proud	maghrur	مغرور
self-centred	khod mehvar	خود محور
sensual	khosh gozarān	خوش گذران
stingy	khasis	خسیس

INTERESTS

Astronomy
ستاره شناسی

Are you interested in astronomy?
[shomā] be setāre shenāsi alāghe dārin?
(شما) به ستاره شناسی علاقه دارید؟

I'm interested in astronomy.
[man] be setāre shenāsi alāghe dāram
(من) به ستاره شناسی علاقه دارم

Do you have a telescope?
[shomā] teleskop dārin?
(شما) تلسکوپ دارید؟

Is there a planetarium/ observatory nearby?
in nazdiki rasadkhāne hast?
این نزدیکی رصدخانه هست؟

Where's the best place to see stars at night?

behtarin jā barāye didan e setārehā dar moghe' e shab kojā st?	بهترین جا برای دیدن ستاره ها در موقع شب کجاست؟

Will it be cloudy tonight?

havā emshab abri khāhad bud?	هوا امشب ابری خواهد بود؟

When can I see ...?	[man] key mitunam ... ro bebinam?	(من) کی می توانم ... را ببینم؟
Mercury	otārod	عطارد
Mars	merrikh	مریخ
Uranus	orānus	اورانوس
Pluto	poloton	پلوتون

Earth	zamin	زمین
Milky Way	rāh e shiri	راه شیری
Ursa Major/The Great Bear/The Big Dipper	dobb e akbar	دب اکبر
The Little Bear	dobb e asghar	دب اصغر
astronaut	fazānavard	فضانورد
astronomer	setāreshenās	ستاره شناس
atmosphere	javv	جو
comet	setāre ye donbāledār	ستاره دنباله دار
full moon	māh e kāmel	ماه کامل
meteor	shahābsang	شهاب سنگ
moon	māh	ماه
nebula	sahāb	سحاب
planet	sayyāre	سیاره
sky	āsemun	آسمان
space	fazā	فضا
space exploration	josteju ye fazā	جستجوی فضا
stars	setāregān	ستارگان
sun	khorshid	خورشید
telescope	teleskop	تلسکوپ
universe	hasti	هستی

What time does it rise?

[un] key tulu' mikone?   (آن) کی طلوع می کند؟

What time does it set?

[un] key ghurub mikone?   (آن) کی غروب می کند؟

Can I see it at this time of year
from here?

[man] mitunam un o in
moghe' e sāl az injā bebinam?   (من) می توانم آن را این موقع سال از اینجا ببینم؟

Which way is north?

[shomāl] kodum taraf e?   (شمال) کدام طرف است؟

Is that Orion?

un setāre ye shekār chi ye?   آن ستاره شکارچی است؟

It's the other way in the Southern
hemisphere.

un dar nimkore ye junubi
dar taraf e dige ast   آن در نیمکره جنوبی در طرف دیگر است

The Unexplained   توجیح نشده ها

Do you believe there's life out there?

[shomā] zendegi dar korāt e
dige ro bāvar mikonin?   (شما) زندگی در کرات دیگر را باور می کنید؟

Do you believe in ...?	[shomā] be ... e'teghād dārin?	(شما) به ... اعتقاد دارید؟
(black) magic	jādu ye (siyāh)	جادوی (سیاه)
extraterrestrials	māvarā'ottabi'e	ماورا الطبیعه
ghosts	arvāh	روح
life after death	zendegi ba'd az marg	زندگی بعد از مرگ
miracles	mo'jezāt	معجزات
telepathy	telepāti	تله پاتی
UFOs	boshghāb parande	بشقاب پرنده

POLITICS

سیاست

Because of various Middle Eastern conflicts and Iran's unique situation in the region, many people are interested in talking about politics. In fact, politics is one of the main themes of conversation in Iran, and most people will be interested in your opinion about current international events.

Although local politics is a hot topic, to be on the safe side it's best to avoid the subject, particularly sensitive and controversial issues.

Did you hear the news about ...?
    [shomā] akhbār e marbut
    be ... ro shenidin?

(شما) اخبار مربوط
به ... را شنیدید؟

What do you think of the
current/new government?
    [shomā] dar mored e dolat
    e jadid chi fekr mikonin?

(شما) در مورد دولت
جدید چه فکر می کنید؟

I agree with their   [man] bā siyāsat e
policy on ...   unā dar mored e
           ... movāfegham

(من) با سیاست آنها
در مورد ... موافقم

drugs	mavādd e mokhadder	مواد مخدر
education	āmuzesh	آموزش
international affairs	masā'el e beynolmelali	مسائل بین المللی
military service	nezām vazife	نظام وظیفه
privatisation	khususi sāzi	خصوصی سازی
social welfare	refāh e ejtemāyi	رفاه اجتماعی
the economy	eghtesād	اقتصاد
the environment	mohit e zist	محیط زیست

candidate's speech	sokhanrāni ye kāndid	سخنرانی کاندید
corrupt	fāsed	فاسد
counting of votes	shomāresh e ārā	شمارش آرا
democracy	domokrāsi	دمکراسی
demonstration	tazāhorāt/rāhpeymāyi	تظاهرات/راهپیمایی
elections	entekhābāt	انتخابات
national	melli	ملی
electorate	hoze ye entekhābāti	حوزه انتخاباتی
exploitation	estesmār/bahrekeshi	استثمار/بهره کشی
legislation	ghānun gozāri	قانون گذاری
parliament	majles	مجلس
policy	siyāsat	سیاست
polls	nazarkhāhi	نظر خواهی
president	ra'is e jumhuri	رئیس جمهوری
prime minister	nakhost vazir	نخست وزیر
racism	nezhād parasti	نژاد پرستی
rally	rāhpeymāyi	راهپیمایی
rip off	ekhtelās	اختلاس
strike	e'tesāb	اعتصاب
term of office	dore	دوره
unemployment	bikāri	بیکاری
vote	ra'y	رای

DID YOU KNOW ...   In Iran, people call each other by their surname. First names,esm e kuchik , are only used with very close friends, family members and children.

ENVIRONMENT

محیط زیست

Pollution is a big problem in Iran, especially in Tehran, which has a population of more than 10 million and thousands of old vehicles. On the other hand, rural areas and the countryside are unpolluted and full of natural beauty.

Does (Iran) have a pollution problem?	(irān) moshkel e āludegi ye havā dāre?	(ایران) مشکل آلودگی هوا دارد؟

Are there any protected ... here?	injā ... e hefāzat shode hast?	اینجا ... حفاظت شده هست؟
parks	pārk	پارک
forests	jangal	جنگل
species	gunehā	گونه ها

Where do you stand on ...?	moze' e shomā dar mored e ... chi ye?	موضع شما در مورد ... چیست؟
pollution	āludegi	آلودگی
deforestation	jangal zodāyi	جنگل زدایی
nuclear testing	āzemāyesh e hasteyi	آزمایش هسته ای

antinuclear group	guruh e zedd e hasteyi	گروه ضد هسته ای
conservation	hefāzat	حفاظت
disposable	dur andākhtani	دور انداختنی
drought	khoshksāli	خشکسالی
ecosystem	ekosistem	اکوسیستم
endangered species	gunehā ye dar hāl e nābudi	گونه های در حال نابودی
industrial pollution	āludegi ye san'ati	آلودگی صنعتی
irrigation	ābyāri	آبیاری
nuclear energy	enerezhi ye hasteyi	انرژی هسته ای
ozone layer	lāye ye ozon	لایه ازون
pesticides	mavādd e hashare kosh	مواد حشره کش
recyclable	ghābel e tabdil	قابل تبدیل
recycling	tabdil	تبدیل
reservoir	manba'	منبع
toxic waste	zobāle ye sammi	زباله سمی
water supply	manābe' e ābi	منابع آبی

SOCIAL ISSUES

مسائل اجتماعی

How do people feel about ...?
   mardom dar mored e ... che
   ehsāsi dārand?

مردم در مورد ... چه
احساسی دارند؟

What do you think about ...?
   [shomā] dar morede ...
   che fekr mikonin?

(شما) در مورد ...
چه فکر می کنید؟

I'm in favour of ...	[man] tarafdār e ... am	(من) طرفدار ... هستم
I'm against ...	[man] mokhālef e ... am	(من) مخالف ... هستم
abortion	seght e janin	سقط جنین
animal rights	hemāyat az heyvānāt	حمایت از حیوانات
immigration	mohājerat	مهاجرت
party politics	siyāsat e hezbi	سیاست حزبی
racism	nezhādparasti	نژاد پرستی
tax	māliyāt	مالیات
unions	ettehādiyehā	اتحادیه ها

TOUGH DEALS

Iran is one of the most active countries in fighting against
drug use, and you won't see drugs being used in public
places. The smallest amount of hashish can carry a minimum
six-month jail sentence. In Iran, all drugs are illegal and
penalties for drug dealing are tough.

This drug is for medical use.
   in dāru barāye
   masraf e tebbi ye

این دارو برای
مصرف طبی است

SHOPPING

Traditional market bazaars are still the main place to shop in Iran. The bazaar in each city is the best place to find local products and crafts. There are also a lot of modern shopping centres and stores which can be found in the city centre.

LOOKING FOR ...

گشتن برای ...

Where can I buy ...?
[man] kojā mitunam ... bekharam?

(من) کجا می توانم ... بخرم؟

Where's the nearest ...?	nazdiktarin ... kojā st?	نزدیکترین ... کجاست؟
barber	ārāyeshgāh	آرایشگاه
bookshop	ketāb furushi	کتاب فروشی
camera shop	durbin furushi	دوربین فروشی
chemist (pharmacy)	dārukhune	داروخانه
clothing store	lebās furushi	لباس فروشی
dry cleaner	khoshk shuyi	خشکشویی
general store	furushgāh	فروشگاه
market	bāzār	بازار
newsagency	ruznāme furushi	روزنامه فروشی
optician	eynak furushi	عینک فروشی
shoe shop	kafsh furushi	کفش فروشی
souvenir shop	kādo furushi	کادو فروشی
stationers	nevesht afzār furushi	نوشت افزار فروشی
travel agency	āzhāns e mosāferati	آژانس مسافرتی

SHOPPING

MAKING A PURCHASE

خرید کردن

Most shops don't have refund or exchange policies. If in doubt, be sure to ask before making a purchase.

How much? che ghadr?

چقدر؟

I'll buy it.
  [man] un o mikharam

(من) آنرا می خرم

I'd like to buy ...
  [man] mikhām ... bekharam

(من) می خواهم ... بخرم

Do you have others?
  [shomā] chizhā ye dige
  ham dārin?

(شما) چیزهای دیگر
هم دارید؟

I don't like it.
  [man] az un khosh am nemiyād

(من) از آن خوشم نمی آید

Can I look at it?
  mishe negāh esh konam?

می شود نگاه اش کنم؟

I'm just looking.
  [man] faghat negāh mikonam

(من) فقط نگاه می کنم

Can you write down the price?
  [shomā] mitunin gheymat
  esh o benevisin?

(شما) می توانید قیمت اش
را بنویسید؟

Do you accept credit cards?
  [shomā] kārt e e'tebāri
  ghabul mikonin?

(شما) کارت اعتباری
قبول می کنید؟

Please wrap it.
  lotfan baste bandish konin

لطفاً بسته بندی اش کنید

Can I have a receipt?
  [shomā] mishe ye resid
  be man bedin?

(شما) می شود یک
رسید به من بدهید؟

Does it have a guarantee?
  in gārānti dāre?

این گارانتی دارد؟

Can I have it sent overseas?
  [shomā] mishe un o barāy
  am be khārej beferestin?

(شما) می شود آنرا برایم
به خارج بفرستید؟

I'd like to return this.
  [man] mikhām in o pas bedam

(من) می خواهم این را پس بدهم

I'd like my money back.

[shomā] mishe pul am o
pas bedin?

(شما) می شود پولم را پس بدهید؟

It's faulty.   [un] kharāb e   (آن) خراب است

It's broken.   [un] shekaste   (آن) شکسته

RAISING THE TONE

When asking a question in Persian, there's no need to change the word order of a sentence. Just raise the intonation towards the end of the sentence.

BARGAINING

چانه زدن

Bargaining is standard practice in most shops and stalls except supermarkets, department stores and food markets. Usually there are no price tags, but even if you see them you can still bargain.

I think it's too expensive.

[man] fekr mikonam un
kheyli gerun e

(من) فکر می کنم آن خیلی
گران است

The price is very high.

gheymat esh kheyli bālā st

قیمت اش خیلی بالا است

Can you lower the price?

mishe gheymat esh
o kamtar konin?

می شود قیمت اش
را کمتر کنید؟

Do you have something cheaper?

[shomā] chiz e arzuntar
ham dārin?

(شما) چیز ارزانتر
هم دارید؟

I don't have much money.

[man] pul e ziyādi nadāram

(من) پول زیادی ندارم

I'll give you (2000) Toman.

[man] (do hezār) toman be
shomā midam

(من) (۲۰۰۰) تومان به
شما می دهم

No more than (2500) Toman.
بیشتر از (۲۵۰۰)
    bishtar az (do hezār o punsad)
تومان نمی شود
    toman nemishe

Give me ...	... be man bedin	... به من بدهید
a kilogram	ye kilo	یک کیلو
a litre	ye litr	یک لیتر
half	ye nesfe	یک نصفه

ESSENTIAL GROCERIES   لوازم خواربار

Where can I find ...?
(من) کجا می توانم ...
    [man] kojā mitunam ...
پیدا کنم؟
    peydā konam?

I'd like (a) ...	[man] ... mikhām	(من) ... می خواهم
batteries	bātri	باطری
bread	nun	نان
butter	kare	کره
cheese	panir	پنیر
chocolate	shokolāt	شکلات
eggs	tokhm e morgh	تخم مرغ
flour	ārd	آرد
gas cylinder	kapsul e gāz	کپسول گاز
honey	asal	عسل
margarine	mārgārin	مارگارین
matches	kebrit	کبریت
milk	shir	شیر
salt	namak	نمک
shampoo	shāmpu	شامپو
soap	sābun	صابون
sugar	shekar	شکر
toilet paper	kāghaz tuvālet	کاغذ توالت
toothpaste	khamir dandun	خمیر دندان
washing powder	pudr e lebās shuyi	پودر لباس شویی
yogurt	māst	ماست

SOUVENIRS

basket	sabad	سبد / هدیه / کادو
brassware	vasāyel e berenji	وسایل برنجی
cane ware/furniture	moblemān	مبلمان
crafts	sanāye' e dasti	صنایع دستی
fretwork	monabbat kāri	منبت کاری
handicraft	sanāye' e dasti	صنایع دستی
jewellery	javāherāt	جواهرات
miniature	miniyātor	مینیاتور
paintings	naghghāshi	نقاشی
posters	puster	پوستر
pottery	vasāyel e sofāli	وسایل سفالی
rug (carpet)	farsh	فرش
silverware	vasāyel e noghreyi	وسایل نقره ای

THEY MAY SAY ...

befarmāyin
  Can I help you?

chiz e dige ham mikhāyin
  Will that be all?

mikhāyin bastebandi sh konam?
  Would you like it wrapped?

mota'essefāne, faghat hamin munde
  Sorry, this is the only one.

cheghadr/chandtā mikhāyin?
  How much/many would you like?

mobārak bāshe
  Blessings! (with the purchase)

CLOTHING لباس

boots	putin/chakme	پوتین/چکمه
chuddar	chādor	چادر
clothes	lebās	لباس
coat	pālto	پالتو
coat (long, worn by women)	mānto	مانتو
dress	pirāhan e zanāne	پیراهن زنانه
jacket	cot	کت
jeans	jin	جین
jumper (sweater)	poliver	پولیور
pants	shalvār	شلوار
pantyhose	jurāb shalvāri	جوراب شلواری
raincoat	bāruni	بارانی
scarf	rusari	روسری
shirt	pirhan	پیراهن
shoes	kafsh	کفش
socks	jurāb	جوراب
stockings	jurāb e zanāne	جوراب زنانه
swimsuit	māyo	مایو
umbrella	chatr	چتر
T-shirt	tishert	تی شرت
underwear	lebās e zir	لباس زیر

Can I try it on? [man] mitunam emtahān esh bekonam?		(من) می توانم امتحانش بکنم؟
My size is ...	sāyz e man ... e	سایز من ... است
It doesn't fit.	andāze nist	اندازه نیست
It's too ...	kheyli ... e	خیلی ... است
big	bozorg	بزرگ
small	kuchik	کوچک
short	kutāh	کوتاه
long	boland	بلند
tight	tang	تنگ
loose	goshad	گشاد

MATERIALS

		مواد
ceramic	serāmik	سرامیک
cotton	katān	کتان
glass	shishe	شیشه
handmade	dast sāz	دست ساز
leather	charm	چرم
metal	felezzi	فلزی
of brass	berenji	برنجی
of gold	talā	طلا
of silver	noghreyi	نقره ای
plastic	pelāstiki	پلاستیکی
silk	abrishami	ابریشمی
stainless steel	istil	استیل
synthetic	masno'i	مصنوعی
wool	pashmi	پشمی
wood	chubi	چوبی

COLOURS

		رنگها
dark ...	... tire	... تیره
light ...	... roshan	... روشن
black	siyāh	سیاه
blue	ābi	آبی
brown	ghahveyi	قهوه ای
green	sabz	سبز
grey	khākestari	خاکستری
orange	nārenji	نارنجی
pink	surati	صورتی
purple	banafsh	بنفش
red	ghermez	قرمز
white	sefid	سفید
yellow	zard	زرد

TOILETRIES

لوازم آرایش

aftershave	āftersheyv	آفتر شیو
comb	shune	شانه
condom	kāndom	کاندوم
dental floss	nakh e dandun	نخ دندان
deodorant	zedd e aragh	ضد عرق
hairbrush	bores	برس
moisturiser	kerem e martub konande	کرم مرطوب کننده
pregnancy test kit	kit e āzemāyesh e hamelegi	کیت آزمایش حاملگی
razor	rish tarāsh	ریش تراش
razor blade	tigh	تیغ
sanitary napkins	navār behdāshti	نوار بهداشتی
shampoo	shāmpu	شامپو
shaving cream	khamir rish	خمیر ریش
soap	sābun	صابون
scissors	gheychi	قیچی
sunblock	kerem e zedd e āftāb	کرم ضد آفتاب
tampon	tāmpon	تامپون
tissues	dastmāl kāghazi	دستمال کاغذی
toothbrush	mesvāk	مسواک

FOR THE BABY

برای نوزاد

baby food	ghazā ye bachche	غذای بچه
baby powder	pudr e bachche	پودر بچه
bib	pishband	پیش بند
disposable nappies	pushak e ye bār masraf	پوشک یکبار مصرف
dummy (pacifier)	pestunak	پستانک
feeding bottle	shishe shir	شیشه شیر
nappy	pushak	پوشک
nappy rash cream	kerem e zedd e sukhtegi ye bachche	کرم ضد سوختگی بچه
powdered milk	shir khoshk	شیر خشک

SHOPPING

STATIONERY & PUBLICATIONS

نوشت افزار و
نشریات

Is there an English-language bookshop here?
   injā ketāb furushi ye
   ingilisi hast?

اینجا کتاب فروشی
انگلیسی هست؟

Where's the English-language section?
   ghesmat e ketābā ye
   ingilisi kojā st?

قسمت کتاب های
انگلیسی کجاست؟

Do you have the latest novel by ...?
   [shomā] ākharin romān e
   ... ro dārin?

(شما) آخرین رمان
... را دارید؟

Do you have a copy of ...?
   [shomā] ketāb e ... ro dārin?

(شما) کتاب ... را دارید؟

Can you recommend a good
Persian book available in English?
   [shomā] mitunin ye ketāb
   e fârsi ye khub pishnahād
   konin ke be ingilisi ham
   tarjome shode bāshe?

(شما) می توانید یک کتاب فارسی
خوب پیشنهاد کنید که به
انگلیسی هم ترجمه شده باشد؟

Is this author translated into English?
   ketābā ye in nevisande be
   ingilisi tarjome shode?

کتاب های این نویسنده
به انگلیسی ترجمه شده؟

DRESS ME UP, DRESS ME DOWN

- chādor
  (lit: tent) an all-encompassing, head-to-toe black covering
  worn by most Iranian women
- hejāb
  (lit: modest dress) the general term for the type of dress
  required, by law, of females over the age of seven
- mānto
  the most common form of dress for middle, and upper,
  class Iranian women. The mānto is a sort of baggy
  trenchcoat, worn below the knee and buttoned to the
  neck. They're normally of a dark, plain colour, worn with
  trousers underneath.

SHOPPING

Do you sell ...?	[shomā] ... mifurushin?	(شما) ... می فروشید؟
magazines	majalle	مجله
newspapers	ruznāme	روزنامه
postcards	kārt postāl	کارت پوستال
dictionaries	diksheneri/ farhang e loghat	دیکشنری/فرهنگ لغت
English-language newspapers	ruznāme ingilisi zabān	روزنامه انگلیسی زبان
envelopes	pākat	پاکت
paper	kāghaz	کاغذ
pens (ballpoint)	khodkār	خودکار
stamps	tambr	تمبر
... maps	naghshe ye ...	نقشه ...
city	shahr	شهر
regional	mantagheyi	منطقه ای
road	jādde	جاده

MUSIC موسیقی

I'm looking for a (traditional music) CD.

  [man] donbāl e ye sidi ye
(musighi ye asil) migardam

(من) دنبال یک سی دی
(موسیقی اصیل) می گردم

Do you have any (Shajariyan) cassettes?

  [shomā] navāri az (shajariyān)
dārin?

(شما) نواری از (شجریان)
دارید؟

Who's the best singer?

  behtarin khānande ki ye?

بهترین خواننده کی هست؟

What's his/her best recording?

  behtarin navār e un kudum e?

بهترین نوار او کدام است؟

What music do you recommend
to take back to (the US)?

  [shomā] che navār e musighi
barāye bordan be (āmrikā)
pishnehād mikonin?

(شما) چه نوار موسیقی
برای بردن به (آمریکا)
پیشنهاد می کنید؟

I'd like the CD of a singer called ...
[man] sidi ye khānandeyi be
esm e ... ro mikhām

(من) سی دی خواننده ای
به اسم ... را می خواهم

Can I listen to this CD here?
[man] mitunam in sidi ro
injā gush konam?

(من) می توانم این سی
دی را اینجا گوش کنم؟

Do you have this on ...?	[shomā] ... ye in o dārin?	(شما) ... ی این را دارید؟
CD	sidi	سی دی
record	safhe	صفحه
cassette	navār	نوار

I need ...	[man] ... mikhām	(من) ... می خواهم
a blank tape	ye navār e khāli	یک نوار خالی
headphones	hedfon	هدفون
batteries	bātri	باطری

PHOTOGRAPHY

عکاسی

How much is it to process this film?
zāher kardan e in film
cheghadr kharj dāre?

ظاهر کردن این فیلم
چقدر خرج دارد؟

When will it be ready?
[un] key hāzer mishe?

(آن) کی حاضر می شود؟

I'd like a film for this camera.
[man] ye film barāye in
durbin mikhām

(من) یک فیلم برای
این دوربین می خواهم

Can you put the film in, please?
lotfan mitunin film o tu
ye durbin bezārin?

لطفاً می توانید فیلم را
توی دوربین بگذارید؟

Do you have one-hour processing?
[shomā] mitunin film o ye
sā'ate zāher konin?

(شما) می توانید فیلم را
یک ساعته ظاهر کنید؟

I'd like to have some passport photos taken.
[man] mikhām chand tā
aks e pāsport begiram

(من) می خواهم چند تا
عکس پاسپورت بگیرم

This film is jammed.
in film jam shode
این فیلم جمع شده

This camera doesn't work.
in durbin kār nemikone
این دوربین کار نمی کند

Can you repair it?
[shomā] mitunin un o ta'mir konin?
(شما) می توانید آنرا تعمیر کنید؟

battery	bātri	باطری
B&W film	film e siyāh o sefid	فیلم سیاه و سفید
camera	durbin	دوربین
colour film	film e rangi	فیلم رنگی
film	film	فیلم
flash (bulb)	felāsh	فلاش
lens	lenz	لنز
light meter	nursanj	نورسنج
slide	eslāyd	اسلاید
videotape	navār e vidiyo	نوار ویدیو

SMOKING   دخانیات

A packet of cigarettes, please.
lotfan ye baste sigār bedin
لطفاً یک بسته سیگار بدهید

Are these cigarettes strong or mild?
in sigārā ghavi hastan yā molāyem?
این سیگار ها قوی هستند یا ملایم؟

Do you have a lighter/matches?
[shomā] fandak/kebrit dārin?
(شما) فندک/کبریت دارید؟

Do you mind if I smoke?
eshkāl nadāre [man] sigār bekesham?
اشکال ندارد (من) سیگار بکشم؟

Please don't smoke.
lotfan sigār nakeshin?
لطفاً سیگار نکشید

Would you like a cigarette?
[shomā] sigār mikhāyin?
(شما) سیگار می خواهید؟

Could I have one?
mishe ye sigār be man bedin?
می شود یک سیگار به من بدهید؟

I'm trying to give up.

(من) سعی می کنم ترک کنم   [man] sa'y mikonam tark konam

cigarettes	sigār	سیگار
cigarette papers	kāghaz e sigār	کاغذ سیگار
filtered	filterdār	فیلتر دار
lighter	fandak	فندک
matches	kebrit	کبریت
pipe	pip	پیپ
tobacco	tanbāku	تنباکو

SIZES & COMPARISONS

اندازه ها و مقایسه ها

also	ham	هم
big	bozorg	بزرگ
enough	kāfi	کافی
heavy	sangin	سنگین
light	sabok	سبک
little (amount)	kam	کم
a little bit	ye kami	یک کمی
many	kheyli	خیلی
more	ziyād	زیاد
small	kuchik	کوچک
too much/many	keyli ziyād	خیلی زیاد

In Iran, lunch and dinner are the principal meals.

Different provinces have their own specialities, but across Iran, bread, rice and meat form the basis of most meals. Serving alcohol is illegal in Iran, fast food isn't common, and you won't find pork because of religious prohibition.

breakfast	sobhune	صبحانه
lunch	nāhār	ناهار
dinner	shām	شام
supper	asrune	عصرانه

BREAKFAST   صبحانه
Breakfast usually consists of cheese, butter, bread, jam, milk, honey, tea and cream, and sometimes scrambled eggs. Iranians prefer their bread homemade and hot.

THE DAYS OF OUR LOAVES

Many bakeries specialise in certain kinds of bread, such as:

barbari
    crisp and salty, with a glazed and finely latticed crust
bātri
    bread
lavāsh
    flat and very thin, folded twice into a square
sangak
    pulpy, oval-shaped break baked on a bed of stones

VEGETARIAN & SPECIAL MEALS

غذاهای سبزیخواری
و مخصوص

Although meat is the main ingredient of most meals in Iran, it is possible to find meals made only with vegetables. In Iran, vegetarianism is unusual, so you should explain what you can and can't eat.

I'm a vegetarian.
[man] sabzikhār am

(من) سبزیخوار هستم

I don't eat meat.
[man] gusht nemikhoram

(من) گوشت نمی خورم

I don't eat chicken or fish.
[man] morgh yā māhi nemikhoram

(من) مرغ یا ماهی
نمی خورم

I can't eat dairy products.
[man] nemitunam labaniyyāt bekhoram

(من) نمی توانم لبنیات
بخورم

Do you have any vegetarian dishes?
[shomā] az ghazāhāye makhsus e sbazikhārā dārin?

(شما) از غذاهای مخصوص
سبزیخوار ها دارید؟

Does this dish have meat?
in ghazā gusht dāre?

این غذا گوشت دارد؟

Can I get this without meat?
mishe bedune gusht e in o be man bedin?

می شود بدون گوشت
این را به من بدهید؟

Does it contain eggs?
[un] tokhm e morgh dāre?

(آن) تخم مرغ دارد؟

I'm allergic to (peanuts).
[man] be (bādum zamini) hassāsiyat dāram

(من) به (بادام زمینی)
حساسیت دارم

Is this organic?
in tabi'i ye?

این طبیعی است؟

without meat	bedun e gusht	بدون گوشت
meatless dish	ghazā ye bedun e gusht	غذای بدون گوشت

EATING OUT

بیرون غذا خوردن

Iran has a variety of places to eat out. They range from traditional restaurants where roasted lamb with rice is the main dish, tea houses serving snacks and light meals, to modern restaurants with western-style food on the menu. Sandwiches, burgers and pizzas are also readily available.

pizza place	**pitzāyi**	پیتزایی
tea house	**ghahve khune**	قهوه خانه
traditional restaurant	**chelo kababi**	چلوکبابی

Table for (five), please.
    miz barāye (panj nafar) lotfan   میز برای (پنج نفر) لطفاً

Can we see the menu?
    mishe [mā] list e ghazā ro   می شود (ما) لیست
    bebinim?   غذا را ببینیم؟

I'd like lunch.
    [man] nāhār mikhām   (من) ناهار می خواهم

Is service included in the bill?
    surat hesāb shāmel e   صورت حساب شامل
    servis ham mishe?   سرویس هم می شود؟

Does the meal come with salad?
    nāhār sālād ham dāre?   ناهار سالاد هم دارد؟

What's the soup of the day?
    sup e emruz chi ye?   سوپ امروز چیست؟

What do you recommend?
    [shomā] chi pishnahād mikonin?   (شما) چه پیشنهاد می کنید؟

What are they eating?
    unā chi mikhoran?   آنها چی می خورند؟

I'll try what s/he's having.
    [man] az ghazāyi ke un   (من) از غذایی که او می
    mikhore mikhām   خورد می خواهم

What's in this dish?
    in ghazā chi ye?   این غذا چیست؟

FOOD

I'd like something to drink.
[man] nushidani mikhām   (من) نوشیدنی می خواهم
Do you have a highchair for the baby?
[shomā] sandali ye bachche dārin?   (شما) صندلی بچه دارید؟

Please bring	lotfān barāye man	لطفاً برای من
me some ...	kami ... biyārin	کمی ... بیاورید
bread	nun	نان
pepper	felfel	فلفل
salt	namak	نمک
water	āb	آب
salad	sālād	سالاد

Should I get it myself or do they
bring it to us?
[man] bāyad khod am bardāram   (من) باید خودم بردارم یا
yā barāmun miyāran?   برایمان می آورند؟

Please bring ...	lotfan ... biyārin	لطفاً ... بیاورید
an ashtray	ye zirsigāri	یک زیر سیگاری
the bill	surat hesāb	صورت حساب
a fork	ye changāl	یک چنگال
a glass of water	ye livān āb	یک لیوان آب
(with/without ice)	(bā/bedun e yakh)	(با/بدون یخ)
a knife	ye chāghu	یک چاقو
a plate	ye boshghāb	یک بشقاب

No ice, please.
lotfan yakh nadāshte bāshe   لطفاً یخ نداشته باشد

USEFUL WORDS   کلمه های مفید

cup	fenjun	فنجان
fresh	tāze	تازه
spicy	tond	تند
sweet	shirin	شیرین
toothpick	khalāl e dandun	خلال دندان
waiter	gārson/	گارسون/پیشخدمت
	pishkhedmat	

FOOD

TYPICAL DISHES

غذاهای معمول

The dish āsh, 'Persian soup', is the most popular soup in Iran. There are many varieties, served as either first course or as a main dish.

Soups		آش ها
āsh e adas		آش عدس
lentil soup		
āsh e ālu		آش آلو
soup with plum, rice and vegetables		
āsh e anār		آش انار

soup made with pomegranate juice, rice, onion, oil, vegetables and seasoned with salt and pepper

āsh e jo   آش جو
   barley soup with cream, butter, parsley and pepper

āsh e māsh   آش ماش
   soup made with chitterlings (intestines), rice and vegetables

āsh e māst   آش ماست
   hot yogurt soup with peas, beans, lentils and vegetables

āsh e reshte   آش رشته
   noodle soup with beans and vegetables

āsh e sabzi	vegetable soup	آش سبزی
kalle pāche	trotter soup	کله پاچه
sirābi	tripe soup	سیرابی
sup e juje	chicken soup	سوپ جوجه

Snacks

عصرانه

Snacks are available throughout the day at a ghahve khune, 'tea house'. Most of the following treats are served in tea houses:

kashk e bādemjun   کشک بادمجان
   vegetable casserole made with eggplants, kashk (thick whey) and mint

FOOD

kuku ye sabzi   کوکوی سبزی
    fried vegetables cooked in eggs and flour

māst-o-khiyār   ماست و خیار
    dip made with yogurt, cucumber, onion, mint, salt and pepper

nun o panir   نان و پنیر
    thin bread and cheese

sālād olviye   سالاد الویه
    chicken salad with egg, dill-pickles, potato, and lime juice

Main Course   غذاهای اصلی

ābgusht   آبگوشت
    lamb stew hash made with meat, peas, potato and tomato
    paste, served with bread

adas polo bā khormā   عدس پلو با خرما
    steamed rice with lentils and dates

ālbālu polo   آلبالو پلو
    chicken and black cherry with steamed rice

bāghāli polo   باقالی پلو
    chicken with broad beans, steamed rice and vegetables

barre ye beryun   بره بریان
    roasted lamb

chelo kabāb   چلو کباب
    spicy broiled lamb or beef with steamed rice

chelo kabāb e kubide   چلو کباب کوبیده
    roasted minced meat with steamed rice

chelo māhi   چلو ماهی
    fried fish served with steamed rice and vegetables

dolme ye barg   دله برگ
    grape leaves stuffed with meat and rice

dolme bādemjun · دله بادنجان
  stuffed eggplant

fesenjun · فسنجان
  chicken and steamed rice flavoured with pomegranate
  paste and grated walnut

ghorme sabzi · قرمه سبزی
  a mix of diced meat, steamed rice, beans, tomato paste
  and vegetables

juje kabāb · جوجه کباب
  barbecued chicken

khoresht e bādemjun · خورشت بادمجان
  stew made with chicken or diced meat, eggplant, tomato
  paste and steamed rice

khoresht e gheyme · خورشت قیمه
  stew made with diced meat, split pea, dried lemon, chips
  and steamed rice

lubiyā polo · لوبیا پلو
  diced meat, beans, tomato paste and steamed rice

mirzā ghāsemi · میرزا قاسمی
  eggplant, tomato and egg with garlic

tahchin · ته چین
  baked chicken or meat, yogurt, rice and eggs

zereshk polo bā morgh · زرشک پلو با مرغ
  roasted chicken served with rice and barberry (a type of fruit)

Desserts · دسرها

In Iran, desserts are light. Fruit forms the main part of dessert,
complemented by different types of sweets and biscuits.

bāghlavā · باقلوا
  flaky pastry, honey and nuts

bāmiye · بامیه
  flour, eggs, sugar and rosewater

FOOD

FOOD

bastani	بستنی
ice cream	
fereni	فرنی
rice-flour, milk, sugar and rosewater	
halvā	حلوا
flour, butter and sugar	
komput	کمپوت
stewed fruit	
kerem kārāmel	کرم کارامل
baked caramel custard	
nun berenji	نان برنجی
rice-flour, sugar, eggs and rosewater	
nunvāyi	نانوایی
bakery	

shir berenji	شیر برنجی
rice, sugar, rosewater, milk and cream	
shole zard	شله زرد
rice, sugar, saffron, rosewater, pistachios, almonds and cinnamon	
ranginak	رنگینک
flour, dates and walnut	
samanu	سمنو
wheat and wheat flour	
yakh dar behesht	یخ در بهشت
rice-flour, starch, sugar, rosewater, milk and pistachios	
zulbiyā	زولبیا
yogurt, sugar, rosewater and starch	

SELF-CATERING
In the Delicatessen

درست کردن غذای خود
در خوار و بار فروشی

FOOD

How much is (a kilo of) ...?
... (kiloyi) chand e?

... (کیلویی) چند است؟

Do you have anything cheaper?
chiz e arzuntari ham dārin?

چیز ارزان تری هم دارید؟

Give me (half a kilo), please.
lotfan (nim kilo) be man bedin

لطفاً (نیم کیلو) به من بدهید

Can I taste it?
mishe uno bechesham?

می شود آنرا بچشم؟

bread	nun	نان
butter	kare	کره
cheese	panir	پنیر
chocolate	shokolāt	شکلات
eggs	tokhm e morgh	تخم مرغ
flour	ārd	آرد
honey	asal	عسل
margarine	mārgārin	مارگارین
milk	shir	شیر
pepper	felfel	فلفل
salt	namak	نمک
sugar	shekar	شکر
yogurt	māst	ماست

THEY MAY SAY ...

befarmāyiyn
You'll hear this phrase often and on different occasions. It's said when offering an invitation, a seat, a meal, and so on. It's the formal equivalent of 'please help yourself' or 'here you are'.

FOOD

AT THE MARKET
Meat & Poultry

در بازار
گوشت ومرغ

beef	gusht e gāv	گوشت گاو
chicken	morgh	مرغ
goat	gusht e boz	گوشت بز
heart	del	دل
kidney	gholve	قلوه
lamb	gusht e gusfand	گوشت گوسفند
liver	jegar	جگر
meat	gusht	گوشت
mutton	gusht e gusfand	گوشت گوسفند
quail	belderchin	بلدرچین
tongue	zabān	زبان
turkey	bughalamun	بوقلمون
veal	gusht e gusāle	گوشت گوساله

Fish & Seafood

ماهی و غذاهای دریایی

Different types of fish are readily available, especially in cities close to the Caspian Sea and the Persian Gulf.

Prawns are the only crustaceans eaten in Iran. While it's unusual to find other crustaceans and shellfish on a menu, it isn't forbidden. Caviar is popular, but expensive.

anchovies	māhi ye koli	ماهی کولی
caviar	khāviyār	خاویار
(fresh) fish	māhi (ye tāze)	ماهی (تازه)
prawns	meygu	میگو
trout	ghezel ālā	قزل آلا
sardines	sārdin	ساردین
tuna	ton e māhi	تن ماهی

Vegetables

سبزیجات

beans	lubiyā	لوبیا
cabbage	kalam	کلم
carrot	havij	هویج
cauliflower	gol e kalam	گل کلم
celery	karafs	کرفس
cucumber	khiyār	خیار
eggplant	bādemjun	بادمجان
green beans	lubiyā sabz	لوبیا سبز
green pepper	felfel sabz	فلفل سبز
lettuce	kāhu	کاهو
okra	bāmiye	بامیه
mushroom	ghārch	قارچ
onion	piyāz	پیاز
peas	nokhod	نخود
potato	sib zamini	سیب زمینی
red beans	lubiyā ghermez	لوبیا قرمز
spinach	esfenāj	اسفناج
tomato	goje farangi	گوجه فرنگی
vegetables	sabzijāt	سبزیجات

FOOD

DID YOU KNOW ...

In spoken Persian, the verb khordan is used to mean both 'drinking' and 'eating'. The word nushidan, 'to drink', which is found in the written style of Persian, is no longer used in the spoken style.

Fruit & Nuts

میوه ها و آجیل

Fruit and nuts are served at almost every function and ceremony, and are commonly served with tea in Iranian homes.

almond	bādum	بادام
apple	sib	سیب
apricot	zard ālu	زرد آلو
banana	moz	موز
berry	tut	توت
cherry	gilās	گیلاس
coconut	nārgil	نارگیل
fig	anjir	انجیر
fruit	mive	میوه
grape	angur	انگور
grapefruit	gripfurut	گریپ فروت
hazelnut	fandogh	فندق
kiwifruit	kivi	کیوی
lemon	limu	لیمو
mandarin	nārengi	نارنگی
melon	kharboze	خربزه
nut	ājil	آجیل
orange	porteghāl	پرتقال
peach	hulu	هلو
pear	golābi	گلابی
peanut	bādum zamini	بادام زمینی
pineapple	ānānās	آناناس
pistachio	peste	پسته
plum	ālu	آلو
pomegranate	anār	انار
strawberry	tut farangi	توت فرنگی
sultana	keshmesh	کشمش
watermelon	hendune	هندوانه

FOOD

Spices & Condiments

ادویه ها و چاشنی ها

cinnamon	dārchin	دارچین
fruit jam	morabbā	مربا
garlic	sir	سیر
lemon	limu	لیمو
mayonnaise	sos e māyonez	سوس مایونز
oil	roghan	روغن
olive	zeytun	زیتون
olive oil	roghan e zeytun	روغن زیتون
pickled vegetables	torshi	ترشی
red peppers	felfel e ghermez	فلفل قرمز
saffron	za'ferān	زعفران
salt	namak	نمک
sugar	shekar	شکر
turmeric	zard chube	زردچوبه
vinegar	serke	سرکه

FOOD

FOOD

DRINKS
نوشیدنی ها

Iran has no bars or bottle shops, and due to Islamic law, no alcoholic drinks are served. The most popular drink in Iran is tea, which is served with cubed sugar instead of plain sugar. Tea is normally drunk black.

coffee	ghahve	قهوه
fruit juice	āb mive	آب میوه
soft drink	nushābe	نوشابه
tea	chāyi	چایی
yogurt drink	dugh	دوغ

... water	āb e ...	آب ...
boiled	jush	جوش
mineral	ma'dani	معدنی
tap	shir	شیر

with/without ...	bā/bedun e ...	با/بدون ش...
milk	shir	شیر
sugar	shekar	شکر

> **DID YOU KNOW ...**
> According to Islamic law, Muslims are forbidden to eat or drink anything containing pork, alcohol, blood or the meat of any animal which has died of natural causes.

Many mountains in Iran are good for hiking, including the Alborz mountains and the volcanic Mt Damāvand. Both these mountains are accessible from Tehran.

CAMPING
چادر زدن

backpack	kule poshti	کوله پشتی
camping	chādor zadan	چادر زدن
campsite	mahall e chādor zadan	محل چادر زدن
can opener	dar bāzkon	در باز کن
compass	ghotb namā	قطب نما
fire wood	ojāgh e hizomi	اجاق هیزمی
hammer	chakkosh	چکش
mat	hasir/pādari	حصیر/پادری
mattress	toshak	تشک
rope	tanāb	طناب
sleeping bag	kise khāb	کیسه خواب
stove	ojāgh	اجاق
tent	chādor	چادر
tent peg	mikh e chādor	میخ چادر
torch (flashlight)	cherāgh ghovve	چراغ قوه
water bottle	botri ye āb	بطری آب

Do you have any campsites available?
  [shomā] jāyi barāye chādor
  zadan dārin?
(شما) جایی برای چادر
زدن دارید؟

How much is it per person/tent?
  barāye har nafar/chādor
  cheghadr migirin?
برای هر نفر/چادر
چقدر می گیرید؟

Where can I hire a tent?
  [man] kojā mitunam ye
  chādor kerāye konam?
(من) کجا می توانم یک
چادر کرایه کنم؟

IN THE COUNTRY

Can we camp here?
  [ma] mitunim injā chādor
  bezanim?

(ما) می توانیم اینجا چادر
بزنیم؟

Who owns this land?
  in zamin māl e ki ye?

این زمین مال کی هست؟

Can I talk to her/him?
  [man] mitunam bā un
  sohbat konam?

(من) می توانم با او
صحبت کنم؟

Are there shower facilities?
  injā dush dāre?

اینجا دوش دارد؟

Can we light a fire here?
  [mā] mitunim injā ātish
  roshan konim?

(ما) می توانیم اینجا آتش
روشن کنیم؟

Where's the electric hookup?
  piriz e bargh kojā st?

پریز برق کجاست؟

Where's the shower/toilet?
  dush/tuvālet kojā st?

دوش/توالت کجاست؟

Where can I have my gas
cylinder filled?
  [man] kojā mitunam kapsul
  e gāz am o por konam?

(من) کجا می توانم کپسول
گازم را پر کنم؟

HIKING

پیاده روی

Are there any tourist attractions
near here?
  in nazdikiyā jāhāye didani
  barāye turistā hast?

این نزدیکی ها جاهای دیدنی
برای توریست ها هست؟

Where's the nearest village?
  nazdik tarin deh kojā st?

نزدیک ترین ده کجاست؟

Is it safe to climb this mountain?
  bālā raftan az in
  kuh bikhatar e?

بالا رفتن از این کوه بی خطر هست؟

Is there a hut up there?
  panāhgāhi dar un bālā hast?

پناهگاهی در آن بالا هست؟

Do we need a guide?
  [mā] rāhnamā lāzem dārim?

(ما) راهنما لازم داریم؟

We'd like to talk to someone
who knows this area.

(ما) می خواهیم با یک نفر که

  [mā] mikhāyim bā ye nafar ke
  in mantaghe ro mishnāse
  sohbat konim

این منطقه را می شناسد
صحبت کنیم

How long is the trail?

این سفر چقدر طول می کشد؟

  in safar cheghdr tul mikeshe?

Is the track well marked?

مسیر خوب علامت

  masir khub alāmat
  gozāri shode?

گذاری شده ؟

How high is the climb?

ارتفاع چقدر است؟

  ertefā cheghadr e?

Which is the shortest/
easiest route?

کوتاه/آسان ترین

  kutāh/āsun tarin
  rāh kodum e?

راه کدام است؟

Is the path open?

مسیر باز است؟

  masir bāz e?

When does it get dark?

هوا کی تاریک می شود؟

  havā key tārik mishe?

Is it very scenic?

(آن) خوش منظره است؟

  [un] khosh manzare ast?

Where can we buy supplies?

(ما) از کجا می توانیم

  [mā] az kojā mitunim
  vasāyel bekharim?

وسایل بخریم؟

On the Path

در طول مسیر

Where have you come from?

(شما) از کجا آمدید؟

  [shomā] az kojā umadin?

How long did this route take you?

این مسیرچقدر برای

  in masir cheghadr barāye
  shomā tul keshid?

شما طول کشید؟

Does this path go to ...?

این راه به ... می رود؟

  in rāh be ... mire?

I'm lost.

(من) گم شده ام

  [man] gom shodam

Where can we spend the night?

[mā] kojā mitunim shab
o bemunim?

(ما) کجا می توانیم شب
را بمانیم؟

Can I leave some things here for a while?

[man] mitunam chizāyi ro
barāye moddati injā bezāram?

(من) می توانم چیزهایی
را برای مدتی اینجا بگذارم؟

altitude	ertefā'	ارتفاع
backpack	kule poshti	کوله پشتی
binoculars	durbin	دوربین
candle	sham'	شمع
to climb	bālā raftan	بالا رفتن
compass	ghotb namā	قطب نما
downhill	sarāziri	سرازیری
first-aid kit	ja'be ye komakhā ye avvaliyye	جعبه کمک های اولیه
gloves	dastkesh	دستکش
guide	rāhnamā	راهنما
guided trek	safar e rāhnamāyi shode	سفر راهنمایی شده
hiking	piyāde ravi	پیاده روی
hiking boots	putin e piyāde ravi	پوتین پیاده روی
hunting	shekār	شکار
ledge	labe	لبه
lookout	cheshm andāz	چشم انداز
map	naghshe	نقشه
mountain climbing	kuh navardi	کوه نوردی
pick	kolang e kuh navardi	کلنگ کوه نوردی
provisions	tadārokāt	تدارکات
rock climbing	sakhre navardi	صخره نوردی
rope	tanāb	طناب
signpost	tāblo ye rāhnamā	تابلوی راهنما
steep	shib	شیب
trek	safar e piyāde ye tulāni	سفر پیاده طولانی
uphill	sar bālāyi	سربالایی
to walk	rāh raftan	راه رفتن

AT THE BEACH

در کنار دریا

There are a few sandy beaches in the north and south, and a few hotels on the coast along the Caspian Sea have private beaches. Men and women must swim and sunbathe in segregated areas.

Can we swim here?
[mā] mitunim injā shenā konim?

(ما) می توانیم اینجا شنا کنیم؟

Is it safe to swim here?
shenā kardan dar injā amn e?

شنا کردن در اینجا امن است؟

What time is high/low tide?
che mogheyi jazromad mishe?

چه موقعی جذر و مد می شود؟

IN THE COUNTRY

coast	sāhel	ساحل
fishing	māhi giri	ماهی گیری
rock	sakhre	صخره
sand	shen	شن
sea	daryā	دریا
snorkelling	ghavvāsi	غواصی
sunblock	kerem e zedd e āftāb	کرم ضد آفتاب
sunglasses	eynak e āftābi	عینک آفتابی
surf	moj	موج
surfing	moj savāri	موج سواری
surfboard	takhte ye moj savāri	تخته ی موج سواری
swimming	shenā	شنا
towel	hole	حوله
waterskiing	eski ru ye āb	اسکی روی آب
waves	amvāj	امواج
windsurfing	bād savāri	باد سواری

IN THE COUNTRY

Diving
غواصی

Are there good diving sites here?
اینجا جاهای خوب برای غواصی هست؟
injā jāhāye khub barāye
ghavvāsi hast?

Can we hire a diving boat/guide?
(ما) می توانیم یک قایق/
[mā] mitunim ye ghāyegh/
rāhnamā ye ghavvāsi kerāye?
راهنمای غواصی کرایه کنیم؟
konim?

We'd like to hire some diving equipment.
(ما) می خواهیم وسایل
[mā] mikhāyim vasāyel e
ghavvāsi kerāye konim
غواصی کرایه کنیم

I'm interested in exploring wrecks.
(من) به جستجوی کشتی های
[man] be josteju ye keshtihā
ye ghargh shode alāghe dāram
علاقه دارمغرق شده

scuba diving	ghavvāsi bā dastgāh e oksizhen	غواصی با دستگاه اکسیژن

WEATHER
هوا

Iran is a country of different climates. In the north and south, the
weather is humid and warm. The west and north-west are cold,
with large snowfalls in winter, while the centre is dry and temperate.
Nevertheless, you can find four distinct seasons in each part of Iran.

What's the weather like?
havā chetore?
هوا چطور است؟

Today it's ...	emruz havā ... e	امروز هوا ... است
cloudy	abri	ابری
cold	sard	سرد
hot	dagh	داغ
warm	garm	گرم
windy	bādi	بادی

It's raining heavily/lightly.
bārun e shadidi/kami miyād
باران شدیدی/کمی می آید

It's flooding.
مثل سیل باران می آید

    mesle seyl bārun miyād

to freeze	yakh zadan	یخ زدن
ice	yakh	یخ
snow	barf	برف
snowy	barfi	برفی
storm	tufān	طوفان
sun	āftāb	آفتاب
typhoon	gerdbād	گردباد
weather	havā	هوا
wind	bād	باد

IN THE COUNTRY

SEASONS		
spring	bahār	بهار
summer	tābestun	تابستان
autumn	pāyiyz	پاییز
winter	zemestun	زمستان

IN THE COUNTRY

GEOGRAPHICAL TERMS

اصطلاحات جغرافیایی

beach	sāhel	ساحل
bridge	pol	پل
cave	ghār	غار
cliff	sakhre	صخره
earthquake	zelzele	زلزله
farm	mazre'e	مزرعه
footpath	radd e pā	رد پا
forest	jangal	جنگل
gap (narrow pass)	shekāf	شکاف
harbour	eskele	اسکله
hill	tappe	تپه
hot spring	cheshme ye āb garm	چشمه آب گرم
house	khune	خانه
island	jazire	جزیره
lake	daryāche	دریاچه
mountain	kuh	کوه
mountain path	masir e kuh	مسیر کوه
pass	ma'bar	معبر
peak	gholle	قله
river	rudkhune	رودخانه
sea	daryā	دریا
valley	darre	دره
waterfall	ābshār	آبشار

FAUNA
Farm Animals

جانوران
حیوانات اهلی

calf	gusāle	گوساله
camel	shotor	شتر
cat	gorbe	گربه
chicken	juje	جوجه
cockerel	juje khurus	جوجه خروس
cow	gāv	گاو
dog	sag	سگ
donkey	olāgh/khar	الاغ/خر
duck	ordak	اردک
goat	boz	بز

goose	ghāz	غاز
hen	morgh	مرغ
horse	asb	اسب
sheep	gusfand	گوسفند
lamb	barre	بره
pigeon	kaftar/kabutar	کفتر/کبوتر

Wildlife

حیوانات وحشی

You'll be able to see most of these animals if you travel to remote countryside or visit a national park.

badger	gurkan	گورکن
bear	khers	خرس
deer	āhu	آهو
fish	māhi	ماهی
fox	rubāh	روباه
ibex (wild goat)	boz e kuhi	بز کوهی
lion	shir	شیر
pig	khuk	خوک
rabbit	khargush	خرگوش
reindeer	gavazn	گوزن
snake	mār	مار
tiger	babr	ببر
wolf	gorg	گرگ

Birds

پرندگان

bird	parande	پرنده
buzzard	lāshkhor	لاشخور
crow	kalāgh	کلاغ
eagle	oghāb	عقاب
harrier (bird of prey)	bāz	باز
owl	joghd	جغد
partridge	kabk	کبک
quail	belderchin	بلدرچین
sparrow	gonjeshk	گنجشک
stork	laklak	لک لک
vulture	karkas	کرکس
woodpecker	dārkub	دارکوب

IN THE COUNTRY

Insects

حشرات

ant	murche	مورچه
butterfly	parvāne	پروانه
cockroach	susk	سوسک
fly	magas	مگس
leech	zālu	زالو
mosquito	pashe	پشه
spider	ankabut	عنکبوت

FLORA & AGRICULTURE

نباتات و کشاورزی

agriculture	keshāvarzi	کشاورزی
barley	jo	جو
corn	zorrat	ذرت
cotton	panbe	پنبه
crops	mahsul	محصول
farmer	keshāvarz	کشاورز
flower	gol	گل
greenhouse	golkhune	گلخانه
to harvest	bardāsht/dero	برداشت/درو
irrigation	ābyāri	آبیاری
leaf	barg	برگ
planting (sowing)	kāshtan	کاشتن
rice field	shālizār	شالیزار
sunflower	āftābgardān	آفتاب گردان
tobacco	tanbāku	تنباکو
tree	derakht	درخت
village(r)	rustā(yi)	روستا(یی)
wheat	gandom	گندم

HEALTH

Every city and town has private and public health services. The bigger the city, the better the health services. Healthcare facilities can't usually be found in villages.

Where's the ...?	... kojā st?	... کجاست؟
chemist	dārukhune	داروخانه
dentist	dandun pezeshk	دندان پزشک
doctor	doktor	دکتر
hospital	bimārestān	بیمارستان

Can the doctor come here?
doktor mitune injā biyād?　　　دکتر می تواند اینجا بیاید؟

AT THE DOCTOR　　　در مطب دکتر

I'm sick.　　　**mariz am**　　　مریض هستم

My friend is sick.　　　**dust am mariz e**　　　دوست ام مریض است

I need a doctor who speaks English.
[man] ye doktor lāzem dāram　　　(من) یک دکتر لازم دارم
ke ingilisi balad bāshe　　　که انگلیسی بلد باشد

It hurts here.
unjā dard mikone　　　آنجا درد می کند

I feel better/worse.
hāl am behtar/badtar e　　　حالم بهتر/بدتر است

HEALTH

THE DOCTOR MAY SAY ...

chi shode?
چی شده؟
What's the matter?

hāletun chetor e?
حالتون چطوره؟
How do you feel?

dard dāri?
درد داری؟
Do you feel any pain?

kojā dard mikone?
کجا درد می کند؟
Where does it hurt?

tab dāri?
تب داری؟
Do you have a temperature?

chand vaghte ke
چند وقته که اینجوری
injuri hasti?
هستی؟
How long have you
been like this?

ghablan injuri shodi?
قبلاً اینجوری شدی؟
Have you had this before?

dāru masraf mikoni?
دارو مصرف می کنی؟
Are you on medication?

sigār mikeshi?
سیگار می کشی؟
Do you smoke?

mashrub mikhori?
مشروب میخوری؟
Do you drink?

mavādde mokhadder
مواد مخدر مصرف می کنی؟
masraf mikoni?
Do you take drugs?

be chizi hassāsiyat dāri?
به چه چیزی حساسیت داری؟
Are you allergic to
anything?

bārdār hasti?
باردار هستی؟
Are you pregnant?

periyod i?
پریودی؟
Are you menstruating?

AILMENTS

بیماری ها

I'm ill.
   [man] mariz am

(من) مریض هستم

I feel nauseous.
   hālat e tahavvo' dāram

حالت تهوع دارم

I've been vomiting.
   estefrāgh mikonam

استفراغ می کنم

I've burnt my (hand).
   [man] (dast) am sukhte

(من) (دست) ام سوخته

My (foot) is infected.
   [man] (pā) yam ufunat karde

(من) (پا) یم عفونت کرده

I've sprained my (ankle).
   [man] (moch e pā)
   yam pich khorde

(من) (مچ پا)
یم پیچ خورده

I have sunburn.
   [man] āftāb sukhte shodam

(من) آفتاب سوخته شده ام

I have a cough.
   [man] sorfe mikonam

(من) سرفه می کنم

I've caught a cold.
   sarmā khordam

سرما خورده ام

I can't sleep.
   nemitunam bekhābam

نمی توانم بخوابم

I feel ...	[man] ehsās e ... mikonam	(من) احساس ... می کنم
dizzy	sargije	سرگیجه
shivery	larz	لرز
weak	za'f	ضعف

HEALTH

AH CHOO!

If somebody sneezes, it's customary to say:
   āfiyat bāshe, 'Bless you!'
   (lit: may it be useful to your health).

The sneezer should say in return:
   kheyli mamnun

e (a/an) ...	[man] ... dāram	(من) ... دارم
allergy	hassāsiyat	حساسیت
anaemia	kam khuni	کم خونی
bite (insect)	nish	نیش
bite (dog)	gāz	گاز
burn	sukhtegi	سوختگی
cancer	saratān	سرطان
cold	sarmā khordegi	سرما خوردگی
constipation	yubusat	یبوست
cystitis	kist	کیست
diarrhoea	es-hāl	اسهال
fever	tab	تب
gastroenteritis	eltehāb e me'de vo rude	التهاب معده و روده
headache	sardard	سردرد
heart condition	nārāhati ye ghalbi	ناراحتی قلبی
indigestion	su' e hāzeme	سو هاضمه
lice	shepesh	شپش
migraine	migren	میگرن
pain	dard	درد
sore throat	galu dard	گلو درد
stomachache	me'de dard	معده درد
toothache	dandun dard	دندان درد
urinary tract infection	ufunat e majāri ye edrāri	عفونت مجاری ادراری
venereal disease	bimāri ye urughi	بیماری عروقی
worms	kerm	کرم

HEALTH

USEFUL PHRASES

عبارات مفید

I feel better/worse.

   hāl am behtar/badtar e

حالم بهتر/بدتر است

I usually take this medicine.

   [man] ma'mulan in dāru
   ro masraf mikonam

(من) معمولاً این دارو را مصرف می کنم

I've been vaccinated.

   [man] vāksan zadam

(من) واکسن زده ام

I don't want a blood transfusion.

[man] tazrigh e khun
nemikhām

(من) تزریق خون
نمی خواهم

Can I have a receipt for my insurance?

mishe barāye bime be man
resid bedin?

می شود برای بیمه به من
رسید بدهید؟

WOMEN'S HEALTH

بهداشت زنان

Could I be examined by a female doctor?

mishe ye doktor e zan man
o mo'āyene kone?

می شود یک دکتر زن
مرا معاینه بکند؟

I'm pregnant.

[man] hāmele/bārdār am

(من)حامله/ باردار هستم

I think I'm pregnant.

fekr mikonam hāmele/bārdār am

فکر می کنم باردار هستم

I'm on the Pill.

[man] ghors e zedd e
hāmelegi mikhoram

(من) قرص ضد
حاملگی می خورم

I haven't had my period for ... weeks.

... hafte ast ke periyod
nashodam

... هفته است که پریود
نشده ام

I'd like to get the Pill.

mikhām ghors e zedd e
hāmelegi begiram

می خواهم قرص ضد
حاملگی بگیرم

abortion	seght e janin	سقط جنین
cystic fibrosis	fibroz e kisti	فیبروز کیستی
cystitis	kist	کیست
diaphragm	diyāfrāgm	دیافراگم
IUD	āyudi	آیودی
mammogram	māmogrām	ماموگرام
menstruation	ādat e māhāne/periyod	عادت ماهانه/پریود
miscarriage	seght	سقط
pap smear	pāp esmeyr	پاپ اسمیر
period pain	dard e periyod	درد پریود
the Pill	ghors e zedd e hāmelegi	قرص ضد حاملگی
ultrasound	sonogerāfi	سونوگرافی

HEALTH

SPECIAL HEALTH NEEDS   نیازهای بهداشتی خاص

I have ...	[man] ... dāram	(من) ... دارم
anaemia	kam khuni	کم خونی
asthma	āsm	آسم
diabetes	diyābet	دیابت
I'm allergic to ...	[man] be ...	(من) به ...
	hassāsiyat dāram	حساسیت دارم
antibiotics	āntibiyutik	آنتی بیوتیک
aspirin	āsperin	آسپرین
bees	zanbur	زنبور
codeine	kode'in	کودئین
dairy products	labaniyyāt	لبنیات
penicillin	penisilin	پنی سیلین
pollen	garde	گرده

I have a skin allergy.
  [man] ye hassāsyat e
  pusti dāram
(من) یک حساسیت
پوستی دارم

I have my own syringe.
  [man] khod am sorang dāram
(من) خودم سرنگ دارم

I'm on medication for ...
  [man] barāye ... dāru masraf
  mikonam
(من) برای ... دارو مصرف می کنم

I need a new pair of glasses.
  [man] ye eynak e tāze
  lāzem dāram
(من) یک عینک تازه
لازم دارم

addiction	e'tiyād	اعتیاد
bleeding	khun rizi	خون ریزی
blood pressure	feshār e khun	فشار خون
(high/low)	(bālā/pāyin)	(بالا/پایین)
blood test	āzemāyesh e khun	آزمایش خون
contraceptive	zedd e hāmelegi	ضد حاملگی
injection	tazrigh	تزریق
injury	jarāhat	جراحت
operation	amal e jarrāhi	عمل جراحی
pill	ghors	قرص
to vomit	estefrāgh	استفراغ
X-ray	aksbardāri	عکسبرداری
wound	zakhm	زخم

ALTERNATIVE TREATMENTS   درمان های جایگزین

acupuncture	tebbe suzani	طب سوزنی
faith healer	shafā bakhsh	شفا بخش
herbalist	doktor e giyāhi	دکتر گیاهی
massage	māsāzh	ماساژ
meditation	mediteyshen	مدیتیشن
yoga	yogā	یوگا

HEALTH

DID YOU KNOW ... Persepolis, the ancient city of Persian kings, was once called Pārsā. Persepolis meant both 'city of Pārsā' and 'Persian city' as well as 'the destroyer of cities'. Persepolis is also known as Takht e Jamshid or the 'Throne of Jamshid'.

PARTS OF THE BODY

اعضای بدن

ankle	moch e pā	مچ پا
appendix	āpāndis	آپاندیس
arm	bāzu	بازو
back	posht	پشت
bladder	masāne	مثانه
blood	khun	خون
bone	ostukhun	استخوان
chest	sine	سینه
ear	gush	گوش
eye	cheshm	چشم
finger	angosht	انگشت
foot	pā	پا
hand	dast	دست
head	sar	سر
heart	ghalb	قلب

kidney	koliye	کلیه
knee	zānu	زانو
leg	sāgh	ساق
liver	kabed	کبد
lung	riye	ریه
mouth	dahan	دهان
muscle	azole	عضله
rib	dande	دنده
shoulder	shune	شانه
skin	pust	پوست
stomach	me'de	معده
tooth	dandun	دندان
throat	galu	گلو
vein	rag	رگ

AT THE CHEMIST

در داروخانه

I need medicine for ...
[man] dāruyi barāye ...
mikhām

(من) دارویی برای ... می خواهم

Does this medicine need a
prescription?
in dāru noskhe lāzem dāre?

این دارو نسخه لازم دارد؟

Are there any side effects?
avārez e jānebi dāre?

عوارض جانبی دارد؟

How many times a day?
chand bār dar ruz?

چند بار در روز؟

THEY MAY SAY ...

har shish sā'at ye bār
Once every six hours.

هر شش ساعت یک بار

(chāhār) bār dar ruz
(Four) times a day.

(چهار) بار در روز

---

antibiotics	āntibiyutik	آنتی بیوتیک
antiseptic	zedd e ufuni konande	ضد عفونی کننده
aspirin	āsperin	آسپرین
bandage	bāndāzh	باندإژ
condom	kāndom	کاندوم
contraceptive	zedd e hāmelegi	ضد حاملگی
cotton ball	panbe	پنبه
cough medicine	dāruye sorfe	داروی سرفه
gauze	gāz	گاز
laxatives	molayyen	ملین
painkillers	mosakken	مسکن
rubbing alcohol	alkol	الکل
sleeping pills	ghors e khāb	قرص خواب
vitamins	vitāminhā	ویتامین ها

HEALTH

AT THE DENTIST

در دندان پزشکی

I have a toothache.
[man] dandun am dard mikone

(من) دندان ام درد می کند

I have a cavity.
dandun am surākh shode

دندان ام سوراخ شده

I've lost a filling.
tu ye dandun e por
shode am oftāde

توی دندان پر
شده ام افتاده

I've broken my tooth.
dandun am shekaste

دندان ام شکسته

My gums hurt.
lase am dard mikone

لثه ام درد می کند

I don't want it extracted.
nemikhām un o bekishin

نمی خواهم آنرا بکشید

Please give me an anaesthetic.
lotfan be man ye bihess
konande bedin

لطفاً به من یک بی حس
کننده بدهید

IT MAY HURT ...		
Ouch!	ākh!	آخ

HEALTH

DISABLED TRAVELLERS

مسافران معلول

Iran has few facilities for disabled people, and these are limited to wheelchair access in government offices and some hotels. However, since the war with Iraq – during which many Iranians were injured – more attention is being given to the needs of the disabled.

I'm disabled/handicapped.
[man] ma'lul am
(من) معلول ام

I need assistance.
[man] komak lāzem dāram
(من) کمک لازم دارم

What services do you have for disabled people?
[shomā] barāye ma'lulin che khademāti dārin?
(شما) برای معلولین چه خدماتی دارید؟

Can I go there by wheelchair?
[man] mitunam bā sandali ye charkhdār unjā beram?
(من) می توانم با صندلی چرخدار آنجا بروم؟

I'm deaf. Speak more loudly, please.
[man] nāshenavā hastam. lotfan bolandtar sohbat konin
(من) ناشنوا هستم. لطفاً بلند تر صحبت کنید

I can lip-read.
[man] mitunam labkhāni konam
(من) می توانم لب خوانی کنم

I have a hearing aid.
[man] sam'ak dāram
(من) سمعک دارم

braille library	ketābkhune ye bereyl	کتابخانه بریل
disabled person	fard e ma'lul	فرد معلول
wheelchair	sandali ye charkhdār	صندلی چرخدار

TRAVELLING WITH A FAMILY

مسافرت با خانواده

Are there facilities for babies?
    tas-hilāti barāye nozādān
    vujud dāre?

تسهیلاتی برای نوزادان
وجود دارد؟

Do you have a child-minding service?
    [shomā] mahalli barāye negahdāri
    ye bachchehā dārin?

(شما) محلی برای نگهداری
بچه ها دارید؟

Where can I find a (English-speaking)
babysitter?
    [man] kojā mitunam kesi ro
    (ke ingilisi balad bāshe)
    barāye negahdāri ye bachche
    peydā konam

(من) کجا می توانم کسی را
(که انگلیسی بلد باشد) برای
نگهداری بچه پیدا کنم؟

Can you put an (extra) bed/cot in
the room?
    mishe ye takht/takht e bachche
    (ezāfe) dar otāgh bezārin?

می شود یک تخت/تخت بچه
(اضافه) در اتاق بگذارید؟

I need a car with a child seat.
    [man] ye māshin mikhām ke
    sandali ye bachche dāshte bāshe

(من) یک ماشین می خواهم
که صندلی بچه داشته باشد

Is it suitable for children?
    un barāye bachchehā
    monāseb e?

آن برای بچه ها مناسب
هست؟

Are there any activities for children?
    barāye bachchehā hich
    sargarmiyi hast?

برای بچه ها هیچ
سرگرمی ای هست؟

Is it a family discount?
    barāye khānevāde
    takhfifi hast?

برای خانواده ها
تخفیفی هست؟

Are children allowed?
    bachehā ro mizārin?

بچه ها را می گذارید؟

Do you have food suitable for
children?
    [shomā] ghazāye monāseb
    barāye bachchehā dārin?

(شما) غذای مناسب
برای بچه ها دارید؟

LOOKING FOR A JOB

گشتن برای شغل

Finding a job is difficult for tourists. But you may find work as a private English tutor.

Where can I find job advertisements?
   [man] kojā mitunam āgahihā
     ye kār o bekhunam

(من) کجا می توانم آگهی
های کار را بخوانم؟

I've come about the position advertised.
   [man] barāye kāri ke āgahi
     kardin umadam

(من) برای کاری که آگهی
کرده اید آمده ام

I'm ringing about the position advertised.
   [man] barāye kāri ke āgahi
     kardin zang mizanam

(من) برای کاری که آگهی
کرده اید زنگ می زنم

Do I need a work permit?
   [man] bāyad ejāze ye kār
     dāshte bāsham?

(من) باید اجازه کار
داشته باشم؟

I've had experience.
   [man] tajrobe ye kār dāram

(من) تجربه کار دارم

What's the wage?
   hughugh esh cheghadr e?

حقوق اش چقدر است؟

Do I have to pay tax?
   [man] bāyad māliyāt bedam?

(من) باید مالیات بدهم؟

I can start ...	[man] mitunam ...	(من) می توانم ...
	shuru' konam	شروع کنم
today	emruz	امروز
tomorrow	fardā	فردا
next week	hafte ye ba'd	هفته بعد

HIP TO BE SQUARE

Because the subject of a sentence is indicated in the verb, subject pronouns are optional. In this phrasebook, subject pronouns appear in square brackets.

SPECIFIC NEEDS

casual	movaghghati	موقتی
employee (office)	kārmand	کارمند
employee (factory)	kārgar	کارگر
employer	kārfarmā	کار فرما
full-time	tamām vaght	تمام وقت
job	shoghl	شغل
occupation/trade	herfe	حرفه
part-time	nime vaght	نیمه وقت
résumé	sharh e savābegh	شرح سوابق
traineeship	kar āmuzi	کار آموزی
work experience	tajrobe ye kār	تجربه کار

ON BUSINESS

برای تجارت

We're attending a ...	mā dar ye ... sherkat	ما در یک ... شرکت
	mikonim	می کنیم
conference	konferāns	کنفرانس
meeting	jalase	جلسه
trade fair	namāyeshgāh	نمایشگاه بازرگانی
	e bāzargāni	

I have an appointment with ...
  [man] bā ... gharār dāram   (من) با ... قرار دارم

Here's my business card.
  in kārt e bāzargāni ye man e   این کارت بازرگانی من است

I need an interpreter.
  [man] ye motarjem lāzem dāram   (من) یک مترجم لازم دارم

I need to use a computer.
  [man] ye kāmpiyuter   (من) یک کامپیوتر
  lāzem dāram   لازم دارم

I need to send a fax/an email.
  [man] mikhām ye faks/   (من) می خواهم یک فاکس/
  imeyl beferestam   ای میل بفرستم

client	arbāb ruju'	ارباب رجوع
colleague	hamkār	همکار
distributor	tozi' konande	توزیع کننده
email	imeyl	ای میل
exhibition	namāyeshgāh	نمایشگاه
manager	modir	مدیر
mobile phone	telfon e hamrāh/	تلفن همراه/
	mobāyl	موبایل
profit	sud	سود
proposal	tarh	طرح

ON TOUR

برای گردش

We're part of a group.
　mā joz' e ye guruh im

ما جزو یک گروه هستیم

We're tourists.
　[mā] jahāngard/turist im

(ما) جهانگرد/توریست هستیم

I'm with the ...　[man] bā ... am

(من) با ... هستم

group	guruh	گروه
band	guruh e musighi	گروه موسیقی
team	tim	تیم
crew	khadame	خدمه

Please speak with our manager.
　lotfan bā modir e mā
　sohbat konin

لطفاً با مدیر ما
صحبت کنید

We've lost our equipment.
　[mā] vasāyel emun
　o gom kardim

(ما) وسایل مان
را گم کرده ایم

We sent equipment　[mā] vasāyel emun
on this ...　　　　o bā in ... ferestādim

(ما) وسایل مان را با
این ... فرستادیم

bus	utubus	اتوبوس
flight	parvāz	پرواز
train	ghatār	قطار

FILM & TV CREWS

گروه فیلم و تلویزیون

We're on location.
  [mā] dar mahall e film
  bardāri hastim

(ما) در محل فیلم
برداری هستیم

We're filming!
  [mā] film migirim

(ما) فیلم می گیریم

Can we film here?
  mishe injā film begirim?

می شود اینجا فیلم بگیریم؟

We're making a ...	mā ye ... misāzim	ما یک ... می سازیم
documentary	film e mostanad	فیلم مستند
film	film	فیلم
TV series	majmu'e ye televiziyoni	مجموعه تلویزیونی

PILGRIMAGE & RELIGION

زیارت و مذهب

Discussing religion is OK, as long as you're respectful toward the local Islamic faith.

What's your religion?	din e shomā chi ye?	دین شما چیست؟

I'm ...	[man] ... am	(من) ... هستم
Buddhist	budāyi	بودایی
Christian	masihi	مسیحی
Hindu	hendu	هندو
Jewish	yahudi	یهودی
Muslim	mosalmun	مسلمان

I'm (Catholic), but not practising.
  [man] (kātolik) am, vali ādāb
  e maz-habi ro anjām nemidam

(من) (کاتولیک) هستم ولی آداب
مذهبی را انجام نمی دهم

I believe in God.
  [man] be khodā mo'taghed am

(من) به خدا معتقدم

I believe in destiny/fate.
[man] be sarnevesht/
taghdir mo'taghed am

(من) به سرنوشت/
تقدیر معتقدم

I'm interested in astrology/
philosophy.
[man] be tāle' bini/falsafe
alāghe dāram

(من) به طالع بینی/فلسفه
علاقه دارم

Can I attend this service/mass?
[man] mitunam dar in
marāsem sherkat konam?

(من) می توانم در این
مراسم شرکت کنم؟

Can I pray here?
[man] mitunam injā ebādat
konam?

(من) می توانم در اینجا
عبادت کنم؟

Where can I pray/worship?
[man] kojā mitunam ebādat
konam?

(من) کجا می توانم
عبادت کنم؟

TOWERS OF SILENCE

Zoroastrianism was the major religion in Iran until it was
lost after the Arab Conquest (637 AD). Founded in the late
seventh or early sixth century BC by the prophet Zoroaster,
it was one of the first religions to follow an omnipotent god.
Today, only around 150,000 people follow the religion,
many of whom still live in or around the city of Yazd.

Some customs and beliefs remain entrenched in modern
Iranian life. Many pre-Islamic monuments display Zoroastrian
symbols, and today this symbolism features in Iranian art.
Fire is worshipped as a symbol of God, and 'eternal' flames
are kept burning in temples.

Believing in the purity of natural elements, Zoroastrians
refused to bury or cremate their dead to avoid polluting the
earth or the atmosphere. Instead, corpses were left exposed
on 'towers of silence' to be disposed of by vultures. These
days, Zoroastrians are often buried in concrete-lined graves
to prevent 'contamination' of the earth.

church	kelisā	کلیسا
funeral	marāsem e tadfin	مراسم تدفین
god	khodā	خدا
monk	rāheb	راهب
prayer	do'ā/ebādat	دعا/عبادت
priest	keshish	کشیش
shrine	maghbare	مقبره

TRACING ROOTS & HISTORY

پیدا کردن
شجره و تاریخچه

(I think) my ancestors came from this area.

    (fekr mikonam) ajdād e man
    az in mantaghe hastan

(فکر می کنم) اجداد من
از این منطقه هستند

I'm looking for my relatives.

    [man] donbāl e aghvām am
    migardam

(من) دنبال اقوام ام
می گردم

I had a relative who lived around here.

    [man] ye fāmili dāshtam ke
    injāhā zendegi mikard

(من) یک فامیلی داشتم ک
ه اینجا ها زندگی می کرد

Is there anyone here with the name of ...?

    injā kesi be esm e ... hast?

اینجا کسی به اسم ... هست؟

I'd like to go to the cemetery/ burial ground.

    [man] mikhām be ghurestān
    e injā beram

(من) می خواهم به
گورستان اینجا بروم

TIME, DATES & FESTIVALS

زمان، تاریخ و جشن ها

TELLING THE TIME

گفتن ساعت

Telling time in Persian is similar to telling time in English. The main difference is that you need to say daghighe, 'minute', after the number of minutes. So, if you want to indicate minutes to the hour, say the number of minutes first, then daghighe, 'minutes', then be, 'to', and lastly, the number of the hour.

five minutes to four
panj daghighe be chāhār
(lit: five minutes to four)

پنج دقیقه به چهار

To indicate minutes past the hour, first say the hour, then o, 'and', then the number of minutes, and lastly daghighe.

45 minutes past five
panj o chehel o panj daghighe
(lit: five and forty and five minutes)

پنج و چهل و پنج دقیقه

What time is it?	sā'at chand e?	ساعت چند است؟
It's one o'clock.	sā'at yek e	ساعت یک است
It's ten o'clock.	sā'at dah e	ساعت ده است
Half past one.	yek o nim	یک و نیم
Half past five.	panj o nim	پنج و نیم

It's 14.15.
sā'at chāhārdah o punzdah daghighe ast

ساعت چهارده و پانزده دقیقه است

It's 20 minutes to 12.
sā'at bist daghighe be davāzdah e

ساعت بیست دقیقه به دوازده است

The bus leaves at 10 past five.
   utubus panj o dah daghighe
   harekat mikone

اتوبوس پنج و ده دقیقه
حرکت می کند

The train should arrive at 18
minutes to six.
   ghatār bāyad hijdah daghighe
   be shish berese

قطار باید هیجده دقیقه
به شیش برسد

alarm clock	sā'at e zangdār	ساعت زنگ دار
clock	sā'at e divāri	ساعت دیواری
hour	sā'at	ساعت
minute	daghighe	دقیقه
second	sāniye	ثانیه
time	vaght/zamān	وقت/زمان
watch	sā'at	ساعت

DAYS

روزهای هفته

In Iran, the week starts on Saturday and ends on Friday, so the
weekend falls on Thursday and Friday. Schools and most state
offices are open on Thursdays.

Saturday	shanbe	شنبه
Sunday	yek shanbe	یک شنبه
Monday	do shanbe	دوشنبه
Tuesday	se shanbe	سه شنبه
Wednesday	chāhār shanbe	چهار شنبه
Thursday	panj shanbe	پنج شنبه
Friday	jom'e	جمعه

TIME, DATE & FESTIVALS

MONTHS

ماه ها

Three calendars are in common use in Iran. The official calendar is the Persian solar calendar, which is in everyday use. The Muslim lunar calendar is used for Islamic religious matters, while the Western (Gregorian) calendar is used when dealing with foreigners.

Persian Calendar

تقویم فارسی

The names of months in the Persian solar calendar originate from Zoroastrian history and the Persian Empire which dates back 2500 years. After the introduction of Islam, the calendar was adjusted to begin with the date of the Prophet Mohammed's migration from Mecca to Medina in 622 AD.

According to this calendar, a solar year has 12 months lasting 30 days each (366 every leap year).

The New Year begins on 21 March – the first day of the month of **farvardin** and the first month of spring. Sometimes 'AHS' is written after dates calculated according to the Persian calendar.

	Month	Begins	
Spring bahār	farvardin	21 March	فروردین
	ordibehesht	21 April	اردیبهشت
بهار	khordād	22 May	خرداد
Summer tābestun	tir	22 June	تیر
	mordād	23 July	مرداد
تابستان	shahrivar	23 August	شهریور
Autumn pāyiyz	mehr	23 September	مهر
	ābān	23 October	آبان
پاییز	āzar	22 November	آذر
Winter zemestun	dey	22 December	دی
	bahman	21 January	بهمن
زمستان	esfand	20 February	اسفند

TIME, DATES
& FESTIVALS

Western (Gregorian) Calendar		تقویم میلادی
January	zhānviye	ژانویه
February	fevriye	فوریه
March	mārs	مارس
April	āvril	آوریل
May	meh	مه
June	zhu'an	ژوئن
July	zhu'iye	ژوئیه
August	ut	اوت
September	septāmr	سپتامبر
October	oktobr	اکتبر
November	novāmr	نوامبر
December	desāmr	دسامبر

Muslim Calendar   تقویم قمری

Religious holidays normally follow the Muslim calendar. Based on the lunar year of 354 or 355 days, it's currently out of step with the Persian solar calendar by some 40 years.

moharram	محرم
safar	صفر
rabi'-ol-Avval	ربیع الا ول
rabi'-ol Akhar	ربیع الا آخر
jamādi-ol-Avval	جمادی الا ول
jamādi-ol-Akhar	جمادی الا آخر
rajab	رجب
sha'bān	شعبان
ramazān	رمضان
shavvāl	شوال
zi-l-Gha'de	ذی القعده
zi-l-Hajje	ذی الحجه

DATES

تاریخ

All official dates in Iran are taken from the Persian solar calendar (see page 169). Because the Persian calendar is completely different from that used in the West, most people won't be able to tell you the date without consulting a calendar. It's a good idea to carry a Persian-English calendar to convert the dates.

What date is it today?
emruz chandom e māh e?   امروز چندم ماه است؟
It's the 10th of Aban.
dahom e ābān e   دهم آبان است

PRESENT

حال

What day is today?	emruz che ruzi ye?	امروز چه روزی است
It's Tuesday.	emruz se shanbe ast	امروز سه شنبه است
now	hālā	حالا
this morning	emruz sob	امروز صبح
today	emruz	امروز
tonight	emshab	امشب
this week	in hafte	این هفته
this month	in māh	این ماه
this year	emsāl	امسال
early/late	zud/dir	زود/دیر
every hour/	har sā'at/	هر ساعت/
day/month	ruz/māh	روز/ماه

PAST

گذشته

(six hours) before	(shish sā'at) ghabl	(شش ساعت) قبل
(nine hours) after	(noh sā'at) ba'd	(نه ساعت) بعد
yesterday	diruz	دیروز
day before yesterday	pariruz	پریروز
yesterday morning	diruz sob	دیروز صبح
last night	dishab	دیشب
last week	hafte ye gozashte	هفته گذشته
last month	māh e gozashte	ماه گذشته
last year	pārsāl	پارسال

TIME, DATES
& FESTIVALS

FUTURE

آینده

in (20 minutes)
dar (bist daghighe)

در (بیست دقیقه)

(three hours) from now
(se sā'at) ba'd az in

(سه ساعت) بعد از این

How many hours/minutes does it take?
chand sā'at/daghighe
tul mikeshe?

چند ساعت/دقیقه
طول می کشد؟

It takes ... hours/minutes.
... sā'at/daghighe tul mikeshe

... ساعت/دقیقه طول می کشد

It takes ... minutes.
... daghighe tul mikeshe

... دقیقه طول می کشد

When will you come back?
[shomā] key bar migardin?

(شما) کی بر می گردید؟

When will it be ready?
[un] key āmāde mishe?

(آن) کی آماده می شود؟

I'll stay for four days/weeks.
[man] chāhār ruz/
hafte mimunam

(من) چهار روز/
هفته می مانم

tomorrow	fardā	فردا
day after tomorrow	pas fardā	پس فردا
tomorrow morning	fardā sob	فردا صبح
tomorrow afternoon	fardā ba'd az zohr	فردا بعد ازظهر
tomorrow evening	fardā shab	فردا شب
next week/month	hafte/māh e ba'd	هفته/ماه بعد
next year	sāl e ba'd	سال بعد
soon; right away	bezudi/foran	بزودی/فوراً

DURING THE DAY

در طول روز

afternoon	ba'd az zohr	بعد ازظهر
dawn	sahar	سحر
day	ruz	روز
early	zud	زود
fast	tond	تند
midnight	nesf e shab	نصف شب
morning	sob	صبح
night	shab	شب
noon	zohr	ظهر
slow	kond	کند
sometimes	ba'zi mavāghe'	بعضی مواقع
sunrise	tulu'	طلوع
sunset	gurub	غروب

FESTIVALS (OFFICIAL NATIONAL HOLIDAYS)

جشن ها/اعیاد
(تعطیلات ملی رسمی)

eyd e fetr   عید فطر
the end of the Islamic fasting month of Ramadan. It occurs
at a different time each year, due to the difference between
the Islamic and Persian calendars.

eyd e ghorbān   عید قربان
like eyd e fetr, it occurs at a different time each year, due to the
difference between the Islamic and Persian calendars. Its origin
is in the story of Abraham, Ishmael and the sacrificial lamb.

eyd e noruz   عید نوروز
the New Year starts on 21 March, which is the first day of spring.
Celebrations last for 13 days. The first three days of the New
Year are official state holidays. Students are on holiday until the
13th day of the New Year. During this time, people visit relatives
and friends, eat sweets, and children receive gifts called eydi

sizdah bedar   سیزده بدر
the 13th of the new year, which is the last day of the festival.
People often go out for a family picnic.

Happy New Year!	sāl e no mobārak!	سال نو مبارک
Happy holiday!	eyd e shomā mobārak	عید شما مبارک
Here's to your health!	sad sāl be in sālhā!	صد سال به این سالها
	(lit: live 100 years like this!)	

ZOROASTRIAN CALENDAR

The Zoroastrian calendar operates around a solar year lasting 12 months of 30 days each (plus five additional days). The concept of the week has no place in this system. Each of the 30 days of the month is named after an angel or archangel. The 1st, 8th, 15th and 23rd of each month are holy days.

As in the Persian calendar, the Zoroastrian year begins in March at the vernal equinox. Many months of the Zoroastrian calendar have the same names as the Persian calendar.

WEDDINGS

عروسی ها

Congratulations!	tabrik migam!	تبریک می گویم
engagement	nāmzadi	نامزدی
honeymoon	māh asl	ماه عسل
wedding	arusi	عروسی
wedding anniversary	sālgard e ezdevāj	سالگرد ازدواج
wedding cake	keyk e arusi	کیک عروسی
wedding present	hedye ye arusi	هدیه عروسی

NUMBERS & AMOUNTS

ارقام و مقادیر

Persian numerals are written in Arabic, not Roman. Unlike Persian script, numbers are written from left to right. As prices and dates are written in Persian numerals, it's a good idea to learn at least the basics.

```
1 2 3 4 5 6 7 8 9 10
۱ ۲ ۳ ۴ ۵ ۶ ۷ ۸ ۹ ۱۰
```

CARDINAL NUMBERS

عددهای اصلی

1	yek	یک
2	do	دو
3	se	سه
4	chāhār	چهار
5	panj	پنج
6	shish	شش
7	haft	هفت
8	hasht	هشت
9	noh	نه
10	dah	ده
11	yāzdah	یازده
12	davāzdah	دوازده
13	sizdah	سیزده
14	chāhārdah	چهارده
15	punzdah	پانزده

NUMBERS

175

NUMBERS

16	shunzdah	شانزده
17	hifdah	هفده
18	hijdah	هیجده
19	nuzdah	نوزده
20	bist	بیست
21	bist o yek	بیست و یک
22	bist o do	بیست و دو
30	si	سی
40	chehel	چهل
50	panjāh	پنجاه
60	shast	شصت
70	haftād	هفتاد
80	hashtād	هشتاد
90	navad	نود
100	sad	صد
200	divist	دویست
300	sisad	سیصد
400	chāhārsad	چهار صد
500	punsad	پانصد
600	shishsad	ششصد
700	haftsad	هفتصد
800	hashtsad	هشتصد
900	nohsad	نهصد
1000	hezār	هزار
2000	do hezār	دو هزار
2200	do hezār o divist	دو هزار و دویست
45	chehel o panj	چهل و پنج
167	sad o shast o haft	صد و شصت و هفت
1320	hezār o sisad o bist	هزار و سیصد و بیست
1999	hezār o nohsad o navad o noh	هزار و نهصد و نود و نه
14800	chāhārdah hezār o hashtsad	چهارده هزار و هشتصد
one million	yek milyon	یک میلیون

ORDINAL NUMBERS

عددهای ترتیبی

To form an ordinal number, the suffix -om comes after the
number. The first three ordinal numbers are irregular.

1st	avval	اول
2nd	dovvom	دوم
3rd	sevvom	سوم
6th	shishom	ششم
13th	sizdahom	سیزدهم
20th	bistom	بیستم
58th	panjāh o hashtom	پنجاه و هشتم
100th	sadom	صدم
188th	sad o hashtād o hashtom	صد و هشتاد و هشتم

NUMBERS

FRACTIONS

كسرها

1/4	chārak/yek chāhārom	چارک/یک چهارم
1/3	sols/yek sevvom	ثلث/ یک سوم
1/2	nesf	نصف
3/4	se chāhārom	سه چهارم

USEFUL WORDS

كلمات مفيد

all	hame	همه
double	dogāne/dobarābar	دوگانه/دوبرابر
a dozen	dojin	دوجین
few	kam	کم
less	kamtar	کمتر
many	kheyli	خیلی
more	bishtar	بیشتر
none	hich	هیچ
some	ba'zi	بعضی

NUMBERS

موارد اضطراری

Help!	komak!	کمک
Stop!	ist!	ایست
Go away!	gom sho!	گم شو
Thief!	dozd!	دزد
Fire!	ātish!	آتش
Watch out!	movāzeb bāsh!	مواظب باش
It's an emergency!	ezterāri ye!	اضطراری است
I'm lost.	[man] gom shodam	(من) گم شده ام
Where's the toilet?	tuvālet kojā st?	توالت کجاست؟
Call the police!	polis o khabar konin!	پلیس را خبر کنید

Could you help us, please?
   mitunin lotfan be mā   می توانید لطفاً به ما
   komak konin?   کمک کنید؟
Could I use the telephone?
   lotfan mishe ye telefon bezanam?   لطفاً می شود یک تلفن بزنم؟
Where's the police station?
   edāre ye polis kojā st?   اداره پلیس کجاست؟

DEALING WITH
THE POLICE

سروکارداشتن با
پلیس

Iranian police are generally helpful toward tourists, so don't hesitate to ask their help when necessary. Remember that Islam doesn't differentiate between the secular and religious lives of people.

We want to report an offence.
   [mā] mikhāyim ye khalāfkāri   (ما) می خواهیم یک خلاف
   ro gozāresh bedim   کاری را گزارش بدهیم
I've been raped/assaulted.
   man mored e tajāvoz/aziyyat   من مورد تجاوز/اذیت
   gharār gereftam   قرار گرفته ام
I've been robbed.
   vasāyel am dozdide shode   وسایل ام دزدیده شده

My ... was/were stolen.   ... am dozdide shode   ... ام دزدیده شده
backpack	kule poshti	کوله پشتی
bags/handbag	kifhhā/kif dasti	کیف ها/کیف دستی
money	pul	پول
papers	madārek	مدارک
travellers cheque	chek e mosāferati	چک مسافرتی
passport	pāsport/gozarnāme	پاسپورت/گذرنامه
wallet	kif e pul	کیف پول

My possessions are insured.
   dārāyi ye man bime ast   دارایی من بیمه است

I'm sorry./I apologise.
   ma'zerat mikham   معذرت می خواهم

I didn't realise I was doing anything wrong.
   [man] nafahmidam ke kār
   e eshtebāhi mikonam   (من) نفهمیدم که کار اشتباهی می کنم

I didn't do it.
   [man] in kār o nakardam   (من) این کار را نکردم

We're innocent.
   mā bigonāh im   ما بیگناه ایم

I want to contact my embassy/consulate.
   [man] mikham bā
   sefārat/konsulgari khod am
   tamās begiram   (من) می خواهم با سفارت/کنسول گری خودم تماس بگیرم

Can I call someone?
   [man] mitunam be kesi zang
   bezanam?   (من) می توانم به کسی زنگ بزنم؟

Can I have a lawyer who speaks English?
   [man] mitunam ye vakil e
   ingilisi zabān begiram?   (من) می توانم یک وکیل انگلیسی زبان بگیرم؟

Is there a fine we can pay to clear this?
   mishe barāye in khalāf jarime
   bedim?   می شود برای این خلاف جریمه بدهیم؟

I know my rights.
   [man] hughugh e khod am
   o midunam   (من) حقوق خودم را می دانم

EMERGENCIES

What am I accused of? [man] be che jormi mottahem am?		(من) به چه جرمی متهم هستم؟
I understand.	mifahmam	می فهمم
I don't understand.	namifahmam	نمی فهمم

THEY MAY SAY ...

[shomā/un] be jorm e ... mohākeme khāhid/khāhad shod You'll/(S)he'll be charged with ...		(شما/آن) به جرم ... محاکمه خواهید شد
fa'āliyat e zedd e dolati anti-government activity		فعالیت ضد دولتی
barham zadan e nazm disturbing the peace		بر هم زدن نظم
dashtan e (mavādd e gheyr e ghānuni) possession (of illegal substances)		داشتن (مواد غیر قانونی)
tamām shodan e vizā/ravādid overstaying your visa		تمام شدن ویزا/روادید
kār e bedun e ejāze working without a permit		کار بدون اجازه

aziyyat	assault	اذیت
vurud e gheyr	illegal entry	ورود غیر قانونی
ghatl	murder	قتل
nadāshtan e vizā/ravādid	not having a visa	نداشتن ویزا/روادید
tajāvoz	rape	تجاوز
dozdi	robbery	سرقت
dozdi az maghāze	shoplifting	دزدی از مغازه
serghat	theft	دزدی
takhallof e rānandegi	traffic violation	تخلف رانندگی

EMERGENCIES

arrested	dastgir shode	دستگیر شده
cell	sellul	سلول
consulate	konsulgari	کنسول گری
embassy	sefārat	سفارت
fine	jarime	جریمه
guilty	moghasser/gonāhkār	مقصر/گناه کار
lawyer	vakil	وکیل
not guilty	bigonāh	بیگناه
police officer	ma'mur e polis	مامور پلیس
police station	edāre ye polis	اداره پلیس
prison	zendān	زندان
trial	dādgāh	دادگاه

HEALTH　بهداشت

Call a doctor!
　ye doktor khabar konin!　یک دکتر خبر کنید
Call an ambulance!
　ye āmbulāns khabar konin!　یک آمبولانس خبر کنید
I'm ill.
　[man] mariz am　(من) مریض هستم
My friend is ill.
　dust e man mariz e　دوست من مریض است
I have medical insurance.
　[man] bime ye darmāni dāram　(من) بیمه درمانی دارم

(See also page 149 for more Health phrases.)

The transliteration of Persian vocabulary is based on the spoken style, while standard Persian is used in the script. When there's more than one Persian entry for an English word, they are separated by a bullet. When two entries are interchangeable, they are separated by a slash.

again	dobāre • bāz	دوباره • باز
to cancel	laghv/kansel kardan	لغو/کنسل کردن
(meaning either laghv kardan or kansel kardan)		

A آ

able (to be); can	tavānestan	توانستن

Can (may) I take your photo?
[man] mitunam aks e shomā ro begiram?

(من) می توانم عکس شما را بگیرم؟

Can you show me on the map?
[shomā] mitunin ru ye naghshe be man neshun bedin?

(شما) می توانید روی نقشه به من نشان بدهید؟

aboard	ru/tu ye	روی/توی
abortion	seght e janin	سقط جنین
above	bālāye • ru ye	بالای • رو ی
abroad	khārej	خارج
to accept	paziroftan • ghabul kardan	پذیرفتن • قبول کردن
accident	tasādof	تصادف
accommodation	mahall e sukunat	محل سکونت
ache	dard	درد
across	arz • sartāsar e	عرض • سرتاسر
actor	bāzigar	بازیگر
activist	amal gerā	عمل گرا
addict	mo'tād	معتاد
addiction	e'tiyād	اعتیاد
address	ādres	آدرس
to admire	tahsin kardan	تحسین کردن
admission	paziresh • ghabul	پذیرش • قبول

to admit	paziroftan • ghabul kardan	پذیرفتن • قبول کردن
adult	bozorgsāl • bālegh	بزرگسال • بالغ
advantage	emtiyāz	امتیاز
advice	tosye	توصیه
aeroplane	havāpeymā	هواپیما
to be afraid	tarsidan az	ترسیدن از
after	ba'd	بعد

[in the] afternoon
ba'd az zohr

بعد از ظهر

[this] afternoon
emuruz ba'd az zohr

امروز بعد از ظهر

again	dobāre • bāz	دوباره • باز
against	moghābel • ruberu	مقابل • روبرو
age	senn	سن
aggressive	parkhāshgar	پرخاشگر

[a while] ago
[chand lahze] pish/ghabl

(چند لحظه) پیش/قبل

[half an hour] ago
[nim sā'at] pish/ghabl

(نیم ساعت) پیش/قبل

[three days] ago
[se ruz] pish/ghabl

(سه روز) پیش/قبل

to agree	movāfegh budan	موافق بودن

I don't agree.
[man] mokhālef am

(من) مخالفم

Agreed!	ghabul e!	قبوله
agriculture	keshāvarzi	کشاورزی
ahead	jelo	جلو
aid (help)	komak	کمک
AIDS	eydz	ایدز
air	havā	هوا
air-conditioned	dārāye tahviye ye matbu'	دارای تهویه مطبوع
air mail	post e havāyi	پست هوایی
airport	furudgāh	فرودگاه
airport tax	avārez e furudgāh	عوارض فرودگاه
alarm clock	sā'at e zangdār	ساعت زنگ دار
all	hame	همه
an allergy	hassāsiyat	حساسیت
to allow	ejāze dādan	اجازه دادن
It's allowed.		
[un] mojāz e	(آن) مجاز است	
It's not allowed.		
[un] mojāz nist	(آن) مجاز نیست	
almost	taghriban	تقریباً
alone	tanhā	تنها
already	pish az in • tā hāl	پیش از این • تا حال
also	ham	هم
altitude	ertefā'	ارتفاع
always	hamishe	همیشه
amateur	gheyr e herfe yi • āmātor	غیر حرفه ای • آماتور
ambassador	safir	سفیر
among	beyn	بین
anaemia	kam khuni • ānemi	کم خونی • آنمی
anarchist	harj o marj talab • ānārshist	هرج و مرج طلب • آنارشیست
ancient	bāstāni	باستانی
and	va	و
and (col)	o	و
angry	asabāni	عصبانی
animal	heyvun	حیوان
ankle	moch e pā	مچ پا
annual	sāliyāne	سالیانه
answer	javāb	جواب
answering	javāb dādan	جواب دادن
ant	murche	مورچه
antenna (TV)	ānten	آنتن
antibiotics	āntibiyutik	آنتی بیوتیک
antinuclear	zedd e haste yi	ضد هسته ای
antique	atighe	عتیقه
antiseptic	zedd e ufuni konande	ضد عفونی کننده
any	har • hich	هر • هیچ
appendix (written)	zamime	ضمیمه
appendix (body part)	āpāndis	آپاندیس
appetisers	eshtehā āvar	اشتهاآور
appointment	garār • va'de	قرار • وعده
April	āvril	آوریل
archaeology	bāstān shenāsi	باستان شناسی
architect	me'mār • ārshitekt	معمار • آرشیتکت
architecture	me'māri	معماری
to argue (reasoning)	estedlāl kardan	استدلال کردن
to argue (fight)	da'vā kardan	دعوا کردن
arm	bāzu	بازو
to arrive	residan	رسیدن
arrival	vurud	ورود
art	honar	هنر
art gallery	namāyeshgāh e honari	نمایشگاه هنری
artist	honar mand	هنرمند
artwork	kār e honari	کار هنری
as big as	be bozorgi ye	به بزرگی
ashtray	zir sigāri	زیر سیگاری
to ask (for something)	khāstan	خواستن
to ask (a question)	porsidan	پرسیدن
aspirin	āsperin	آسپرین
asthmatic	āsmi	آسمی

B

astronaut	fazā navard	فضانورد
astronomer	setāre shenās	ستاره شناس
atmosphere	javv	جو
August	ut	اوت
aunt		
(maternal)	khāle	خاله
(paternal)	amme	عمه
automatic teller machine (ATM)	āber bānk	عابر بانک
autumn	pāyiz	پاییز
avenue (street)	bulvār	بلوار
awful	vahshatnāk	وحشتناک

B ب

baby	nozād	نوزاد
baby food	ghazā ye nozād	غذای نوزاد
baby powder	pudr e bachche	پودر بچه
babysitter	morāgheb e bachche	مراقب بچه
back (body)	posht	پشت
at the back (behind)	dar posht	در پشت
backpack	kule poshti	کوله پشتی
bad	bad	بد
badger	gurkan	گورکن
bag	kif	کیف
baggage	bār	بار
baggage claim	tahvil gereftan e bār	تحویل گرفتن بار
bakery	nunvāyi	نانوایی
balcony	bālkon	بالکن
ball	tup	توپ
ballet	bāle	باله
band (music)	guruh e musighi	گروه موسیقی
bandage	bāndāzh	باندا‌ژ
bank	bānk	بانک
banknote	eskenās	اسکناس
a bar; café	ghahve khune	قهوه خانه
basket	sabad	سبد

basketball	basketbāl	بسکتبال
bath	hamum • dush	حمام • دوش
bathing suit	māyo	مایو
bathroom	dast shuyi	دستشویی
battery	bātri	باطری
to be	budan	بودن
beach	sāhel	ساحل
beautiful	ghashang	قشنگ
because	chon	چون
bed	takht khāb	تختخواب
bedroom	otāgh khāb	اتاق خواب
bee	zanbur	زنبور
before	ghablan • ghabl az	قبلاً • از قبل
beggar	gedā	گدا
to begin	shuru' kardan	شروع کردن
behind	posht • aghab	پشت • عقب
below	zir • pāyin	زیر • پایین
beside	kenār • pahlu	کنار • پهلو
best	behtarin	بهترین
a bet	shart	شرط
better	behtar	بهتر
between	beyn • vasat	بین • وسط
bib	pishband	پیش بند
the Bible	enjil	انجیل
bicycle	docharkhe	دوچرخه
big	bozorg	بزرگ
bike (motor)	motorsiklet	موتورسیکلت
bill		
(shopping)	surat hesāb	صورت حساب
(electricity, phone, etc)	ghabz	قبض
billiards	bilyārd	بیلیارد
binoculars	durbin	دوربین
biography	sharh e hāl	شرح حال
bird	parande	پرنده
birth certificate	shenāsnāme	شناسنامه
birthday	ruz e tavallod	روز تولد
birthday cake	keyk e tavallod	کیک تولد
bite (dog)	gāz	گاز
bite (insect)	nish	نیش
black	siyāh	سیاه
B&W (film)	siyāh o sefid	سیاه و سفید

B

D
I
C
T
I
O
N
A
R
Y

blanket	patu	پتو
to bleed	khunrizi kardan	خونریزی کردن
to bless	do'ā ye kheyr kardan	دعای خیر کردن
Bless you! (when sneezing) āfiyat bāshe!		
		عافیت باشه
blind	nābinā • kur	نابینا • کور
a blister	tāval	تاول
blood	khun	خون
blood group	guruh e khuni	گروه خونی
blood pressure	feshār e khun	فشار خون
blood test	āzemāyesh e khun	آزمایش خون
blue	ābi	آبی
to board (ship, etc)	savār shodan	سوار شدن
boarding pass	kārt e savār shodan	کارت سوار شدن
boat	ghāyegh	قایق
body	badan	بدن
Bon appetit! nush e jān!		نوش جان
Bon voyage! safar be kheyr!		سفر بخیر
bone	ostukhun	استخوان
book	ketāb	کتاب
to book (make a booking)	rezerv kardan	رزرو کردن
bookshop	ketāb furushi	کتاب فروشی
boots	putin • chakme	چکمه • پوتین
border	marz	مرز
bored	khaste	خسته
boring	khaste konande	خسته کننده
to borrow	gharz kardan	قرض کردن
both	har do	هر دو
bottle	botri	بطری
bottle opener	dar bāz kon	در باز کن
[at the] bottom	tah	ته

box	ja'be	جعبه
boxing	boks • mosht zani	بکس • مشت زنی
boy	pesar	پسر
boyfriend	dost pesar	دوست پسر
bra	korset	کرست
brake	tormoz	ترمز
branch	shākhe	شاخه
of brass	berenji	برنجی
brave	shojā'	شجاع
bread	nun	نان
to break	shekastan	شکستن
breakfast	subhune	صبحانه
breast	pestun	پستان
to breathe	nafas keshidan	نفس کشیدن
a bribe	reshve	رشوه
to bribe	reshve dādan	رشوه دادن
bridge	pol	پل
brilliant	fogholāde • āli	فوق العاده • عالی
to bring	āvordan	آوردن
broken	shekaste	شکسته
broken (out of order)	kharāb	خراب
bronchitis	boronshit • zātorriye	برونشیت • ذات الریه
brother	barādar	برادر
brown	ghahveyi	قهوه ای
a bruise	kuftegi	کوفتگی
bucket	satl	سطل
Buddhist	budāyi	بودایی
bug	hashare	حشره
to build	sākhtan	ساختن
building	sākhtemun	ساختمان
bus	utubus	اتوبوس
bus station	termināl	ترمینال
bus stop	istgāh e utubus	ایستگاه اتوبوس
business	tejārat • bāzargāni	تجارت • بازرگانی
business person	tājer • bāzargān	تاجر • بازرگان
busy (crowded)	shulugh	شلوغ
busy (engaged)	mashghul	مشغول

C

but	ammā • vali	اما • ولی
butterfly	parvāne	پروانه
button	dogme	دکمه
to buy	kharidan	خریدن

I'd like to buy ...
[man] mikhām ... be kharam

(من) می خواهم ... بخرم

Where can I buy a ticket?
[man] kojā mitunam ye belit
bekharam?

(من) کجا می توانم یک بلیط بخرم؟

C
س

cake shop	keyk furushi	کیک فروشی
calendar	taghvim	تقویم
calf	gusāle	گوساله
camera	durbin	دوربین
camera shop	durbin furushi	دوربین فروشی
to camp	chādor zadan	چادر زدن

Can we camp here?
[mā] mitunim injā chādor bezanim?

(ما) می توانیم اینجا چادر بزنیم؟

can (to be able)	tavānestan	توانستن

We can do it.
[mā] mitunim in kār o bekonim

(ما) می توانیم این کار را بکنیم

I can't do it.
[man] nemitunam in kār o bekonam

(من) نمی توانم این کار را بکنم

can (aluminum)	ghuti	قوطی
can opener	dar bāz kon	در باز کن
canary	ghanāri	قناری
to cancel	laghv/kansel kardan	لغو/کنسل کردن
candle	sham'	شمع
candy	shirni	شیرینی
car	māshin	ماشین

car registration	avārez e māshin	عوارض ماشین
to care (about something)	morāghebat karadan	مراقبت کردن
to care (for someone)	alāghemand budan	علاقه مند بودن
card	kārt	کارت

Careful!
movāzeb bāshin!

مواظب باشید

caring	mehrabun	مهربان
carpet	farsh	فرش
to carry	haml kardan	حمل کردن
carton	kārton	کارتن
cartoons	kārtun	کارتون
cash register	sandugh	صندوق
cashier	sandughdār	صندوقدار
cassette	navār • kāset	نوار • کاست
castle	ghal'e	قلعه
cat	gorbe	گربه
cathedral	kelisā	کلیسا
Catholic	kātolik	کاتولیک
cave	ghār	غار
CD	sidi	سی دی
to celebrate	jashn gereftan	جشن گرفتن
cemetery	ghabrestun • gurestān	قبرستان • گورستان
centimetre	sāntimetr	سانتیمتر
ceramic	serāmik	سرامیک
certificate	gavāhināme	گواهینامه
chair	sandali	صندلی
champagne	shāmpāyn	شامپاین
championship	ghahremāni	قهرمانی
chance	forsat	فرصت
to change	taghyir dādan • avaz kardan	عوض کردن • تغییردادن
change (coins)	khurd	خرد
channel	kānāl	کانال
charming	faribande	فریبنده

to chat up	gap zadan	گپ زدن
cheap hotel	hotel e arzun	هتل ارزان
a cheat	taghallob	تقلب
Cheat!		
taghallob!		تقلب!
to check	kontorol •	کنترل •
	chek kardan	چک کردن
check-in	paziresh	پذیرش
(desk)		
Checkmate!		
kish māt!		کیش مات!
checkpoint	mahall e	محل
	bāzrasi	بازرسی
cheese	panir	پنیر
chemist	dārukhune	داروخانه
chess	shatranj	شطرنج
chessboard	safhe ye	صفحه
	shatranj	شطرنج
chest	sine	سینه
chewing gum	ādāms	آدامس
chicken	juje	جوجه
child	bachche	بچه
childminding	morāghebat	مراقبت
	az bachche	از بچه
children	bachchehā	بچه ها
chocolate	shokolāt	شکلات
to choose	entekhāb	انتخاب کردن
	kardan	
Christian	masihi	مسیحی
christian name	esm e kuchik	اسم کوچک
church	kelisā	کلیسا
cigarette	kāghaz	کاغذ سیگار
papers	e sigar	
cigarettes	sigār	سیگار
cinema	sinemā	سینما
circus	sirk	سیرک
citizenship	tāba'iyyat	تابعیت
city	shahr	شهر
city bus	utubus	اتوبوس
city centre	markaz e	مرکز شهر
	shahr	

civil rights	hughugh e	حقوق مدنی
	madani	
class	tabaghe	طبقه
classical art	honar e	هنر کلاسیک
	kelāsik	
classical	te'ātr e	تئاتر سنتی
theatre	sonnati	
clean	tamiz	تمیز
clean hotel	hotel e tamiz	هتل تمیز
cleaning	nezāfat	نظافت
client	arbāb ruju'	ارباب رجوع
cliff	sakhre	صخره
to climb	bālā raftan	بالا رفتن
cloak	abā	عبا
cloakroom	rakhtkan	رختکن
clock	sā'at e divāri	ساعت دیواری
to close	bastan	بستن
closed	baste	بسته
clothing	lebās	لباس
clothing store	lebās furushi	لباس فروشی
cloud	abr	ابر
cloudy	abri	ابری
clown	dalghak	دلقک
clutch (car)	kelāj	کلاج
coach (trainer)	morabbi	مربی
coast	sāhel	ساحل
coat	pālto	پالتو
cocaine	kokā'in	کوکائین
cockerel	juje khurus	جوجه خروس
cockroach	susk	سوسک
coin	sekke	سکه
a cold	sarmā	سرما خوردگی
	khordegi	
cold (adj)	sard	سرد
It's cold.		
(havā) sard e		هوا سرد است
to have a cold	sarmā	سرما خوردن
	khordan	
cold water	āb e sard	آب سرد
colleague	hamkār	همکار
college	kālej	کالج

C

colour	rang	رنگ
colour (film)	rangi	رنگی
comb	shune	شانه
to come	umadan	آمدن
comedy	komedi	کمدی
comfortable	rāhat	راحت
comics	kārikātor	کاریکاتور
communist	komonist	کمونیست
companion	hamrāh	همراه
company	sherkat	شرکت
compass	ghotb namā	قطب نما
computer game	bazi ye kāmpiyuteri	بازی کامپیوتری
a concert	konsert	کنسرت
confession (religious)	e'terāf	اعتراف
to confirm (a booking)	ta'yiyd kardan	تایید کردن

Congratulations!
mobārak e! — مبارک است

conservative	mohāfezekār	محافظه کار
to be constipated	yubusat dāshtan	یبوست داشتن
constipation	yubusat	یبوست
construction work	kār e sākhtemāni	کار ساختمانی
consulate	konsulgari	کنسول گری
contact lens	lenz e tamāsi • kāntakt lenz	لنز تماسی • کانتکت لنز
contraception	jelogiri az bārdāri	جلو گیری از بارداری
contraceptive	zedd e bārdāri	ضد بارداری
contract	gharārdād	قرارداد
convent	some'e	صومعه
to cook	pokhtan	پختن
corner	gushe	گوشه
corrupt	fāsed	فاسد
to cost	kharj dāshtan	خرج داشتن

How much does it cost to go to ...?
raftan be ... cheghadr kharj dāre?

رفتن به ... چقدر خرج دارد؟

It costs a lot.
kheyli kharj dāre — خیلی خرج دارد

cotton	katun	کتان
country	keshvar	کشور
countryside	yeylāgh	ییلاق
a cough	sorfe	سرفه
to count	shomordan	شمردن
coupon	kopon • zheton	کپن • ژتون
court (legal)	dādgāh	دادگاه
court (tennis)	meydun	میدان
cow	gāv	گاو
crafts	sanāye' e dasti	صنایع دستی
crafty	māher	ماهر
crag (wall of rock)	sakhre	صخره
crazy	divune	دیوانه
credit card	kārt e e'tebāri	کارت اعتباری
creep (slang)	murmur	مورمور
cricket (insect)	jirjirak	جیرجیرک
cross (religious)	salib	صلیب
(angry)	asabāni	عصبانی
a cuddle	baghal	بغل
cup	fenjun	فنجان
cupboard	ghafase ye lebās	قفسه لباس
curator	negahbun	نگهبان
current affairs	masā'el e jāri	مسائل جاری
customs	gomrok	گمرک
to cut	boridan	بریدن
to cycle	docharkhe savāri kardan	دوچرخه سواری کردن
cycling	docharkhe savāri	دوچرخه سواری
cyclist	docharkhe savār	دوچرخه سوار
cystitis	kist	کیست

DICTIONARY

D

dad	bābā	بابا
daily	ruzāne	روزانه
dairy products	labaniyyāt	لبنیات
to dance	raghsidan	رقصیدن
dancing	raghs	رقص
dangerous	khatarnāk	خطرناک
dark		
(light)	tārik	تاریک
(colour)	tire	تیره
date		
(appointment)	gharār • va'de	قرار • وعده
(time)	tārikh	تاریخ
to date (someone)	gharār dāshtan	قرار داشتن
date of birth	tārikh e tavallod	تاریخ تولد
daughter	dokhtar	دختر
dawn	sahar	سحر
day	ruz	روز
day after tomorrow pas fardā		پس فردا
day before yesterday pariruz		پریروز
in (six) days dar (shish) ruz		در (شش) روز
dead	morde	مرده
deaf	nāshenavā • kar	ناشنوا • کر
to deal (trade)	mo'āmele kardan	معامله کردن
to deal with	residegi kardan	رسیدگی کردن
death	marg	مرگ
December	desāmr	دسامبر
to decide	tasmim gereftan	تصمیم گرفتن
deck (of cards)	dast (e varagh)	دست (ورق)
deep	amigh	عمیق

deer	āhu	آهو
deforestation	jangal zodāyi	جنگل زدایی
degree	daraje	درجه
delay	ta'khir	تاخیر
delicatessen	khār o bār furushi	خوار و بار فروشی
delirious	hazyān gu	هزیان گو
democracy	demokrāsi	دمکراسی
demonstration	tazāhorāt • rāhpeymāyi	تظاهرات • راهپیمایی
dental floss	nakh e dandun	نخ دندان
dentist	dandun pezeshk	دندان پزشک
to deny	enkār kardan	انکار کردن
deodorant	zedd e aragh	ضد عرق
to depart (leave)	tark kardan	ترک کردن
department store	furushgāh e zanjireyi	فروشگاه زنجیره ای
departure	harekat	حرکت
descendent	olād • nasl	اولاد • نسل
desert	biyābun	بیابان
design	tarh	طرح
destination	maghsad	مقصد
to destroy	kharāb kardan	خراب کردن
detail	joz'iyyāt	جزئیات
diabetic	diyābeti	دیابتی
dial tone	zang	زنگ
diarrhoea	es-hāl	اسهال
diary	daftar e khāterāt	دفتر خاطرات
dice/die	takhte nard	تخته نرد
dictionary	diksheneri • farhang e loghat	دیکشنری • فرهنگ لغت
to die	mordan	مردن
different	motafāvet	متفاوت
difficult	moshkel	مشکل
dining room (in a home)	otāgh e ghazākhori	اتاق غذا خوری
dinner	shām	شام
direct	mostaghim	مستقیم

director	modir	مدیر
dirty	kasif	کثیف
disabled	nātavān • ma'lul	ناتوان • معلول
disadvantage	mahrumiyat	محرومیت
discount	takhfif	تخفیف
to discover	kashf kardan	کشف کردن
discrimination	tab'iz	تبعیض
disease	bimāri	بیماری
distributor	tozi' konande	توزیع کننده
diving	ghavvāsi	غواصی
diving equipment	vasāyel e ghavvāsi	وسایل غواصی
dizzy	gij	گیج
to do	kardan	کردن

What are you doing?
chikār mikonin? چکار می کنید؟
I didn't do it.
[man] un kār o nakardam (من) آن کار و نکردم

doctor	doktor	دکتر
a documentary	mostanad	مستند
dog	sag	سگ
doll	arusak	عروسک
door	dar	در
double	dogāne • dobarābar	دوگانه • دوبرابر
double bed	takht e do khābe	تخت دو خوابه
double room	otāgh e do khābe	اتاق دو خوابه
a dozen	dojin	دوجین
drama	derāmā	دراما
dramatic	barjaste • derāmātik	برجسته • دراماتیک
draught	khoshk sāli	خشکسالی
to draw	keshidan	کشیدن
to draw (a drawing)	naghghāshi kardan	نقاشی کردن
to dream	khāb didan	خواب دیدن
dress	lebās	لباس
a drink	nushābe	نوشابه
to drink (pol)	nushidan	نوشیدن

to drink (inf)	khordan	خوردن
to drive	rāndan	راندن
driver's licence	gavāhināme ye rānandegi	گواهینامه رانندگی
drum	tabl	طبل
to be drunk	mast budan	مست بودن
to dry (clothes)	khoshk kardan	خشک کردن
duck	ordak	اردک
dummy (baby's)	pestunak	پستانک

E / ای

each	har kodum • har yek	هرکدوم • هر یک
eagle	oghāb	عقاب
ear	gush	گوش
early	zud	زود

It's early.
zud e زود است

to earn	kasb kardan	کسب کردن
earrings	gushvāre	گوشواره
ear	gush	گوش
Earth	kore ye zamin	کره زمین
earth (soil)	zamin	زمین
earthquake	zelzele	زلزله
east	shargh	شرق
easy	āsun	آسان
to eat	khordan	خوردن
economy	eghtesād	اقتصاد
editor	virāstār	ویراستار
editor (in charge)	sardabir	سردبیر
education	āmuzesh	آموزش
eight	hasht	هشت
eighteen	hijdah	هجده
eighth	hashtom	هشتم
eighty	hashtād	هشتاد
elections	entekhābāt	انتخابات
electorate	hoze ye entekhābāti	حوزه انتخاباتی
electricity	bargh	برق
elevator	āsānsor	آسانسور

eleven	yāzdah	یازده
embarrassed	sharmande	شرمنده
embarrassment	sharmandegi	شرمندگی
embassy	sefārat	سفارت
emergency	ezterāri	اضطراری
employee (office)	kārmand	کارمند
(factory)	kārgar	کارگر
employer	kārfarmā	کارفرما
empty	khāli	خالی
end	ākhar • pāyān	آخر • پایان
to end	tamum shodan	تمام شدن
endangered species	gunehā ye dar hāl e nābudi	گونه های در حال نابودی
engagement (relations)	nāmzadi	نامزدی
engagement	mashguliyat	مشغولیت
engine	motor	موتور
engineer	mohandes	مهندس
engineering	mohandesi	مهندسی
England	ingilis	انگلیس
English	ingilisi	انگلیسی
to enjoy (oneself)	lezzat bordan	لذت بردن
enough	kāfi • bas	کافی • بس
Enough!	kāfiye!	کافی است
to enter	vāred shodan • tu raftan	شدن وارد • تو رفتن
entertaining	sargarm konande	سرگرم کننده
envelope	pākat	پاکت
environment	mohit	محیط
epileptic	sar'i	سرعی
equal	forsat e mosāvi	فرصت مساوی
opportunity		
equality	barābari • tasāvi	برابری • تساوی
equipment	vasile	وسیله
European	urupāyi	اروپایی
evening	shab	شب
every day	har ruz	هر روز
example	mesāl	مثال

For example, ...	barāye mesāl, ...	برای مثال ...
excellent	āli	عالی
exchange	tabdil • ta'viz	تبدیل • تعویض
to exchange	tabdil kardan	تبدیل کردن
exchange rate	nerkh e arz	نرخ ارز
to exclude	kenār gozāshtan	کنار گذاشتن
Excuse me. bebakhshid		ببخشید
to exhibit	neshun dādan	نشان دادن
exhibition	namāyeshghāh	نمایشگاه
exit	khuruj	خروج
expensive	gerun	گران
exploitation	bahrekeshi • estesmār	بهره کشی • استثمار
express	sari'	سریع
express mail	post e sari' • osseyr • ekspres	پست سریع • السیر • اکسپرس
eye	cheshm	چشم

F
اف

face	surat	صورت
factory	kārkhune	کارخانه
factory worker	kārgar	کارگر
fall (autumn)	pāyiyz	پاییز
family	khānevāde	خانواده
famous	mashhur • ma'ruf	مشهور • معروف
fan (hand-held)	panke	پنکه
fan (machine)	kuler	کولر
fans (of a team)	havādārān	هواداران
fantastic	āli	عالی
far	dur	دور
farm	mazre'e	مزرعه
farmer	keshāvarz	کشاورز

fast	tond	تند
fat (food)	charbi	چربی
fat (build)	chāgh	چاق
father	pedar	پدر
father-in-law		
(wife's side)	pedar zan	پدر زن
(husband's side)	pedar shohar	پدر شوهر
fault (someone's)	taghsir	تقصیر
faulty (equipment)	kharāb	خراب
fear	tars	ترس
February	fevriye	فوریه
to feel	ehsās kardan	احساس کردن
feelings	ehsāsāt	احساسات
fence	narde • hesār	حصار • نرده
fencing	shamshir bāzi	شمشیر بازی
festival	jashnvāre • eyd	جشنواره • عید
fever	tab	تب
few	kam	کم
fiancé(e)	nāmzad	نامزد
fiction	khiyāli	خیالی
field	mahdude • meydun	محدوده • میدان
fight	jang • da'vā	جنگ • دعوا
to fight	jang kardan	جنگ کردن
figures	arghām • ashkāl	ارقام • اشکال
to fill	por kardan	پر کردن
film (negatives/ cinema/ camera)	film	فیلم
film speed	sor'at e film	سرعت فیلم
films (movies)	film	فیلم
filtered	tasfiye shode	تصفیه شده
to find	peydā kardan	پیدا کردن
a fine	jarime	جریمه

finger	angosht	انگشت
fire	ātish	آتش
to fire	ekhrāj	اخراج
firewood	hizom	هیزم
first	avval	اول
first-aid kit	ja'be ye komakhā ye avvaliyye	جعبه کمک های اولیه
fish	māhi	ماهی
fish shop	māhi furushi	ماهی فروشی
five	panj	پنج
flag	parcham	پرچم
flat (land, etc)	sāf	صاف
flea	kak	کک
flashlight	cherāgh ghovve	چراغ قوه
flight	parvāz	پرواز
floor	kaf e zamin	کف زمین
floor (storey)	tabaghe	طبقه
flour	ārd	آرد
flower	gol	گل
flower seller	gol furush	گل فروش
fly	magas	مگس

It's foggy.
(havā) mehālud e (هوا) مه آلود است

to follow	donbāl/ peyravi kardan	دنبال/ پیروی کردن
food	ghazā	غذا
foot	pā	پا
football (soccer)	futbāl	فوتبال
footpath	radd e pā	رد پا
foreign	khāreji	خارجی
forest	jangal	جنگل
forever	hamishe	همیشه
to forget	farāmush kardan	فراموش کردن

I forgot.
[man] farāmush kardam (من) فراموش کردم

Forget about it! • Don't worry!
farāmush esh konin! فراموش اش کنید

G

to forgive	bakhshidan	بخشیدن
fortnight	do hafte	دو هفته
fortune teller	fālbin	فال بین
forty	chehel	چهل
four	chāhār	چهار
fourteen	chāhārdah	چهارده
fourth	chāhārom	چهارم
fox	rubāh	روباه
free		
(not bound)	āzād	آزاد
(of charge)	majjāni/moft	مجانی/مفت
to freeze	yakh zadan	یخ زدن
Friday	jom'e	جمعه
friend	dust	دوست
frozen food	ghazā ye yakh zade	غذای یخ زده
fruit	mive	میوه
fruit picking	mive chini	میوه چینی
full	por	پر
fun	sargarmi • tafrih	سرگرمی • تفریح

for fun
baraye sargarmi   برای سرگرمی
to have fun
tafrih kardan   تفریح کردن
to make fun of
maskhare kardan   مسخره کردن

| funeral | marāsem e tadfin | مراسم تدفین |
| future | āyande | آینده |

G · جی

game		
(games)	bāzi	بازی
(sport)	bāzi • mosābeghe	بازی • مسابقه
a game show	mosābeghe	مسابقه
garage	mekāniki	مکانیکی
garbage	āshghāl	آشغال
gardening	bāghbuni	باغبانی
garden	bāgh	باغ
gate	darvāze	دروازه

| gay | hamjes bāz e mard | همجنس باز مرد |
| general | umumi • hamegāni | عمومی • همگانی |

Get lost!
gom sho!   گم شو!

gift	hedye • kādo	هدیه • کادو
girl	dokhtar	دختر
girlfriend	dost dokhtar	دوست دختر
to give	dādan	دادن

Could you give me ...?
mishe be man ... bedin?
می شود به من ... بدهید؟

glass	shishe	شیشه
gloves	dastkesh	دستکش
to go	raftan	رفتن

Let's go.
berim   برویم
We'd like to go to ...
[mā] mikhāyim be ... berim
(ما) می خواهیم به ... برویم
Go straight ahead.
mostaghim berin   مستقیم بروید

goal	gol	گل
goalkeeper	darvāzebān	دروازه بان
goat	boz	بز
God	khodā	خدا
of gold	talāyi	طلایی

Good afternoon.
asr bekheyr   عصر بخیر
Good evening/night.
shab bekheyr   شب بخیر

| good hotel | hotel e khub | هتل خوب |

Good luck!
movaffagh bāshid!   موفق باشید
Good morning.
sob bekheyr   صبح بخیر
Goodbye.
khodā hāfez   خدا حافظ

goose	ghāz	غاز
gorilla	guril	گوریل
government	dolat	دولت
gram	geram	گرم
grandchild	nave	نوه
grandfather	pedar bozorg	پدر بزرگ
grandmother	mādar bozorg	مادر بزرگ
grapes	angur	انگور
graphic arts	honarhā ye tarsimi	هنرهای ترسیمی
grass	chaman	چمن
grave	ghabr • gur	قبر • گور
great	bozorg	بزرگ

Great!
āli ye! — عالیه!

green	sabz	سبز
greengrocer	sabzi furush	سبزی فروش
grey	khākestari	خاکستری
to guess	hads zadan	حدس زدن
guide (person/ audio)	rāhnamā	راهنما
guidebook	ketāb e rāhnamā	کتاب راهنما
guidedog	sag e rāhnamā	سگ راهنما
guinea pig	khukche ye di	خوکچه هندی
guitar	gitār	گیتار
gum	lūse	لثه
gym	sālon e varzesh	سالن ورزش
gymnastics	zimnāstik	ژیمناستیک

H
اچ

hair	mu	مو
hairbrush	bores	برس
half	nesf • nim	نصف • نیم
half a litre	nim litr	نیم لیتر
to halluci- nate	hazyān goftan	هذیان گفتن
ham	gusht e khuk	گوشت خوک

hammer	chakkosh	چکش
hammock	nanu	ننو
hand	dast	دست
handbag	kif dasti	کیف دستی
handicrafts	sanāye' e dasti	صنایع دستی
handmade	dast sāz	دست ساز
handsome	khosh ghiyāfe	خوش قیافه
happy	shād • khoshhāl	شاد • خوشحال

Happy birthday!
tavallod et mobārak! — تولدت مبارک!

harbour	langargāh	لنگرگاه
hard	seft	سفت
hard (not easy)	sakht	سخت
harrassment	āzār • aziyat	آزار • اذیت
to have	dāshtan	داشتن

Do you have ...?
[shoma] ... dārin? — (شما) ... دارید؟
I have ...
[man] ... dāram — (من) ... دارم

hayfever	tab e yonje	تب یونجه
he	u	او
head	sar	سر
a headache	sar dard	سردرد
health	salāmati • behdāsht	سلامتی • بهداشت
to hear	shenidan	شنیدن
hearing aid	sam'ak	سمعک
heart	ghalb	قلب
heat	garmā	گرما
heater	hiter • bokhāri	هیتر • بخاری
heavy	sangin	سنگین

Hello.
salām — سلام
Hello! (answering telephone)
alo! — الو

| helmet | kolāh e imani | کلاه ایمنی |

Help!
komak! — کمک!

to help	komak kardan	کمک کردن
hen	morgh	مرغ
hepatitis	hipātit	هیاتیت
herb	giyāh • alaf	گیاه • علف
herbalist	doktor e giyāhi	دکتر گیاهی
here	injā	اینجا
high	boland • bālā	بلند • بالا
high blood pressure	feshār e khun e bālā	فشار خون بالا
high school	dabirestān	دبیرستان
to hike	piyāde ravi kardan	پیاده روی کردن
hiking	piyāde ravi	پیاده روی
hiking boots	putin e piyāde ravi	پوتین پیاده روی
hiking routes	masirhā ye piyāde ravi	مسیر های پیاده روی
hill	tappe	تپه
Hindu	hendu	هندو
to hire	ejāre • kerāye kardan	اجاره • کرایه کردن
HIV positive	dārā ye eydz	دارای ایدز
holiday	ta'tili	تعطیلی
holidays	ta'tilāt	تعطیلات
homelessness	bikhānemāni	بی خانمانی
homosexual	hamjesbāz	همجنس باز
honey	asal	عسل
honeymoon	māh e asal	ماه عسل
horn	shākh	شاخ
horrible	vahshatnāk	وحشتناک
horse	asb	اسب
horse riding	asb savāri	اسب سواری
hospital	bimārestān	بیمارستان
hot	garm	گرم

It's hot.
(havā) garm e (هوا) گرم است

to be hot	garm budan	گرم بودن
hot water	āb e garm	آب گرم
house	khune	خانه
housework	kār e khune	کار خانه
how	chetor	چطور

How do I get to ...?
[man] chetor be ... beram?
(من) چطور به ... بروم؟

How do you say ...?
chetori migin ...?
چطوری می گویید ...؟

hug	baghal	بغل
human rights	hughugh e bashar	حقوق بشر
a hundred	sad	صد
to be hungry	gorosne budan	گرسنه بودن
husband	shohar	شوهر

I
آی

I	man	من
ice	yakh	یخ
ice axe	kolang e yakhshekan	کلنگ یخ شکن
ice cream	bastani	بستنی
identification	hoviyyat	هویت
identification card	kārt e shenāsāyi	کارت شناسایی
idiot	ahmagh	احمق
if	agar	اگر
ill	mariz • bimār	مریض • بیمار
immigration	mohājerat	مهاجرت
important	mohemm	مهم

It's important.
mohemm e مهم است
It's not important.
mohemm nist مهم نیست

in a hurry	ajale dashtan	عجله داشتن
in front of	dar jelo ye	در جلوی
to include	shāmel budan	شامل بودن
income tax	māliyāt bar darāmad	مالیات بر در آمد
incomprehensible	ghyr e ghābel e fahm	غیر قابل فهم
indicator	rāhnamā	راهنما

indigestion	su' e hāzeme	سوء هاضمه
industry	san'at	صنعت
inequality	nābarābari	نابرابری
to inject	tazrigh kardan	تزریق کردن
injection	tazrigh	تزریق
injury	zakhm	زخم
inside	dākhel	داخل
instructor	morabbi	مربی
insurance	bime	بیمه
intense	foshorde • shadid	فشرده • شدید
interesting	jāleb	جالب
intermission	vaghfe • maks	وقفه • مکث
international	beynolmelali	بین المللی
interview	mosāhebe	مصاحبه
Ireland	irland	ایرلند
island	jazire	جزیره
itch	khāresh	خارش
itinerary	safarnāme	سفرنامه
IUD	āyudi	آیودی

J

jack (for car)	jak	جک
jacket	cot	کت
jail	zendān	زندان
January	zhānviye	ژانویه
jar	shishe morabbā	شیشه مربا
jealous	hasud	حسود
jeans	jin	جین
jeep	jip	جیپ
jewellery	javāherāt	جواهرات
Jewish	yahudi	یهودی
job	shoghl • kār	شغل • کار
job advertisement	āgahi ye kār	آگهی کار
job centre	edāre ye kāryābi	اداره کاریابی
job description	sharh e vazāyef	شرح وظایف
jockey	asbsavār e herfeyi	اسب سوار حرفه ای

joke	jok • latife	جوک • لطیفه
to joke	shukhi kardan	شوخی کردن
journalist	ruznāme negār	روزنامه نگار
journey	mosāferat	مسافرت
judge	ghāzi	قاضی
juice	āb e mive	آب میوه
to jump	paridan	پریدن
jumper	poliver	پولیور
June	zhu'an	ژوئن
justice	edālat	عدالت

K

kebab shop	kabābi	کبابی
key	kelid	کلید
keyboard	safhe kelid	صفحه کلید
kick	lagad	لگد
kick off	shuru' e mosābeghe	شروع مسابقه
kidney	koliye	کلیه
to kill	koshtan	کشتن
kilogram	kilogeram	کیلو گرم
kilometre	kilometr	کیلو متر
kind	mehrabun	مهربان
kindergarten	kudakestān	کودکستان
king	shāh	شاه
kiss	buse	بوسه
kiss (inf)	māch	ماچ
to kiss	busidan • māch kardan	بوسیدن • ماچ کردن
kitchen	āshpazkhune	آشپزخانه
kitten	bachche gorbe	بچه گربه
knapsack	kule poshti	کوله پشتی
knee	zānu	زانو
knife	chāghu	چاقو
to know (someone)	shenākhtan	شناختن
(something)	dunestan	دانستن

I don't know.
[man] nemidunam   (من) نمی دانم

L
الـ

lace	band e kafsh	بند کفش
lake	daryāche	دریاچه
lamb	barre	بره
land	zamin	زمین
language	zabān	زبان
large	bozorg • vasi'	بزرگ • وسیع
last	ākhar • gozashte	آخر • گذشته
last month	māh e gozashte	ماه گذشته
last night	dishab • shab e gozashte	دیشب • شب گذشته
last week	hafte ye gozashte	هفته گذشته
last year	pārsāl • sāl e gozashte	پارسال • سال گذشته
late	dir	دیر
laugh	khande	خنده
launderette	māshin e lebās shuyi umumi	ماشین لباسشویی عمومی
law	ghānun	قانون
lawyer	vakil	وکیل
laxative	molayyen	ملین
laziness	tanbali	تنبلی
lazy	tanbal	تنبل
leaded (petrol/gas)	sorb dār	سرب دار
leader	rahbar	رهبر
league	jām e varzeshi	جام ورزشی
to learn	yād gereftan	یاد گرفتن
leather	charm	چرم
leather goods	vasāyel e charmi	وسایل چرمی
ledge	labe	لبه
to be left (behind/over)	jā mundan	جا ماندن
left (not right)	chap	چپ
left luggage	bār e jā munde	بار جا مانده
left-wing	jenāh e chap	جناح چپ

leg	sāgh e pā	ساق پا
legalisation	ghānuni sāzi	قانونی سازی
legislation	ghānun gozāri	قانون گذاری
lens	lenz • adasi	لنز • عدسی
lesbian	hamjensbāz e zan	همجنس باز زن
less	kam	کم
letter	nāme	نامه
letter (alphabet)	harf	حرف
liar	durugh gu	دروغ گو
library	ketābkhune	کتابخانه
lice	shepesh	شپش
to lie	durugh goftan	دروغ گفتن
life	zendegi	زندگی
lift (elevator)	āsānsor	آسانسور
light (n)	cherāgh	چراغ
light (adj)	sabok	سبک
light (sun/lamp)	nur	نور
light (clear)	roshan	روشن
light bulb	lāmp	لامپ
light meter	nur sanj	نور سنج
lighter	fandak	فندک
to like	dust dāshtan	دوست داشتن
line	khat	خط
lip	lab	لب
lipstick	rozh e lab • mātik	رژ لب • ماتیک
to listen	gush kardan	گوش کردن
little (small)	kuchik	کوچک
a little (amount)	kami • meghdāri	کمی • مقداری
a little bit	ye zarre	یک ذره
to live	zendegi kardan	زندگی کردن

Long live ...!
zende bād ...!
زنده با د ...

local	mahalli	محلی
local bus	utubus	اتوبوس
location	mahall	محل
lock	ghofl	قفل
to lock	ghofl kardan	قفل کردن

long	derāz •	دراز •
	tulāni	طولانی
long distance	rāh e dur	راه دور
long-distance bus	utubus e beyn e shahri	اتوبوس بین شهری
to look	negāh kardan	نگاه کردن
to look after	morāghebat kardan	مراقبت کردن
to look for	josteju kardan	جستجو کردن
lookout point	noghte ye cheshm andāz	نقطه چشم انداز
loose	shol	شل
to lose	bākhtan • shekast khordan	باختن • شکست خوردن
loser	bāzande	بازنده
loss	bākht • shekast	باخت • شکست
a lot	ziyād	زیاد
loud	boland	بلند
to love	dust • dāshtan āshegh budan	دوست داشتن عاشق بودن
lover	ma'shughe	معشوقه
low	pāyin	پایین
low blood pressure	feshār e khun e pāyin	فشار خون پایین
loyal	vafādār	وفادار
luck	shāns	شانس
lucky	khosh shāns	خوش شانس
luggage	bār	بار
lump	godde	غده
lunch	nāhār	ناهار
lunchtime	vaght e nāhār	وقت ناهار
luxury	khosh gozarāni • tajammol	خوش گذرانی • تجمل

M

macaroni/ noodles	mākāroni	ماکارونی
machine	dastgāh	دستگاه
mad	divune	دیوانه

made (of)	jens	جنس
magazine	majalle	مجله
magician	sho'bade bāz	شعبده باز
mail	post	پست
mailbox	sandogh e post	صندوق پست
main road	jadde ye asli	جاده اصلی
main square	meydun e asli	میدان اصلی
majority	aksariyyat	اکثریت
to make	sākhtan • dorost kardan	ساختن • درست کردن
make-up	ārāyesh	آرایش
man	mard	مرد
manager	modir	مدیر
manual worker (pol)	kārgar	کارگر
(inf)	amale	عمله
many	kheyli	خیلی
map	naghshe	نقشه

Can you show me on the map?
mitunin tu naghshe be man neshun bedin?

می توانید توی نقشه به من نشان بدهید؟

March	mārs	مارس
margarine	mārgārin	مارگارین
marital status	vaz'iyyat e ta'ahhol	وضعیت تاهل
market	bāzār	بازار
marriage	ezdevāj	ازدواج
to marry	ezdevāj kardan	ازدواج کردن
marvellous	āli	عالی
massage	māsāzh	ماساژ
mat	hasir	حصیر
match	mosābeghe	مسابقه
matches	kebrit	کبریت

[It doesn't] matter.
eyb nadāre

عیب ندارد

[What's the] matter?
chi shode?

چه شده؟

| mattress | toshak | تشک |
| maybe | shāyad | شاید |

May	meh	مه
mayor	shahr dār	شهردار
mechanic	mekānik	مکانیک
medal	medāl • neshān	مدال • نشان
medicine (degree)	pezeshki	پزشکی
(drug)	dāru	دارو
meditation	mediteyshen	مدیتیشن
to meet	molāghāt kardan	ملاقات کردن
member	ozv	عضو
menstruation	periyod • ādat e māhāne	پریود • عادت ماهانه
menu	list e ghazā	لیست غذا
message	peyghām	پیغام
metal	felezzi	فلزی
meteor	shahābsang	شهاب سنگ
metre	metr	متر
midnight	nime shab • nesf e shab	نیمه شب • نصف شب
migraine	migren	میگرن
military service	khedmat e sarbāzi • nezā vazife	خدمت سربازی • نظام وظیفه
milk	shir	شیر
millimetre	milimetr	میلی متر
million	milyon	میلیون
mind	zehn	ذهن
mineral water	āb ma'dani	آب معدنی
a minute	ye daghighe	یک دقیقه

Just a minute.
ye daghighe sabr konin

یک دقیقه صبر کنید

in [five] minutes
dar (panj) daghighe

در (پنج) دقیقه

mirror	āyne	آینه
miscarriage	seght	سقط
to miss (feel absence)	del tang shodan	دل تنگ شدن
mistake	eshtebāh • khatā	اشتباه • خطا

to mix	makhlut kardan	مخلوط کردن
to mix (col)	ghāti kardan	قاطی کردن
mobile phone	telefon e hamrāh • mobāyl	تلفن همراه • موبایل
modem	modem	مودم
moisturiser	kerem e narm konande	کرم نرم کننده
monastery	some'e • khāneghāh	صومعه • خانقاه
Monday	doshanbe	دوشنبه
money	pul	پول
monk	rāheb	راهب
monkey	meymun	میمون
month	māh	ماه
this month	in māh	این ماه
monument	banā ye yādbud	بنای یادبود
moon	māh	ماه
more	bishtar	بیشتر
morning (6 am – 1 pm)	sob	صبح
mosque	masjed	مسجد
mother	mādar	مادر
mother-in-law (husband's)	mādar shohar	مادر شوهر
(wife's)	mādar zan	مادر زن
motorboat	ghāyegh motori	قایق موتوری
motorcycle	motorsiklet	موتور سیکلت
motorway (tollway)	utubān	اتوبان
mountain	kuh	کوه
mountain hut	panāhgāh	پناهگاه
mountain path	masir e kuh	مسیر کوه
mountain range	reshte kuh	رشته کوه
mountaineering	kuh navardi	کوهنوردی
mouse	mush	موش
mouth	dahan	دهان
movie	film	فیلم
mud	gel	گل

Mum	māmān	مامان
muscle	azole	عضله
museum	muze	موزه
music	musighi	موسیقی
musician	musighi dān	موسیقی دان
Muslim	mosalmun	مسلمون
mute	bisedā • lāl	بی صدا • لال

N
ان

name	esm • nām	اسم • نام
nappy	pushak	پوشک
national park	pārk e melli	پارک ملی
nationality	meliyyat	ملیت
nature	tabi'at	طبیعت
nausea	tahavvo'	تهوع
near	nazdik	نزدیک
nearby hotel	hotel e nazdik	هتل نزدیک
necessary	lāzem • zaruri	لازم • ضروری
necklace	gardan band	گردنبند
to need	lazem dāshtan	لازم داشتن
needle (sewing)	suzan	سوزن
(syringe)	suzan	سوزن
neither	hich kodum	هیچ کدام
net	tur	تور
never	hich vaght	هیچ وقت
new	tāze • jadid	تازه • جدید
news	akhbār	اخبار
newsagency	ruznāme furushi	روزنامه فروشی
newspaper	ruznāme	روزنامه
English-language newspaper	ruznāmehā ye ingilisi	روزنامه انگلیسی
New Year's Day	ruz e sāl e no	روز سال نو
New Year's Eve	shab e sāl e no	شب سال نو
New Zealand	nyuziland • zelānd e no	نیوزیلند • زلاند نو
next	ba'd • ba'di • āyande	بعد • بعدی • آینده

next month	māh e ba'd	ماه بعد
next to	nazdik e	نزدیک
next week	hafte ye ba'd	هفته بعد
next year	sāl e ba'd	سال بعد
nice	khub	خوب
night	shab	شب
nine	noh	نه
nineteen	nuzdah	نوزده
ninety	navad	نود
ninth	nohom	نهم
noise	sar o sedā	سر و صدا
noisy	por sar o sedā	پر سر و صدا
non-direct	gheyr e mostaghim	غیر مستقیم
none	hich	هیچ
noon	zohr	ظهر
north	shomāl	شمال
nose	bini	بینی
nose (inf)	damāgh	دماغ
notebook	daftarche	دفترچه
nothing	hich chiz	هیچ چیز
not yet	hanuz na	هنوز نه
novel (book)	roman	رمان
November	novāmr	نوامبر
now	hālā	حالا
nuclear energy	enerezhi ye hasteyi	انرژی هسته ای
nuclear testing	āzemāyesh e hasteyi	آزمایش هسته ای
nun	rāhebe	راهبه
nurse	parastār	پرستار

O
او

obvious	vāzeh • ashkār	واضح • آشکار
ocean	oghyānus	اقیانوس
October	oktobr	اکتبر
offence	tohin	توهین
office	edāre	اداره
office work	kār e edāri	کار اداری
office worker	kārmand	کارمند
offside (soccer)	āfsāyd	آفساید

often	aghlab	اغلب
oil		
(cooking)	roghan	روغن
(crude)	naft	نفت
OK	bāshe	با شه
old	kohne •	کهنه • قدیمی
	ghadimi	
old city	shahr e	شهر قدیمی
	ghadimi	
olive oil	roghan e	روغن زیتون
	zeytun	
olives	zeytun	زیتون
Olympic	bāzihā ye	بازیهای المپیک
Games	olampik	
on	dar • ru ye	در • روی
on time	be moghe'	به موقع
once	ye bār •	یک بار • موقع
(one time)	moghe'	
one million	ye milyon	یک میلیون
one-way	ye sare	یک سره
(ticket)		
only	faghat	فقط
open	bāz	باز
to open	bāz kardan	باز کردن
opening	majrā	مجرا
opera	operā	اپرا
operation	amal e	عمل جراحی
(surgery)	jarrāhi	
operator	operātor	اپراتور
opinion	aghide	عقیده
opposite	mokhālef	مخالف
optician	cheshm	چشم پزشک
	pezeshk	
or	yā	یا
oral	dahāni	دهانی
orange	nārenji	نارنجی
(colour)		
orange (fruit)	porteghāl	پرتقال
orchestra	orkestr	ارکستر
order	dastur	دستور
(command)		
order	sefāresh	سفارش
(request)		
order	nazm	نظم

to order	dastur •	دستور • سفارش دادن
	sefāresh	
	dādan	
ordinary	āddi •	عادی • معمولی
	ma'muli	
to organise	sazemān	سازمان دادن
	dādan	
original	asli	اصلی
other	digar	دیگر
outgoing	mo'āsherati	معاشرتی
(personality)		
outside	birun	بیرون
over	ru ye •	روی • بالای
	bālā ye	
overcoat	overkot	اورکت
overdose	masraf e	مصرف افراطی
	efrāti	
to owe	gharz dāshtan	قرض داشتن
owner	sāheb •	صاحب • مالک
	mālek	
oxygen	oksizhen	اکسیژن
ozone layer	lāye ye ozon	لایه اوزون

P

pacifier	pestunak	پستانک
(baby's)		
package	baste	بسته
packet of cigarettes		
baste sigār		بسته سیگار
padlock	ghofl e zanjir	قفل زنجیر
page	safhe	صفحه
a pain	dard	درد
painful	dardnāk	دردناک
pain in	mozāhem	مزاحم
the neck		
painkiller	mosakken	مسکن
to paint	rang kardan	رنگ کردن
painter	naghghāsh	نقاش
painting	naghghāshi	نقاشی
(the art)		
pair	joft	جفت
(of gloves)	(dastkesh)	(دستکش)
(a couple)	zoj	زوج

English	Transliteration	Persian
palace	ghasr	قصر
pan	māhi tābe	ماهی تابه
pap smear	pāp ismeyr	پاپ اسمیر
paper	kāghaz	کاغذ
paraplegic	falaj e dast o pā	فلج دست و پا
parcel	baste ye posti	بسته پستی
parents	pedar o mādar • vālideyn	پدر و مادر • والدین
a park	pārk	پارک
to park	pārk kardan	پارک کردن
parliament	majles	مجلس
part	ghesmat	قسمت
party	mehmuni	مهمانی
party (politics)	hezb	حزب
pass	javāz e ubur	جواز عبور
passenger	mosāfer	مسافر
passive	geyr e fa'āl	غیر فعال
passport	gozarnāme • pāsport	گذرنامه • پاسپورت
passport number	shomāre ye pāsport	شماره پاسپورت
past	gozashte	گذشته
path	masir	مسیر
patient (adj)	sabur	صبور
to pay	pardākhtan	پرداختن
payment	pardākht	پرداخت
peace	solh	صلح
peak	oj	اوج
pedestrian	āber	عابر
pen (ballpoint)	khodkār	خودکار
pencil	medād	مداد
penicillin	penisilin	پنی سیلین
penis	ālat (e tanāsoli ye mard)	آلت (تناسلی مرد)
penknife	chāghu ye jibi	چاقوی جیبی
pensioner	mostamerri begir	مستمری بگیر
people	mardom	مردم
pepper	felfel	فلفل
per cent	darsad	درصد

English	Transliteration	Persian
performance	bāzdeh e kār	بازده کار
period pain	dard e periyod	درد پریود
permanent	dā'emi • hamishegi	دائمی • همیشگی
permission	ejāze	اجازه
permit	mojavvez	مجوز
person	fard • shakhs	فرد • شخص
personality	shakhsiyat	شخصیت
to perspire	aragh kardan	عرق کردن
petition	shekāyat	شکایت
petrol	benzin	بنزین
pharmacy	dārukhune	داروخانه
phone book	dafter e telefon	دفتر تلفن
phone box	bāje ye telefon	باجه تلفن
phonecard	kārt e telefon	کارت تلفن
photo	aks	عکس

Can (May) I take a photo?
mishe ye aks begiram?
می شود یک عکس بگیرم؟

English	Transliteration	Persian
photographer	akkās	عکاس
photography	akkāsi	عکاسی
pick; pickaxe	kolang	کلنگ
to pick up	bardāshtan • jam kardan	برداشتن • جمع کردن
piece	tikke • ghat'e	تکه • قطعه
pig	khuk	خوک
pill	ghors	قرص
the Pill	ghors e zedd e hāmelegi	قرص ضد حاملگی
pillow	bālesh	بالش
pillowcase	rubāleshi	روبالشی
pink	surati	صورتی
pipe (tube)	lule	لوله
pipe (tobacco)	pip	پیپ
pizza	pitzā	پیتزا
place	mahall • jā	محل • جا
place of birth	mahall e tavallod	محل تولد

English	Transliteration	Persian
plain	sāde	ساده
plane	havāpeymā	هواپیما
planet	sayyāre	سیاره
plant	giyāh	گیاه
to plant	kāshtan	کاشتن
plastic	pelāstik	پلاستیک
plate	boshghāb	بشقاب
plateau	falāt	فلات
platform	sakku	سکو
play (theatre)	namāyesh nāme	نمایشنامه
to play		
(a game)	bazi kardan	بازی کردن
(music)	navākhtan	نواختن
player (sports)	bāzikon	بازیکن
playing cards	varagh	ورق
to play cards	varagh bāzri kardan	ورق بازی کردن
plug (electricity)	doshākhe	دوشاخه
pocket	jib	جیب
poetry	she'r	شعر
point		
(tip)	noghte	نقطه
(in game)	emtiyāz	امتیاز
to point	eshāre kardan	اشاره کردن
poker	poker	پوکر
police	polis	پلیس
politics	siyāsat	سیاست
political speech	sokhanrāni ye siyāsi	سخنرانی سیاسی
politician	siyāsat madār	سیاست مدار
pollen	garde	گرده
polls	ārā' e umumi	آرا عمومی
pollution	āludegi	آلودگی
pool		
(swimming)	estakhr	استخر
(game)	bilyārd	بیلیارد
poor	faghir • bichāre	فقیر • بیچاره
popular	mashhur • ma'ruf	مشهور • معروف
port	bandar	بندر

English	Transliteration	Persian
possible	momken	ممکن
It's possible.	momken e	ممکن است
It's not possible.	momken nist	ممکن نیست
postcard	kārt e postāl	کارت پستال
postcode	kod e posti	کد پستی
postage	hazine ye posti	هزینه پستی
poster	puster	پوستر
post office	edāre ye post	اداره پست
pottery	sofāl gari	سفال گری
poverty	faghr	فقر
power	ghodrat	قدرت
prayer	do'ā • namāz	دعا • نماز
prayer book	ketāb e do'ā	کتاب دعا
to prefer	tarjih dādan	ترجیح دادن
pregnant	hāmele • bārdār	حامله • باردار
prehistoric art	asar e mā ghabl e tārkhi	اثر ما قبل تاریخی
to prepare	āmāde kardan	آماده کردن
present		
(gift)	hedye • kādo	هدیه • کادو
(time)	hāl	حال
presentation	erā'e • mo'arrefi	ارائه • معرفی
presenter (TV, etc)	mojri	مجری
president	ra'is	رئیس
(of a state)	ra'is (e jumhur)	رئیس (جمهور)
pressure	feshār	فشار
pretty	khoshgel	خوشگل
to prevent	jelogiri kardan	جلوگیری کردن
price	nerkh • gheymat	نرخ • قیمت
pride	ghurur	غرور
priest	keshish	کشیش
prime minister	nakhost vazir	نخست وزیر
prison	zendān	زندان

prisoner	zendāni	زندانی
prisoner (of war)	asir	اسیر
private	khus_usi	خصوصی
private hospital	bimārestān e khus_usi	بیمارستان خصوصی
privatisation	khus_usi sāzi	خصوصی سازی
to produce	tolid kardan	تولید کردن
producer	tolid konande	تولید کننده
profession	herfe • shoghl	حرفه • شغل
profit	sud • naf'	سود • نفع
profitability	sud dehi	سود دهی
program	barnāme	برنامه
projector	porozhektor	پروژکتور
promise	va'de • ghol	وعده • قول
proposal	tarh • pishnahād	طرح • پیشنهاد
to protect	mohāfezat kardan	محافظت کردن
protected forest	jangal e hefāzat shode	جنگل حفاظت شده
protected species	gunehā ye hefāzat shode	گونه های حفاظت شده
protest	e'terāz	اعتراض
to protest	e'terāz kardan	اعتراض کردن
public toilet	tuvālet e umumi	توالت عمومی
to pull	keshidan	کشیدن
pump	tolombe	تلمبه
puncture	panchari	پنچری
to punish	tanbih kardan	تنبیه کردن
puppy	tule sag	توله سگ
pure	khāles	خالص
purple	nārenji	نارنجی
to push	hol dādan	هول دادن
to put	gozāshtan	گذاشتن

Q کیو

qualification	madrak	مدرک
quality	keyfiyyat	کیفیت
quarantine	gharantine	قرنطینه

quarrel	da'vā	دعوا
quarter	chārak • rob'	چارک • ربع
queen	malake	ملکه
question	so'āl • porsesh	سوال • پرسش
question (topic)	so'āl	سوال
to question	porsidan	پرسیدن
queue	saf	صف
quick	tond • sari'	تند • سریع
quiet (adj)	sāket	ساکت
to quit	tark kardan	ترک کردن
to quit (a job)	este'fā dādan	استعفا دادن

R آر

rabbit	khargush	خرگوش
race (breed)	nezhād	نژاد
(sport)	mosābeghe	مسابقه
racing bike	docharkhe ye mosābeghe	دوچرخه مسابقه
racism	nezhād parasti	نژاد پرستی
radiator	rādiyātor	رادیاتور
railroad	rāh āhan	راه آهن
railway station	istgāh e rāh āhan	ایستگاه راه آهن
rain	bārun	باران

It's raining.
bārun miyād باران می آید

rally	rāhpeymāyi	راهپیمایی
rape	tajāvoz	تجاوز
rare	kamyāb • nāder	کمیاب • نادر
a rash	jush	جوش
rat	mush	موش
rate of pay	mizān e hughugh	میزان حقوق
raw	khām	خام
razor	rish tarāsh	ریش تراش
razor blade	tigh e rishtarāshi	تیغ ریش تراشی
to read	khundan	خواندن

R

ready	hāzer • āmāde	حاضر • آماده
to realise	dark kardan • fahmidan	درک کردن • فهمیدن
reason	dalil • ellat	دلیل • علت
receipt	resid	رسید
to receive	daryāft kardan	دریافت کردن
recent	akhir	اخیر
recently	akhiran	اخیراً
to recognise	shenākhtan • tashkhis dādan	شناختن • تشخیص دادن
to recommend	pishnahād kardan	پیشنهاد کردن
recording	zabt	ضبط
red	ghermez	قرمز
referee	dāvar	داور
reference	marja'	مرجع
reflection (mirror)	en'ekās • bāztāb	انعکاس • بازتاب
reflection (thinking)	bāztāb	بازتاب
refrigerator	yakhchāl	یخچال
refugee	panāhande	پناهنده
refund	baz pardākht	بازپرداخت
to refund	pas dādan	پس دادن
to refuse	khoddāri kardan	خودداری کردن
regional	mantagheyi	منطقه ای
registered mail	post e sefāreshi	پست سفارشی
to regret	pashimun shodan	پشیمان شدن
relationship	rābete	رابطه
to relax	esterāhat kardan	استراحت کردن
religion	maz-hab • din	مذهب • دین
religious	maz-habi	مذهبی
to remember	be yād āvordan	بیاد آوردن
remote	dur	دور
remote control	kontorol az rāh e dur	کنترل از راه دور

rent	ejāre • kerāye	اجاره • کرایه
to rent	ejāre kardan	اجاره کردن
to repeat	tekrār kardan	تکرار کردن
republic	jumhuri	جمهوری
reservation (booking)	zakhire	ذخیره
reservation (seat)	rezerv	رزرو
to reserve (a seat)	rezerv kardan	رزرو کردن
resignation	este'fā	استعفا
respect	ehterām	احترام
rest (relaxation)	esterāhat	استراحت
rest (what's left)	baghiyye	بقیه
to rest	esterāhat kardan	استراحت کردن
restaurant	resturān	رستوران
résumé	sābeghe ye kār	سابقه کار
retired	bāzneshaste	بازنشسته
to return	bargashtan	برگشتن
return (ticket)	belit e bargasht	(بلیط) برگشت
review	barrasi • murur	بررسی • مرور
rhythm	vazn • ritm	وزن • ریتم
rib	dande	دنده
rice	berenj	برنج
rich (wealthy)	servatmand • poldār	ثروتمند • پولدار
rich (food)	ghani	غنی
to ride (a horse)	savāri kardan	سواری کردن
right (correct)	dorost	درست
right (not left)	rāst	راست
to be right	hagh dāshtan	حق داشتن

You're right.
hagh bā shomā st حق با شماست

| rights (civil) | hughugh e madani | حقوق مدنی |

206

English	Transliteration	Persian
right now	hamin al'ān	همین الان
right-wing	jenāh e rāst	جناح راست
ring		
(on finger)	angoshtar	انگشتر
(of phone)	zang	زنگ

I'll give you a ring.
[man] be shomā zang mizanam
(من) به شما زنگ می زنم

English	Transliteration	Persian
ring (sound)	zang	زنگ
rip-off	chāpidan • ekhtelās	چاپیدن • اختلاص
risk	khatar	خطر
river	rudkhune	رودخانه
road (main)	jādde (ye asli)	جاده (اصلی)
road map	naghshe ye jādde	نقشه جاده
to rob	dozdidan	دزدیدن
rock (climbing)	sakhre (navardi)	صخره (نوردی)
rock group	guruh e rāk	گروه راک
rolling	charkhesh	چرخش
romance	āsheghāne	عاشقانه
room	otāgh	اتاق
room number	shomāre ye otāgh	شماره اتاق
rope	tanāb	طناب
round	gerd	گرد
[at the] roundabout	(dar) meydun	(در) میدان
rubbish	ashghāl	آشغال
rug	farsh	فرش
ruin	kharābe	خرابه
rules	mogarrarāt • gava'ed	مقررات • قواعد
to run	dovidan	دویدن

S
اس

English	Transliteration	Persian
sad	ghamgin • nārāhat	غمگین • ناراحت
saddle	zin	زین

English	Transliteration	Persian
safe (adj)	amn • bikhatar	امن • بی خطر
safe (n)	gāv sandugh	گاو صندوق
saint	gheddis	قدیس
salary	hughugh	حقوق
(on) sale	harāj	حراج
sales department	daftar e furush	دفتر فروش
salt	namak	نمک
same	mosāvi • barābar	مساوی • برابر
sand	shen	شن
sandwich	sandvich	ساندویچ
sanitary napkin	navār behdāshti	نوار بهداشتی
Saturday	shanbe	شنبه
to save (money)	pas andāz kardan	پس انداز کردن
(rescue)	nejāt dādan	نجات دادن
to say	goftan	گفتن
to scale	bālā raftan •	بالا رفتن •
(climb)	su'ud kardan	صعود کردن
scarf	rusari	روسری
school	madrese	مدرسه
science	elm	علم
scientist	dāneshmand	دانشمند
scissors	gheychi	قیچی
to score	emtiyāz gereftan	امتیاز گرفتن
scoreboard	jadval e emtiyāzāt	جدول امتیازات
screen	safhe	صفحه
scriptwriter	film nāme (nevis)	فیلمنامه (نویس)
sculptor	peykar tarāsh	پیکر تراش
sculpture	peykare • mojassame	پیکره • مجسمه
sea	daryā	دریا
seasick	daryāzade	دریا زده
seaside	kenār e daryā	کنار دریا
seat	sandali • jā	صندلی • جا
seatbelt	kamarband	کمربند
a second	sāniye	ثانیه

second	dovvom	دوم
secondary school	dabirestān	دبیرستان
secretary	monshi	منشی
to see	didan	دیدن
We'll see!	khāhim did	خواهیم دید
I see. [understand]	mifahmam	می فهم
See you later.	ba'dan mibinam et	بعداً می بینمت
See you tomorrow.	fardā mibinam et	فردا می بینمت
self-employment	shoghl e āzād	شغل آزاد
selfish	khodkhāh	خود خواه
self-service	self servis	سلف سرویس
to sell	furukhtan	فروختن
to send	ferestādan	فرستادن
sensible	mahsus	محسوس
sentence (words)	jomle	جمله
(prison)	hokm	حکم
to separate	jodā kardan	جدا کردن
September	septāmr	سپتامبر
series	majmu'e	مجموعه
serious (not funny)	jeddi	جدی
(intense)	shadid	شدید
service (assistance)	khedmat	خدمت
(religious)	marāsem	مراسم
several	chandin	چندین
to sew	khayyāti • kardan • dukhtan	خیاطی • کردن • دوختن
sex (gender)	jensiyyat	جنسیت
(intercourse)	amizesh e jensi	آمیزش جنسی
sexism	tab'iz e jensi	تبعیض جنسی
shade	sāye	سایه
shadow	sāye	سایه
shampoo	shāmpu	شامپو
shape	shekl	شکل
to share (with)	bā ham estefāde kardan	با هم استفاده کردن
to share a dorm	ham otāgh shodan	هم اتاق شدن
to shave	tarāshidan • eslāh kardan	تراشیدن • اصلاح کردن
she	un	او
sheep	gusfand	گوسفند
sheet (bed)	malāfe	ملافه
(of paper)	safhe	صفحه
shell	puste	پسته
shelf	ghafase	قفسه
ship	keshti	کشتی
to ship	bā keshti ferestādan	با کشتی فرستادن
shirt	pirhan	پیراهن
shoe shop	kafsh furushi	کفش فروشی
shoes	kafsh	کفش
to shoot (gun)	tir andāzi kardan	تیر اندازی کردن
(film)	filmbardāri kardan	فیلمبرداری کردن
shop	maghāze • furushgāh	مغازه • فروشگاه
to go shopping	kharid raftan	خرید رفتن
short (length/ height)	kutāh	کوتاه
short film/ story	film/dāstān e kutāh	فیلم/داستان کوتاه
shortage	kambud	کمبود
short	shalvārak	شلوارک
shoulder	shune	شانه
to shout	dād zadan	داد زدن
a show	namāyesh	نمایش
to show	neshun dādan	نشان دادن

Can you show me on the map?
mitunin tu ye naghshe be man
neshun bedin?

می توانید توی نقشه به من نشان بدهید؟

English	Persian	
shower	dush	دوش
showers	ragbār	رگبار
shrine	maghbare •	مقبره •
	ārāmgāh	آرامگاه
to shut	bastan	بستن
shy	khejālati	خجالتی
sick	mariz	مریض
a sickness	marizi	مریضی
side	taraf	طرف
a sign	alāmat	علامت
to sign	emzā	امضا کردن
	karadn	
signature	emzā	امضا
silk	abrisham	ابریشم
of silver	noghreyi	نقره ای
similar	shabih	شبیه
simple	sāde	ساده
sin	gonāh	گناه
since (May)	az (meh)	از (مه)
to sing	avāz	آواز خواندن
	khundan	
singer	khānande	خواننده
singer-	khānande-	خواننده-
songwriter	tarānesarā	ترانه ساز
single		
(person)	mojarrad	مجرد
(unique)	tak	تک
single room	otāgh e taki	اتاق تکی
sister	khāhar	خواهر
to sit	neshastan	نشستن
size		
(of anything)	andāze	اندازه
(clothes)	sāyz	سایز
(shoes)	sāyz	سایز
skiing	eski	اسکی
to ski	eski kardan	اسکی کردن
skin	pust	پوست
skirt	dāman	دامن
sky	āsemun	آسمان
to sleep	khābidan	خوابیدن

English	Persian	
sleeping bag	kise khāb	کیسه خواب
sleeping pill	ghors e khāb	قرص خواب
sleepy	khāb ālud	خواب آلود
slide (film)	eslāyd	اسلاید
slow	āheste	آهسته
slowly	yavāsh	یواش
small	kuchik	کوچک
a smell	bu	بو
to smell	buyidan	بوییدن
to smile	labkhand	لبخند زدن
	zadan	
to smoke	sigār	سیگار کشیدن
	keshidan	
snake	mār	مار
snow	barf	برف
soap	sābun	صابون
soccer	futbāl	فوتبال
social-	sosyāl	سوسیال
democratic	domokrāt	دموکرات
social ...	... e ejtemāyi	... اجتماعی
sciences	ulum	علوم
security	ta'min	تامین
welfare	refāh	رفاه
socialist	sosyālist	سوسیالیست
socks	jurāb	جوراب
solid (shape)	jāmed	جامد
solid (strong)	mohkam	محکم
some	ba'zi	بعضی
somebody	kesi	کسی
someone	yeki	یکی
something	chizi	چیزی
sometimes	ba'zi	بعضی وقت ها
	vaghtā	
son	pesar	پسر
song	āvāz	آواز
soon	bezudi •	بزودی •
	zud	زود
sore throat	galu dard	گلو درد
I'm sorry.		
mota'assefam		متاسفم
sound	seda	صدا
south	junub	جنوب

English	Transliteration	Persian
souvenir	kādo • hedye	کادو • هدیه
souvenir shop	kādo furushi	کادو فروشی
space	fazā	فضا
to speak	sohbat kardan • harf zadan	صحبت کردن • حرف زدن
special	makhsus	مخصوص
specialist	motakhasses	متخصص
speed	sor'at	سرعت
speed limit	hadd e aksar e sor'at	حد اکثر سرعت
spicy (hot)	tond	تند
spider	ankabut	عنکبوت
spine	nokhā'	نخاع
sport	varzesh	ورزش
sports person	varzeshkār	ورزشکار
a sprain	rag be rag shodegi	رگ به رگ شدگی
spring (season)	bahār	بهار
(coil)	fanar	فنر
square (shape)	morabba'	مربع
(in town)	meydun	میدان
stadium	estādiyom	استادیوم
stage (period)	marhale	مرحله
stage (play)	sahne	صحنه
stairway	rāh pelle	راه پله
stamp	tambr	تمبر
standard (usual)	estāndārd • ma'mul	استاندارد • معمول
standard of living	sath e zendegi	سطح زندگی
stars	setāregān	ستارگان
to start	shoru' kardan	شروع کردن
station	istgāh	ایستگاه
stationer	nevesht afzār furushi	نوشت افزار فروشی
statue	mojassame	مجسمه

English	Transliteration	Persian
to stay (remain)	mundan	ماندن
(somewhere)	eghāmat kardan	اقامت کردن
to steal	dozdidan	دزدیدن
steam	bokhār	بخار
steep	sarāziri	سرازیری
stepbrother	barādar khānde	برادر خوانده
stepfather	nā pedari	ناپدری
stepmother	nā mādari	نامادری
stepsister	khāhar khānde	خواهر خوانده
stewed fruit	komput	کمپوت
stockings	jorāb e boland	جوراب بلند
stomach	me'de	معده
stomachache	me'de dard	معده درد
stone	sang	سنگ
stop	istgāh	ایستگاه
to stop	tavāghghof kardan	توقف کردن
Stop!	ist!	ایست
stork	laklak	لک لک
storm	tufān	طوفان
story	dāstān • ghesse	داستان • قصه
stove	ojāgh	اجاق
straight	mostaghim	مستقیم
strange	ajib	عجیب
stranger	gharibe	غریبه
stream	jarayān	جریان
street	khiyābun	خیابان
street demonstration	tazāhorāt e khiyābāni	تظاهرات خیابانی
street-seller	dast furush	دست فروش
strength	ghovvat	قوت
a strike	e'tesāb	اعتصاب
string	rismān • zanjir	ریسمان • زنجیر
stroll (walk)	gardesh	گردش
strong	ghavi	قوی

English	Persian	
stubborn	kalle shagh •	که شق •
	lajbāz	لجباز
student		
(university)	danesh ju	دانشجو
(school)	danesh āmuz	دانش آموز
studio	istādiyo •	استودیو •
	kārgāh	کارگاه
stupid	ahmagh	احمق
style	sabk	سبک
subtitle	zir nevis	زیر نویس
suburb	home	حومه
suburbs	home ye ...	حومه ...
of ...		
subway	istgāh e zir	ایستگاه زیر
station	zamini	زمینی
success	movaffaghiyyat	موفقیت
to suffer	ranj bordan	رنج بردن
sugar	shekar	شکر
suitcase	chamedun	چمدان
summer	tābestun	تابستان
sun	āftāb	آفتاب
sunblock	zedd e āftāb	ضد آفتاب
sunburn	āftāb	آفتاب
	sukhtegi	سوختگی
Sunday	yek shanbe	یکشنبه
sunflower	roghan e	روغن آفتاب
oil	āftāb gardān	گردان
sunglasses	eynak āftābi	عینک آفتابی
sunny	āftābi	آفتابی
sunrise	tulu'	طلوع
sunset	ghurub	غروب
Sure.		
hatman		حتماً
surface	post e zamini	پست زمینی
mail		
surfboard	takhte ye	تخته موج سواری
	moj savāri	
surname	esm e kuchik	اسم کوچک
a surprise	ta'ajjob	تعجب
to survive	zende mundan	زنده ماندن
sweater	poliver	پلیور
sweet	shirin	شیرین
to swim	shenā kardan	شنا کردن
swimming	shenā	شنا

English	Persian	
swimming	estakhr e	استخر شنا
pool	shenā	
swimsuit	māyo	مایو
sword	shamshir	شمشیر
sympathetic	delsuz	دلسوز
synagogue	kanise	کنیسه
synthetic	masno'i	مصنوعی
syringe	sorang	سرنگ

T
تی

English	Persian	
table	miz	میز
table football	futbāl dasti	فوتبال دستی
table tennis	tenis e ru	تنیس روی میز
	ye miz	
table tennis	pinkponk	پینگ پونک
(col)		
tail	dom • aghab	دم • عقب
to take		
(away)	bordan	بردن
(food; the	gereftan	گرفتن
train)		
photographs	aks gereftan	عکس گرفتن
to talk	harf zadan	حرف زدن
tall	boland ghad	بلند قد
tampon	tampān	تامپون
tasty	khoshmaze	خوشمزه
tax	māliyāt	مالیات
taxi stand	istgāh e	ایستگاه تاکسی
	tāksi	
teacher	mo'allem	معلم
teaching	tadris	تدریس
team	tim	تیم
tear (crying)	ashk	اشک
technique	fann • teknik	فن •
		تکنیک
telegram	telgerāf	تلگراف
telephone	telefon	تلفن
to telephone	telefon	تلفن کردن
	kardan	
telephone	markaz e	مرکز تلفن
office	telefon	
telescope	teleskop	تلسکوپ
television	televiziyon	تلویزیون
to tell	goftan	گفتن

English	Transliteration	Persian
temperature		
(fever)	tab	تب
(weather)	damā	دما
temple	ma'bad	معبد
ten	dah	ده
tennis (court)	(meydun e) tenis	(میدان) تنیس
tent	chādor	چادر
tent peg	mikh e chādor	میخ چادر
tenth	dahom	دهم
term of office	dore	دوره
terrible	vahshatnāk	وحشتناک
test	test • āzemāyesh	تست • آزمایش
to thank	tashakkor kardan	تشکر کردن
Thank you.		
motashakkeram		متشکرم
theatre	te'ātr	تئاتر
they	unā	آنها
thick	zakhim • koloft	ضخیم • کلفت
thief	dozd • sāregh	دزد • سارق
thin (things)	nāzok	نازک
thin (build)	lāghar	لاغر
to think	fekr kardan	فکر کردن
third	sevvom	سوم
thirsty	teshne	تشنه
thirteen	sizdah	سیزده
thirty	si	سی
thought	fekr	فکر
three-quarters	se chāhārom	سه چهارم
throat	galu	گلو
Thursday	panj shanbe	پنج شنبه
ticket ...	... e belit	... بلیط
collector	ma'mur	مامور
office	daftar furush	دفتر فروش
tide	moj	موج
tight	seft	سفت
time	vaght • zamān	وقت • زمان

English	Transliteration	Persian
timetable	jadval e zamāni	جدول زمانی
tin (can)	ghuti	قوطی
tin opener	dar bāz kon	در باز کن
tip (gratuity)	an'ām	انعام
tired	khaste	خسته
tissues	dastmāl kāghazi	دستمال کاغذی
toad	vazagh	وزغ
toast (bread)	nun e tost	نان توست
tobacco	tanbāku	تنباکو
tobacco kiosk	dakke ye sigār furushi	دکه سیگار فروشی
today	emruz	امروز
together	bāham	باهم
toilet (paper)	(kāghaz e) tuvālet	(کاغذ) توالت
toll-free motorway	bozorg rāh	بزرگراه
tollway	utubān	اتوبان
tomorrow ...	fardā ...	فردا ...
afternoon	ba'd az zohr	بعد از ظهر
morning	sob	صبح
tonight	emshab	امشب
too (as well)	hamchenin • hamintor	همچنین • همینطور
too expensive		
kheyli gerun		خیلی گران
too much; many		
kheyli ziyād		خیلی زیاد
tooth	dandun	دندان
toothache	dandun dard	دندان درد
toothbrush	mesvāk	مسواک
toothpaste	khamir dandun	خمیر دندان
torch (flashlight)	cherāgh ghovve	چراغ قوه
to touch	lams kardan	لمس کردن
tour	gardesh • tur	گردش • تور
tourist	jahāngard • turist	جهانگرد • توریست

tourist information office	markaz e ettelā'āt o jahāngardi	مرکز اطلاعات و جهانگردی
towards	be taraf e	به طرف
towel	hole	حوله
tower	borj	برج
town	shahr	شهر
toxic waste	zobāle ye sammi	زباله سمی
track (footprints)	radd e pā	رد پا
(path)	masir	مسیر
trade union	ettehādiye ye bāzagāni	اتحادیه بازرگانی
traffic	raft o āmad • terāfik	رفت و آمد • ترافیک
traffic light	cherāgh e rāhnamāyi	چراغ راهنمایی
train (station)	(istgāh e) ghatār	(ایستگاه) قطار
tram	ghatār barghi	قطار برقی
transit lounge	sālon e parvāz	سالن پرواز
to translate	tarjome kardan	ترجمه کردن
to travel	safar kardan	سفر کردن
travel agency	āzhāns e mosāferati	آژانس مسافرتی
travel sickness	māshin gereftegi	ماشین گرفتگی
traveller	mosāfer	مسافر
travellers cheque	chek mosāferati	چک مسافرتی
tree	derakht	درخت
trek	safar e piyāde ye tulāni	سفر پیاده طولانی
trip	safar	سفر
trousers	shalvār	شلوار
truck	kāmiyon	کامیون
It's true. dorest e		درست است
trust	e'temād	اعتماد
to trust	e'temād kardan	اعتماد کردن

truth	haghighat	حقیقت
to try	emtahān kardan	امتحان کردن
to try (to attempt)	sa'y kardan	سعی کردن
T-shirt	tishert	تی شرت
Tuesday	se shanbe	سه شنبه
tune	tanzim	تنظیم
Turn left. bepichin chap		بپیچید چپ
Turn right. bepichin rāst		بپیچید راست
TV (set)	(dastgāh e) televiziyon	(دستگاه) تلویزیون
twelve	davāzdah	دوازده
twenty	bist	بیست
twice	dobār	دوبار
twin beds	takht e do khābe	تخت دو خوابه
twins	doghulu	دوقلو
to type	tāyp kardan	تایپ کردن
typical	āddi • nemune	عادی • نمونه
tyre	charkh • tāyer	چرخ • تایر

U یو

ultrasound	sonogerāfi • ulterāsānd	سونو گرافی • اولتراساند
umbrella	chatr	چتر
uncle (paternal)	amu	عمو
(maternal)	dāyi	دایی
underpant	lebās e zir	لباس زیر
to understand	fahmidan	فهمیدن
unemployed	bikār	بیکار
unemployment	bikāri	بیکاری
union	ettehādiye	اتحادیه
universe	hasti	هستی
university	dāneshgāh	دانشگاه
unleaded	bedun e sorb	بدون سرب

unsafe	nā amn	نا امن
until (June)	tā (zhu'an)	تا (ژوئن)
unusual	gheyr e āddi	غیر عادی
up	bālā	بالا
uphill	sarbālāyi	سر بالایی
urgent	ezterāri	اضطراری
US	iyālāt e	ایالات متحده
	mottahede ye	آمریکا
	āmrikā	
useful	mofid	مفید

V وی

vacant	khāli	خالی
vacation	ta'tilāt	تعطیلات
vaccination	vāksināsyon	واکسیناسیون
valley	darre	دره
valuable	bā ārzesh	باارزش
value (price)	gheymat	قیمت
van	vānet	وانت
vegetable	sabzi	سبزی
vegetarian	sabzi khār	سبزی خوار

I'm vegetarian.
[man] sabzi khār am hastam
من سبزی خوار هستم

vegetation	zendegi ye giyāhi	زندگی گیاهی
vein	rag	رگ
venereal disease	bimāri ye urughi	بیماری عروقی
very	kheyli	خیلی
video tape	navār e vidiyo	نوار ویدیو
view	did • manzare	دید • منظره
village	rustā • deh	روستا • ده
vine	mo • tāk	مو • تاک
vineyard	tākestān	تاکستان
virus	virus	ویروس
visa	vizā • ravādid	ویزا • روادید
to visit	didār kardan	دیدار کردن
vitamin	vitāmin	ویتامین
voice	sot	صوت

volume (voice)	bolandi	بلندی
(quantity)	hajm	حجم
to vote	ra'y dādan	رای دادن

W دبلیو

Wait!	sabr kon!	صبر کن
waiter	gārson • pishkhedmat	گارسون • پیشخدمت
waiting room	otāgh e entezār	اتاق انتظار
to walk	rāh raftan	راه رفتن
wall	divār	دیوار
to want	khāstan	خواستن
war	jang	جنگ
wardrobe	ghafase ye lebās	قفسه لباس
warm	garm	گرم
to warn	ekhtār dādan	اخطار دادن
to wash	shostan	شستن
washing machine	māshin e lebās shuyi	ماشین لباس شویی
watch	sā'at	ساعت
to watch	tamāshā kardan	تماشا کردن
water	āb	آب
mineral water	āb e ma'dani	آب معدنی
water bottle	botri ye āb	بطری آب
waterfall	ābshār	آبشار
wave	moj	موج
way	rāh	راه

Please tell me the way to ...
lotafan rāh e ... ro be man begin
لطفاً راه ... را به من بگویید

Which way?
kodum rāh?
کدام راه؟

| we | mā | ما |
| weak | za'if | ضعیف |

W

wealthy	servatmand • puldār	ثروتمند • پولدار
to wear	pushidan	پوشیدن
weather	havā	هوا
wedding ...	... e arusi	... عروسی
anniversary	sālgard	سالگرد
cake	keyk	کیک
present	hedye	هدیه
Wednesday	chāhār shanbe	چهار شنبه
week	hafte	هفته
this week	in hafte	این هفته
weekend	ākhar e hafte	آخر هفته
to weigh	vazn kardan	وزن کردن
weight	vazn	وزن
welcome!	khosh āmadin	خوش آمدین
welfare	refāh • āsāyesh	رفاه • آسایش
well	khub	خوب
west	gharb	غرب
wet	khis	خیس
what	chi	چه

What's he saying?
un chi mige? — او چه می گوید؟

What time is it?
sā'at chand e? — ساعت چند است؟

wheel	charkh	چرخ
wheelchair	sandali ye charkh dār	صندلی چرخدار
when	key • che moghe'	کی • چه موقع

When does it leave?
un key harekat mikone? — آن کی حرکت می کند؟

| where | kojā | کجا |

Where's the bank?
bānk kojā st? — بانک کجاست؟

| white | sefid | سفید |
| who | ki • che kesi | کی • چه کسی |

Who is it?
ki ye? — کیه؟

Who are they?
unā ki yan? — آنها کی هستند؟

| whole | tamām • hame | تمام • همه |
| why | cherā | چرا |

Why is the museum closed?
cherā muze baste ast? — چرا موزه بسته است؟

wide	vasi' • goshād	وسیع • کشاد
wife	zan	زن
wild animal	heyvun e vahshi	حیوان وحشی
to win	bordan	بردن
wind	bād	باد
window	panjere	پنجره
windscreen	shishe ye jelo	شیشه جلو
wine	sharāb	شراب
winery	sharāb sāzi	شراب سازی
wing (bird)	bāl	بال
(politics)	jenāh	جناح
winner	barande	برنده
winter	zemestun	زمستان
wire	sim	سیم
wise	āghel	عاقل
to wish	arezu kardan	آرزو کردن
with	bā	با
within	dar • tu ye	در • توی

within an hour
dar ye sā'at — در یک ساعت

without	bedun e	بدون
without filter	bedun e filter	بدون فیلتر
wolf	gorg	گرگ
woman	zan	زن
wonderful	āli	عالی
wood	chub	چوب
wool	pashm	پشم
word	kalame	کلمه
work	kār	کار

W

to work	kār kardan	کار کردن
workout	tamrin	تمرین
work permit	ejāze ye kār	اجازه کار
workshop	kārgāh	کارگاه
world	donyā • jahān	دنیا • جهان
World Cup	jām e jahāni	جام جهانی
worm	kerm	کرم
worried	negarān	نگران
worship	ebādat	عبادت
worth	arzesh	ارزش
wound	zakhm	زخم
to write	neveshtan	نوشتن
writer	nevisande	نویسنده
wrong	ghalat • eshtebāh	غلط • اشتباه

I'm wrong. (my fault)
taghsir e man e   تقصیر من است
I'm wrong. (not right)
man eshtebāh mikonam

من اشتباه می کنم

Y   **وای**

year	sāl	سال
this year	emsāl	امسال
yellow	zard	زرد
yesterday ...	diruz ...	دیروز ...
afternoon	ba'd az zohr	بعد ازظهر
morning	sob	صبح
yet	hanuz	هنوز
you (pl)	shomā	شما
you (sg, pol)	shomā	شما
you (sg, inf)	to	تو
young	javun	جوان
youth (collective)	javuni	جوانی

Z   **زد**

zebra	gurekhar	گورخر
zero	sefr	صفر
zoo	bāgh e vahsh	باغ وحش

Ā

In this dictionary, we've included ā, ch, gh, kh, sh and zh as separately listed letters. The letter ā is always listed as the first letter of the alphabet, before a. So, if you're looking for a word that starts with the 'a' sound, look under both ā and a. The same applies to the letter ā when it appears within a word. So, for example, dāshtan is listed before dahan. Similarly, ch comes before c, gh before g, kh before k, sh before s, and zh before z.

Ā

Remember that a comes after ā

āb	water	آب
āb e garm	hot water	آب گرم
āb e ma'dani	mineral water	آب معدنی
āb e mive	juice	آب میوه
āb e sard	cold water	آب سرد
āber	pedestrian	عابر
āber bānk	automatic teller machine (ATM)	عابر بانک
ābi	blue	آبی
ābshār	waterfall	آبشار
ādāms	chewing gum	آدامس
āddi	typical	عادی
ādres	address	آدرس

āfiyat bāshe!
Bless you! (when sneezing) — عافیت باشه

āfsāyd	offside	آفساید
āftāb	sun	آفتاب
āftāb sukhtegi	sunburn	آفتاب سوختگی
āftābi	sunny	آفتابی
āghel	wise	عاقل
āgahi ye kār	job advertisement	آگهی کار
āheste	slow • slowly	آهسته
āhu	deer	آهو
ākhar e hafte	weekend	آخر هفته
ākhar	last	آخر
ālat	penis	آلت
āli	excellent	عالی

āliye!
Great! — عالیه

āludegi	pollution	آلودگی
āmāde kardan	to prepare	آماده کردن
āmuzesh	education	آموزش
ānten	antenna (TV)	آنتن
āntibiyutiks	antibiotics	آنتی بیوتیک
āpāndis	appendix (body part)	آپاندیس
ārā' e umumi	polls	آرا عمومی
ārāyesh	make-up	آرایش
ārd	flour	آرد
āsheghāne	romance	عاشقانه
āshghāl	garbage	آشغال
āshpazkhune	kitchen	آشپز خانه
āsānsor	elevator	آسانسور
āsemun	sky	آسمان
āsmi	asthmatic	آسمی
āsperin	aspirin	آسپرین
āsun	easy	آسان
ātish	fire	آتش
āvaz	song	آواز
āvordan	to bring	آوردن
āvril	April	آوریل
āyande	future	آینده
āyne	mirror	آینه
āyudi	IUD	آیودی
āzhans e mosāferati	travel agency	آژانس مسافرتی
āzād	free (not bound)	آزاد
āzār	harrassment	آزار
āzemāyesh e hasteyi	nuclear testing	آزمایش هسته ای
āzemāyesh e khun	blood test	آزمایش خون

A

Remember that ā comes before a

abā	cloak	عبا
abr	cloud	ابر
abri	cloudy	ابری
abrisham	silk	ابریشم
aghide	opinion	عقیده
aghlab	often	اغلب
agar	if	اگر
ahmagh	idiot	احمق
ajale dāshtan	in a hurry	عجله داشتن
ajib	strange	عجیب
akhbār	news	اخبار
akhir	recent	اخیر
akhiran	recently	اخیراً
akkās	photographer	عکاس
akkāsi	photography	عکاسی
aks	photo	عکس
aks gereftan	to take photographs	عکس گرفتن
aksariyyat	majority	اکثریت
alāghemand budan	to care (for someone)	علاقمند بودن
alāmat	a sign	علامت
alo!	Hello! (answering telephone)	الو
amal	operation	عمل
amal garā	activist	عمل گرا
amigh	deep	عمیق
ammā	but	اما
amme	aunt (father's side)	عمه
amn	safe (adj)	امن
an'ām	tip (gratuity)	انعام
andāze	size (of anything)	اندازه
angosht	finger	انگشت
angoshtar	ring (on finger)	انگشتر
angur	grapes	انگور
ankabut	spider	عنکبوت
aragh kardan	to perspire	عرق کردن
arbāb ruju'	client	ارباب رجوع
arghām	figures	ارقام

arusak	doll	عروسک
arusi	wedding	عروسی
arz e	across	عرض
arzesh	worth	ارزش
arzidan	to cost	ارزیدن
ashk	tear (crying)	اشک
asabāni	angry	عصبانی
asal	honey	عسل
asb	horse	اسب
asb savāri	horse riding	اسب سواری
asbsavār e herfeyi	jockey	اسب سوار حرفه ای
asli	original	اصلی
asr bekheyr	Good afternoon.	عصر بخیر
atighe	antiques	عتیقه
avārez e furudgāh	airport tax	عوارض فرودگاه
avārez e māshin	car registration	عوارض ماشین
avval	first	اول
az (meh)	since (May)	از (مه)
azole	muscle	عضله

B

bā	with	با
bā ārzesh	valuable	با ارزش
bā ham estefāde kardan	to share (with)	با هم استفاده کردن
bā keshti ferestādan	to ship	با کشتی فرستادن
bābā	dad	بابا
bād	wind	باد
bāgh	garden	باغ
bāghbuni	gardening	باغبانی
bāgh e vahsh	zoo	باغ وحش
bāham	together	باهم
bāje ye telefon	phone box	باجه تلفن
bākht	loss	باخت

bākhtan	to lose	باختن
bāl	wing	بال
bālā	up	بالا
bālā raftan	to climb	بالا رفتن
bālāye	above	بالای
bāle	ballet	باله
bālesh	pillow	بالش
bālkon	balcony	بالکن
bāndāzh	bandage	بانداژ
bānk	bank	بانک

bānk kojā st?
بانک کجاست؟
Where's the bank?

bār	baggage	بار
bār e jā mānde	left luggage	بار جا مانده
bārun	rain	باران

bārun miyād
باران می آید
It's raining.

bāshe
باشه
OK.

bāstāni	ancient	باستانی
bāstān shenāsi	archaeology	باستان شناسی
bātri	battery	باطری
bāz	open	باز
bāz kardan	to open	باز کردن
bāzār	market	بازار
bāzande	loser	بازنده
bāzi	game (games)	بازی
bāzigar	actor	بازیگر
bāzihā ye olampik	Olympic Games	بازیهای المپیک
bāzikon	player (sports)	بازیکن
bāzneshaste	retired	بازنشسته
bāztāb	reflection (thinking)	بازتاب
bāzu	arm	بازو
bachche	child	بچه
bachche gorbe	kitten	بچه گربه
bachchehā	children	بچه ها
bad	bad	بد

ba'd	after	بعد
badan	body	بدن
ba'd az zohr	[in the] afternoon	بعد ازظهر
ba'di	next	بعدی

ba'dan mibinametun
بعداً می بینمتان
See you later.

baghal	a cuddle	بغل
baghiyye	rest (what's left)	بقیه
bahār	spring (season)	بهار
bahrekeshi	exploitation	بهره کشی
bakhshidan	to forgive	بخشیدن
banā ye yādbud	monument	بنای یاد بود
band e kafsh	lace	بند کفش
bandar	port	بندر
barābari	equality	برابری
barādar	brother	برادر
barādar khānde	stepbrother	برادر خوانده

barāye mesāl, ...
برای مثال ...
For example, ...

barāye sargarmi	for fun	برای سرگرمی
barande	winner	برنده
bardāshtan	to pick up	برداشتن
barf	snow	برف
bargh	electricity	برق
bargashtan	to return	برگشتن
barnāme	program	برنامه
barrasi	review	بررسی
basketbāl	basketball	بسکتبال
bastan	to close	بستن
bastani	ice cream	بستنی
baste	closed	بسته
baste ye posti	parcel	بسته پستی
ba'zi	some	بعضی
ba'zi vaghthā	sometimes	بعضی وقتها
be bozorgi ye	as big as	به بزرگی
be moghe'	on time	به موقع

be salāmati		بسلامتی
Good health! • Cheers!		
be taraf e	towards	به طرف
be yād āvordan	to remember	بیاد آوردن
bebakhshid		ببخشید
Excuse me.		
bedun e	without	بدون
bedun e filter	without filter	بدون فیلتر
bedun e sorb	unleaded	بدون سرب
behtar	est (comparative)	بهتر
behtarin	best (superative)	بهترین
belit	ticket	بلیط
belit jamkon	ticket collector	بلیط جمع کن
benzin	petrol	بنزین
bepichin chap		بپیچید چپ
Turn left.		
bepichin rāst		بپیچید راست
Turn right.		
berenji	of brass	برنجی
berim		برویم
Let's go.		
beyn	among	بین
beynolmelali	international	بین المللی
bezudi	soon	بزودی
bikhānemāni	homelessness	بی خانمانی
bikār	unemployed	بیکار
bikāri	unemployment	بیکاری
bilyārd	billiards	بیلیارد
bimārestān	hospital	بیمارستان
bimārestān e khususi	private hospital	بیمارستان خصوصی
bimāri	disease	بیماری
bimāri ye urughi	venereal disease	بیماری عروقی
bime	insurance	بیمه
bini	nose	بینی

birun	outside	بیرون
bishtar	more	بیشتر
bisedā	mute	بی صدا
bist	twenty	بیست
biyābun	desert	بیابان
bokhār	steam	بخار
boks	boxing	بوکس
boland	loud	بلند
boland ghad	tall	بلند قد
bolandi	volume (voice)	بلندی
bordan	to take (away)	بردن
bores	hairbrush	برس
boridan	to cut	بریدن
borj	tower	برج
boshghāb	plate	بشقاب
botri	bottle	بطری
botri ye āb	water bottle	بطری آب
boz	goat	بز
bozorg	big	بزرگ
bozorg rāh	toll-free motorway	بزرگراه
bozorgsāl	adult	بزرگسال
boronshit	bronchitis	برونشیت
bu	a smell	بو
budāyi	Buddhist	بودایی
budan	to be	بودن
bulvār	avenue (street)	بلوار
buse	kiss	بوسه
busidan	to kiss	بوسیدن
buyidan	to smell	بوییدن

CH

Remember that c comes after ch

chādor	tent	چادر
chādor zadan	to camp	چادر زدن
chāgh	fat (build)	چاق
chāghu	knife	چاقو
chāhār	four	چهار
chāhārom	fourth	چهارم
chāhār shanbe	Wednesday	چهارشنبه

C

chāhārdah	fourteen	چهارده
chārak	quarter	چارک
chakkosh	hammer	چکش
chaman	grass	چمن
chamedun	suitcase	چمدان
chandin	several	چندین
chap	left (not right)	چپ
charbi	fat (food)	چربی
charkh	wheel	چرخ
charkhesh	rolling	چرخش
charm	leather	چرم
chatr	umbrella	چتر
chehel	forty	چهل
chek e mosaferati	travellers cheques	چک مسافرتی
cherā	why	چرا

cherā muze baste ast?
چرا موزه بسته است؟
Why is the museum closed?

cherāgh	a light	چراغ
cherāgh e rāhnamāyi	traffic lights	چراغ راهنمایی
cherāgh ghovve	flashlight	چراغ قوه
cheshm	eye	چشم
cheshm pezeshk	optician	چشم پزشک
chetor	how	چطور

chetori migin ...?
چطوری می گویید ...؟
How do you say ...?

chi	what	چه

chi shode?
چه شده؟
What's the matter?
chikār mikonin?
چکار می کنید؟
What are you doing?

chizi	something	چیزی
chon	because	چون
chub	wood	چوب

C

Remember that ch comes before c

cot	jacket	کت
culer	fan (machine)	کولر

D

dādan	to give	دادن
dād zadan	to shout	داد زدن
dādgāh	court (legal)	دادگاه
dā'emi	permanent	دائمی
dākhel	inside	داخل
dāman	skirt	دامن
dāneshgāh	university	دانشگاه
dārā ye eydz	HIV positive	دارای ایدز
dārāye tahviye ye matbu'	air-conditioned	دارای تهویه مطبوع
dāru	drug	دارو
dārukhune	chemist/ pharmacy	دارو خانه
dāshtan	to have	داشتن
dāstān	story	داستان
dāstānhā ye kutāh	short stories	داستان های کوتاه
dāvar	referee	داور
dabirestān	high/secondary school	دبیرستان
daftar e furush	sales department	دفتر فروش
daftar e furush e belit	ticket office	دفتر فروش بلیط
daftarche	notebook	دفترچه
dafter e khāterāt	diary	دفتر خاطرات
dafter e telefon	phone book	دفتر تلفن
dah	ten	ده
dahāni	oral	دهانی
dahan	mouth	دهان
dahom	tenth	دهم

DICTIONARY

dakke ye sigār furushi	tobacco kiosk	دکه سیگار فروشی
dalghak	clown	دلقک
dalil	reason	دلیل
damā	temperature (weather)	دما
dandehā	ribs	دنده ها
dandun	tooth	دندان
dandun dard	toothache	دندان درد
dandun pezeshk	dentist	دندان پزشک
danesh ...	... student	دانش ...
āmuz	school	دانش آموز
ju	university	دانشجو
daneshmand	scientist	دانشمند
dar	door	در
dar	on	در
dar ...	in ...	در ...
(panj) daghighe (five) minutes		(پنج) دقیقه
(shish) ruz (six) days		(شش) روز
daraje	degree	درجه
dar bāz kon	bottle opener	در باز کن
dard	ache	درد
dardnāk	painful	دردناک
dard e me'de	stomachache	درد معده
dard e periyod	period pain	درد پریود
dar jelo ye	in front of	در جلوی
dark kardan	to realise	درک کردن
dar posht	at the back (behind)	در پشت
darre	valley	دره
darsad	per cent	درصد
darun	within	درون
darvāze	gate	دروازه
darvāzebān	goalkeeper	دروازه بان
daryā	sea	دریا
daryāche	lake	دریاچه

daryāft kardan	to receive	دریافت کردن
dast	hand	دست
dastbord zadan	to rob	دستبرد زدن
daste (varagh)	deck (of cards)	دسته (ورق)
dast furush	street-seller	دست فروش
dastgāh	machine	دستگاه
dastgāh e teliviziyon	TV set	دستگاه تلویزیون
dastkesh	gloves	دستکش
dastmāl kāghazi	tissues	دستمال کاغذی
dast sāz	handmade	دست ساز
dastshuyi	bathroom	دستشویی
dastur dādan	to order	دستور دادن
da'vā	quarrel	دعوا
da'vā kardan	to argue (fight)	دعوا کردن
davāzdah	twelve	دوازده
del tang shodan	to miss (feel absence)	دلتنگ شدن
delsuz	sympathetic	دلسوز
demokrāsi	democracy	دمکراسی
derāz	long	دراز
derakht	tree	درخت
derakht e mo	vine	درخت مو
desāmr	December	دسامبر
did	view	دید
didār kardan	to meet	دیدار کردن
didan	to see	دیدن
digar	other	دیگر
diksheneri	dictionary	دیکشنری
dir	late	دیر
diruz ...	yesterday ...	دیروز ...
ba'd az zohr	afternoon	بعد ازظهر
sob	morning	صبح
dishab	last night	دیشب
divār	wall	دیوار
divune	crazy	دیوانه

diyābeti	diabetic	دیابتی
do'ā	prayer	دعا
dobār	twice	دوبار
dobāre	again	دوباره
docharkhe	bicycle	دوچرخه
docharkhe savāri kardan	to cycle	دوچرخه سواری کردن
docharkhe ye mosābeghe	racing bike	دوچرخه مسابقه
docharkhe savār	cyclist	دوچرخه سوار
docharkhe savāri	cycling	دوچرخه سوار
doghulu	twins	دوقلو
dogāne	double	دوگانه
dogme	button	دکمه
do hafte	fortnight	دو هفته
dojin	a dozen	دوجین
dokhtar	daughter	دختر
doktor	doctor	دکتر
doktor e giyāhi	herbalist	دکتر گیاهی
dolat	government	دولت
dolme	stuffed leaves	دله
dolme bādemjun	stuffed eggplant	دله بادنجان
dom	tail	دم
donbāl kardan	to follow	دنبال کردن
donyā	world	دنیا
dore	term of office	دوره
dorost e It's true.		درست است
dorost	right (correct)	درست
doshākhe	plug (electricity)	دوشاخه
do shanbe	Monday	دوشنبه
dovidan	to run	دویدن
dovvom	second	دوم
dozd	thief	دزد
dozdidan	to steal	دزدیدن

dunestan	to know (something)	دانستن
dur	far	دور
durbin	binoculars	دوربین
durbin furushi	camera shop	دوربین فروشی
durugh gu	liar	دروغگو
durugh goftan	to lie	دروغ گفتن
dust	friend	دوست
dust dāshtan	to like	دوست داشتن

E

ebādat	worship	عبادت
edālat	justice	عدالت
edāre	office	اداره
edāre ye kāryābi	job centre	اداره کار یابی
edāre ye mokhāberāt	telephone office	اداره مخابرات
edāre ye post	post office	اداره پست
eghāmat kardan	to stay (somewhere)	اقامت کردن
eghtesād	economy	اقتصاد
ehsās kardan	to feel	احساس کردن
ehsāsāt	feelings	احساسات
ehterām	respect	احترام
ejāre kardan	to rent	اجاره کردن
ejāre	rent	اجاره
ejāze	permission	اجازه
ejāze ye kār	work permit	اجازه کار
ejāze dādan	to allow	اجازه دادن
ekhrāj	dismissal (to fire)	اخراج
emruz	today	امروز
emshab	tonight	امشب
emsāl	this year	امسال
emtahān kardan	to try	امتحان کردن
emtiyāz	advantage	امتیاز
emtiyāz gereftan	to score	امتیاز گرفتن
emruz ba'd az zohr	this afternoon	امروز بعد ازظهر

F

emzā	signature	امضا
emzā karadn	to sign	امضا کردن
en'ekās	reflection (mirror)	انعکاس
enerezhi ye hasteyi	nuclear energy	انرژی هسته ای
enjil	the Bible	انجیل
enkār kardan	to deny	انکار کردن
entekhāb kardan	to choose	انتخاب کردن
entekhābāt	elections	انتخابات
erā'e	presentation	ارائه
ertefā'	altitude	ارتفاع
eshā e rabbāni	mass (Catholic)	عشا ربانی
eshāre kardan	to point	اشاره کردن
eshetehā āvar	appetisers	اشتهاآور
eshtebāh	mistake	اشتباه
eskenās	banknotes	اسکناس
eski	skiing	اسکی
eski kardan	to ski	اسکی کردن
eslāyd	slide (film)	اسلاید
esm e kuchik	christian name	اسم کوچک
esm	name	اسم
estādiyom	stadium	استادیوم
estāndārd	standard (usual)	استاندارد
estakhr e shenā	swimming pool	استخر شنا
este'fā	resignation	استعفا
estedlāl kardan	to argue (a point)	استدلال کردن
esterāhat	rest (relaxation)	استراحت
esterāhat kardan	to relax	استراحت کردن
e'temād	trust	اعتماد
e'terāf	confession (religious)	اعتراف
e'terāz	protest	اعتراض
e'tesāb	a strike	اعتصاب
e'tiyād	addiction	اعتیاد
ettehādiyehā	unions	اتحادیه ها
ettehādiye ye bāzargāni	trade union	اتحادیه بازرگانی

eyb nadāre		عیب ندارد
It doesn't matter.		
eyd e kirismas	Christmas Eve	عید کریسمس
eyd e pāk	Easter	عید پاک
eydz	AIDS	ایدز
eynak āftābi	sunglasses	عینک آفتابی
ezdevāj	marriage	ازدواج
ezdevāj kardan	to marry	ازدواج کردن
ezterāri	urgent	اضطراری

F

fālbin	fortune teller	فال بین
fāsed	corrupt	فاسد
faghat	only	فقط
faghir	poor	فقیر
faghr	poverty	فقر
fahmidan	to understand	فهمیدن
falāt	plateau	فلات
falaj e dast o pā	paraplegic	فلج دست و پا
fanar	spring (coil)	فنر
fandak	lighter	فندک
fann	technique	فن
farāmush kardan	to forget	فراموش کردن
farāmushesh kon!		فراموش اش کن
Forget about it!; Don't worry!		
fard	person	فرد
fardā	tomorrow	فردا
fardā ba'd az zohr	tomorrow afternoon	فردا بعد ازظهر
fardā mibinametun		فردا می بینمتان
See you tomorrow.		
fardā sob	tomorrow morning	فردا صبح
faribande	charming	فریبنده
farsh	carpet/rug	فرش

fazā	space	فضا
fazānavard	astronaut	فضانورد
fejun	cup	فنجان
fekr	thought	فکر
fekr kardan	to think	فکر کردن
felezzi	metal	فلزی
felfel	pepper	فلفل
ferestādan	to send	فرستادن
feshār	pressure	فشار
feshār e khun	blood pressure	فشار خون
feshār e khun (e pāyin/bālā)	blood pressure (low/high)	فشار خون (بالا/پایین)
fevriye	February	فوریه
film	film	فیلم
filmbardāri kardan	to shoot (film)	فیلم برداری کردن
filmhā ye kutāh	short films	فیلم های کوتاه
filmnāme	script	فیلم نامه
filmnāme nevis	scriptwriter	فیلم نامه نویس
fogholāde	brilliant	فوق العاده
forsat	chance	فرصت
forsat e mosāvi	equal opportunity	فرصت مساوی
foshorde	intense	فشرده
furudgāh	airport	فرودگاه
furukhtan	to sell	فروختن
furushgāh e zanjireyi	department store	فروشگاه زنجیره ای
futbāl	football (soccer)	فوتبال
futbāl dasti	table football	فوتبال دستی

GH

Remember that g comes after gh

ghānun	law	قانون
ghānun gozāri	legislation	قانون گذاری
ghānuni sāzi	legalisation	قانونی سازی
ghār	cave	غار
ghāyegh	boat	قایق
ghāyegh motori	motorboat	قایق موتوری
ghāz	goose	غاز
ghāzi	judge	قاضی
ghablan	before	قبلاً
ghabr	grave	قبر
ghabrestun	cemetery	قبرستان
ghabul e! Agreed!		قبول است
ghabz	bill (account)	قبض
ghafase	shelf	قفسه
ghahremāni	championships	قهرمانی
ghahve khune	bar • cafe	قهوه خانه
ghahveyi	brown	قهوه ای
ghal'e	castle	قلعه
ghalat	wrong	غلط
ghalb	heart	قلب
ghamgin	sad	غمگین
ghanāri	canary	قناری
ghani	rich (food)	غنی
gharārdād	contract	قرارداد
gharantine	quarantine	قرنطینه
gharār dāshtan	to date (someone)	قرار داشتن
gharār	appointment	قرار
gharb	west	غرب
gharibe	stranger	غریبه
gharz dāshtan	to owe	قرض داشتن
gharz kardan	to borrow	قرض کردن
ghashang	beautiful	قشنگ
ghasr	palace	قصر
ghatār	train	قطار
ghatār barghi	tram	قطار برقی
ghavvāsi	diving	غواصی
ghavi	strong	قوی
ghazā	food	غذا
ghazā ye nozād	baby food	غذای نوزاد
ghazā ye yakh zade	frozen food	غذای یخ زده

gheddis	saint	قدیس
ghermez	red	قرمز
ghesmat	part	قسمت
gheychi	scissors	قیچی
gheymat	value (price)	قیمت
gheyr e āddi	unusual	غیر عادی
gheyr e herfe yi	amateur	غیر حرفه ای
gheyr e ghābel e fahm	incomprehensible	غیر قابل فهم
gheyr e mostaghim	non-direct	غیر مستقیم
ghodrat	power	قدرت
ghofl	lock	قفل
ghofl e zanjir	padlock	قفل زنجیر
ghofl kardan	to lock	قفل کردن
ghors	pill	قرص
ghors e khāb	sleeping pill	قرص خواب
ghors e zedd e hāmelegi	the Pill	قرص ضد حاملگی
ghorur	pride	غرور
ghotb namā	compass	قطب نما
ghovvat	strength	قوت
ghurub	sunset	غروب
ghuti	can (aluminium)	قوطی

G

Remember that gh comes before g

gārson	waiter	کارسن
gāv	cow	گاو
gāv sandugh	safe (n)	گاو صندوق
gāz	bite (dog)	گاز
galu	throat	گلو
galu dard	sore throat	گلو درد
gap zadan	to chat up	گپ زدن
gardan band	necklace	گردن بند
garde	pollen	گرده
gardesh	stroll • walk	گردش
garm	warm	گرم
garm kardan	to warm	گرم کردن

garmā	heat	گرما
garm e It's hot.		گرم است.
gavāhināme	certificate	گواهینامه
gavāhināme ye rānan degi	driver's licence	گواهینامه رانندگی
gedā	beggar	گدا
gel	mud	گل
geram	gram	گرم
gerd	round	گرد
gereftan	to take (food; the train)	گرفتن
gerun	expensive	گران
gij	dizzy	گیج
gitār	guitar	گیتار
giyāh	plant	گیاه
goftan	to say	گفتن
gol	flower	گل
gol furush	flower seller	گل فروش
gom sho! Get lost!		کم شو
gomrok	customs	کمرک
gonāh	sin	گناه
gorbe	cat	گربه
gorg	wolf	گرگ
gorosne budan	to be hungry	گرسنه بودن
gozāshtan	to put	گذاشتن
gozarnāme	passport	گذرنامه
gozashte	past	گذشته
gunehā ye ... mohāfezat shode	... species protected	گونه های ... محافظت شده
dar hāl e nādudi	endangered	در حال نابودی
guril	gorilla	گوریل
gurkhar	zebra	گورخر
gurkan	badger	گورکن
guruh (musighi)	band (music)	گروه (موسیقی)

H

guruh e khuni	blood group	گروه خونی
guruh e rāk	rock group	گروه راک
gush	ear	گوش
gush kardan	to listen	گوش کردن
gushe	corner	گوشه
gusht e khuk	ham	گوشت خوک
gushvāre	earrings	گوشواره
gusāle	calf	گوساله
gusfand	sheep	گوسفند

H

hāl	present (time)	حال
hāla	now	حالا
hāmele	pregnant	حامله
hāzer	ready	حاضر
hadde aksar e sor'at	speed limit	حد اکثر سرعت
hads zadan	to guess	حدس زدن
hafte	week	هفته
hafte ye ba'd	next week	هفته بعد
hafte ye gozashte	last week	هفته گذشته

hagh bā shomāst حق با شماست
You're right.

hagh budan	to be right	حق بودن
haghighat	truth	حقیقت
hajm	volume (quantity)	حجم
ham	also	هم

ham otāgh budan هم اتاق بودن
to share a dorm

hamchenin	too (as well)	همچنین
hame	all	همه
hamin al'ān	right now	همین الان
hamishe	always	همیشه
hamjens bāz e mard	gay	همجنس باز مرد
hamjensbāz	homosexual	همجنس باز
hamkār	colleague	همکار
haml kardan	to carry	حمل کردن

hamrāh	companion	همراه
hamum	bath	حمام
hamjensbāz e zan	lesbian	همجنس باز زن
hanuz	yet	هنوز
hanuz na	not yet	هنوز نه
har do	both	هردو
har kodum	each	هر کدام
har ruz	every day	هر روز
har	any	هر
harāj	[on] sale	حراج
harekat	departure	حرکت
harf zadan	to talk	حرف زدن
harj o marj talab	anarchist	هرج و مرج طلب
hashare	bug	حشره
hasht	eight	هشت
hashtād	eighty	هشتاد
hashtom	eighth	هشتم
hasir	mat	حصیر
hassāsiyat	an allergy	حساسیت
hasti	universe	هستی
hasud	jealous	حسود
hatman	Sure.	حتماً
havā	air	هوا

havā mehālud e هوا مه‌آلود است
It's foggy.

havādārān	fans (of a team)	هواداران
havāpeymā	aeroplane	هواپیما
hazine ye posti	postage	هزینه پستی
hazyān goftan	to hallucinate	هذیان گفتن
hazyān gu	delirious	هذیان گو
hedye	gift	هدیه
hendu	Hindu	هندو
herfe	profession	حرفه
hedye ye arusi	wedding present	هدیه عروسی
heyvun e vahshi	wild animal	حیوان وحشی

227

DICTIONARY

English	Persian		

I

heyvun	animal	حیوان
hich	none	هیچ
hich chiz	nothing	هیچ چیز
hich kodum	neither	هیچ کدام
hich vaght	never	هیچ وقت
hipātit	hepatitis	هپاتیت
hiter	heater	هیتر
hizom	firewood	هیزم
hoghugh	salary	حقوق
hoghugh e madani	civil rights	حقوق مدنی
hokm	sentence (prison)	حکم
hol dādan	to push	هل دادن
hole	towel	حوله
home	suburb	حومه
home ye ...	suburbs of ...	... حومه
honar	art	هنر
honar e kelāsik	classical art	هنر کلاسیک
honar e pish tārikhi	prehistoric art	هنر پیش تاریخی
honarhā ye tarsimi	graphic art	هنر های ترسیمی
honar mand	artist	هنر مند
hotel e ...	... hotel	هتل ...
arzun	cheap	ارزان
khub	good	خوب
tamiz	clean	تمیز
zadik	nearby	نزدیک
hoviyyat	identification	هویت
hoze ye entekhābiye	electorate	حوزه انتخابیه
hughugh e bashar	human rights	حقوق بشر

I

in hafte	this week	این هفته
in māh	this month	این ماه
ingilis	England	انگلیس

ingilisi	English	انگلیسی
injā	here	اینجا
irland	Ireland	ایرلند
ist!	Stop!	ایست
istādiyo	studio	استودیو
istgāh e ghatār	train station	ایستگاه قطار
istgāh	station	ایستگاه
istgāh e zir zamini	subway station	ایستگاه زیر زمینی
istgāh e tāksi	taxi stand	ایستگاه تاکسی
istgāh utubus	bus stop	ایستگاه اتوبوس
iyālāt e mottahed e āmrikā	US	ایالات متحده آمریکا

J

jā mundan	to be left (behind/over)	جا ماندن
jādde (e asli)	road (main)	جاده (اصلی)
jāleb	interesting	جالب
jām e jahāni	World Cup	جام جهانی
jām e varzeshi	league	جام ورزشی
jāmed	solid	جامد
ja'be ye komakhā ye avvaliyye	first-aid kit	جعبه کمکهای اولیه
ja'be	box	جعبه
jadval e emtiyāzāt	scoreboard	جدول امتیازات
jadval e zamāni	timetable	جدول زمانی
jahāngard	tourist	جهانگرد
jak	jack (for car)	جک
jang	war	جنگ
jang kardan	to fight	جنگ کردن
jangal	forest	جنگل
jangal e mohāfezat shode	protected forest	جنگل محافظت شده
jangal zodāyi	deforestation	جنگل زدایی

jarayān	stream	جریان
jarime	a fine	جریمه
jashn gereftan	to celebrate	جشن گرفتن
jashnvāre	festival	جشنواره
javāb	answer	جواب
javāb dādan	answering	جواب دادن
javāherāt	jewellery	جواهرات
javān	young	جوان
javāni	youth (collective)	جوانی
javāz e ubur	pass	جواز عبور
javv	atmosphere	جو
jazire	island	جزیره
jeddi	serious	جدی
jelo	ahead	جلو
jelogiri az bārdāri	contraception	جلو گیری از بارداری
jelogiri kardan	to prevent	جلو گیری کردن
jenāh e chap	left-wing	جناح چپ
jenāh e rāst	right-wing	جناح راست
jens gerāyi	sexism	جنس گرایی
jensiyyat	sex	جنسیت
jib	pocket	جیب
jin	jeans	جین
jip	jeep	جیپ
jirjirak	cricket (insect)	جیرجیرک
jodā kardan	to separate	جدا کردن
joft (dastkesh)	pair (of gloves)	جفت (دستکش)
jok	joke	جوک
jom'e	Friday	جمعه
jomhuri	republic	جمهوری
jomle	sentence (words)	جمله
josteju kardan	to look for	جستجو کردن
joz'iyyāt	detail	جزییات
juje	chicken	جوجه
juje khurus	cockerel	جوجه خروس
junub	south	جنوب
jurāb	socks	جوراب
jurāb e boland	stockings	جوراب بلند
jush	a rash	جوش

KH

Remember that k comes after kh

khāb ālud	sleepy	خواب الود
khāb didan	to dream	خواب دیدن
khāhar	sister	خواهر
khāhar khānde	stepsister	خواهر خوانده
khāhim did! We'll see!		خواهیم دید
khākestari	grey	خاکستری
khāle	aunt (mother's side)	خاله
khāles	pure	خالص
khāli	empty • vacant	خالی
khām	raw	خام
khānande	singer	خواننده
khānande-tarānesarā	singer-songwriter	خواننده-ترانه سرا
khārej	abroad	خارج
khāreji	foreign	خارجی
khāresh	itch	خارش
khārobār furushi	delicatessen	خوار و بار فروشی
khāstan	to ask (for something) • to want	خواستن
khamir dandun	toothpaste	خمیر دندان
khande	laugh	خنده
kharāb	broken (out of order) • faulty (equipment)	خراب
kharāb kardan	to destroy	خراب کردن
kharābehā	ruins	خرابه ها
kharid raftan	to go shopping	خرید رفتن
kharidan	to buy	خریدن
khaste	bored • tired	خسته
khaste konande	boring	خسته کننده
khat	line	خط

khatar	risk	خطر
khatarnāk	dangerous	خطرناک
khargush	rabbit	خرگوش
khayyāti kardan	to sew	خیاطی کردن
khedmāt	service (assistance)	خدمت
khedmat e sarbāzi	military service	خدمت سربازی
khejālāt	embarrassment	خجالت
khejālat zade	embarrassed	خجالت زده
khejālati	shy	خجالتی
kheyli	many • very	خیلی
kheyli gerun	too expensive	خیلی گران

kheyli kharj dāre خیلی خرج دارد
It costs a lot.

kheyli ziyād	too much • too many	خیلی زیاد
khis	wet	خیس
khiyābun	street	خیابان
khiyāl	fiction	خیال
khodā	God	خدا

khodā hāfez خدا حافظ
Goodbye.

khoddāri kardan	to refuse	خودداری کردن
khodkhāh	selfish	خودخواه
khodkār	pen (ballpoint)	خودکار
khordan	to eat	خوردن
khosh āmadin	welcome!	خوش آمدید
khosh ghiyāfe	handsome	خوش قیافه
khosh gozarāni	luxury	خوش گذرانی
khosh shāns	lucky	خوش شانس
khoshk kardan	to dry (clothes)	خشک کردن
khoshksāli	draught	خشکسالی
khoshmaze	tasty	خوشمزه
khub	nice • well	خوب
khukche ye hendi	guinea pig	خوکچه هندی

khuk	pig	خوک
khun	blood	خون
khunavāde	family	خانواده
khundan	to read	خواندن
khune	house	خانه
khunrizi kardan	to bleed	خونریزی کردن
khord	change (coins)	خرد
khuruj	exit	خروج
khusuforce	private	خصوصی
khususi	private	خصوصی
khusuci sāzi	privatisation	خصوصی سازی

K

Remember that kh comes before k

kādo	souvenir	کادو
kādo furushi	souvenir shop	کادو فروشی
kāfi	enough	کافی

kāfiye! کافی است
Enough!

kāghaz	paper	کاغذ
kāghaz e sigar	cigarette papers	کاغذ سیگار
kāghaz e tuvālet	toilet paper	کاغذ توالت
kālej	college	کالج
kāmiyon	truck	کامیون
kānāl	channel	کانال
kār	work	کار
kār e edāri	office work	کار اداری
kār e honari	artwork	کار هنری
kār e khune	housework	کار خانه
kār e sākhtemāni	construction work	کار ساختمانی
kār kardan	to work	کار کردن
kārfarmā	employer	کارفرما
kārgāh	workshop	کارگاه
kārgar	factory • manual worker	کارگر
kārkhune	factory	کار خانه
kārikātor	comics	کاریکاتور

kārmand	office worker	کارمند
kārt	card	کارت
kārt e e'tebāri	credit card	کارت اعتباری
kārt e postāl	postcard	کارت پستال
kārt e shenāsāyi	identification card	کارت شناسایی
kārt e savār shodan	boarding pass	کارت سوار شدن
kārt e telefon	phonecard	کارت تلفن
kārton	carton	کارتن
kārtun	cartoons	کارتون
kāshtan	to plant	کاشتن
kātolik	Catholic	کاتولیک
kabābi	kebab shop	کبابی
kaf e zamin	floor	کف زمین
kafsh	shoes	کفش
kafsh furushi	shoe shop	کفش فروشی
kak	flea	کک
kalame	word	کلمه
kalle shagh	stubborn	کله شق
kam	few • less	کم
kam khuni	anaemia	کم خونی
kamarband	seatbelt	کمر بند
kambud	shortage	کمبود
kami	a little (amount)	کمی
kamyāb	rare	کمیاب
kanise	synagogue	کنیسه
kardan	to do	کردن
kashf kardan	to discover	کشف کردن
kasb kardan	to earn	کسب کردن
kasif	dirty	کثیف
kebrit	matches	کبریت
kelāj	clutch (car)	کلاج
kelid	key	کلید
kelisā	cathedral • church	کلیسا
kenār e daryā	seaside	کنار دریا
kenār gozāshtan	to exclude	کنار گذاشتن
kenār	beside	کنار
kerem e narm konande	moisturiser	کرم نرم کننده
kerm	worm	کرم

keshāvarz	farmer	کشاورز
keshāvarzi	agriculture	کشاورزی
keshidan	to draw	کشیدن
keshish	priest	کشیش
keshti	ship	کشتی
keshvar	country	کشور
kesi	somebody • someone	کسی
ketāb	book	کتاب
ketāb e do'ā	prayer book	کتاب دعا
ketāb e rāhnamā	guidebook	کتاب راهنما
ketāb furushi	bookshop	کتاب فروشی
ketābkhune	library	کتابخانه
key	when	کی
keyfiyyat	quality	کیفیت
keyk e arusi	wedding cake	کیک عروسی
keyk e tavallod	birthday cake	کیک تولد
keyk furushi	cake shop	کیک فروشی
ki ye? Who is it?		کی هست؟
ki	who	کی
kif	bag	کیف
kif dasti	handbag	کیف دستی
kilogeram	kilogram	کیلو گرم
kilometre	kilometre	کیلومتر
kise khāb	sleeping bag	کیسه خواب
kist	cystitis	کیست
kod e posti	postcode	کد پستی
kodum rāh? Which way?		کدام راه؟
kohne	old	کهنه
kojā	where	کجا
kokā'in	cocaine	کوکائین
kolāh e imani	helmet	کلاه ایمنی
kolāh bardāri	rip-off	کلاهبرداری
kolang	pickaxe	کلنگ
koliye	kidney	کلیه
komak	aid (help)	کمک

komak kardan	to help	کمک کردن
komak!	Help!	کمک
komedi	comedy	کمدی
komod	cupboard	کمد
komonist	communist	کمونیست
komput	stewed fruit	کمپوت
konsert	a concert	کنسرت
konsulgari	consulate	کنسولگری
kotorol az rāh e dur	remote control	کنترل از راه دور
kontorol kardan	to check	کنترل کردن
kopon	coupon	کوپن
kore ye zamin	Earth	کره زمین
korset	bra	کرست
koshtan	to kill	کشتن
kuchik	little (small)	کوچک
kudakestān	kindergarten	کودکستان
kuftegi	a bruise	کوفتگی
kuh	mountain	کوه
kuh navardi	mountaineering	کوهنوردی
kule poshti	backpack	کوله پشتی
kutāh	short	کوتاه

lāghar	thin (build)	لاغر
lāmp	light bulb	لامپ
lāye ye ozon	ozone layer	لایه اوزون
lāzem	necessary	لازم
lāzem dāshtan	to need	لازم داشتن
lab	lip	لب
labaniyyāt	dairy products	لبنیات
labe	ledge	لبه
labkhand zadan	to smile	لبخند زدن
laghv kardan	to cancel	لغو کردن
lagad	kick	لگد

laklak	stork	لک لک
lams kardan	to touch	لمس کردن
langargāh	harbour	لنگرگاه
lase	gum	لثه
lebās	clothing	لباس
lebās e zir	underpants	لباس زیر
lebās furushi	clothing store	لباس فروشی
lenz e tamāsi	contact lenses	لنز تماسی
lenz	lens	لنز
lezzat bordan	to enjoy (oneself)	لذت بردن
list e ghazā	menu	لیست غذا

lotafan rāh e ... ro be man begin
Please tell me the way to ...

لطفاً راه ... را به من بگویید

M

mā	we	ما
mādar	mother	مادر
mādar bozorg	grandmother	مادر بزرگ
mādar shohar	mother-in-law (man's)	مادر شوهر
mādar zan	mother-in-law (woman's)	مادر زن
māh	month, moon	ماه
māh e asal	honeymoon	ماه عسل
māh e ba'd	next month	ماه بعد
māh e gozashte	last month	ماه گذشته
māher	crafty	ماهر
māhi	fish	ماهی
māhi furushi	fish shop	ماهی فروشی
māhi tābe	pan	ماهیتابه
māhi ye tāze	fresh fish	ماهی تازه
māliyāt	tax	مالیات
māliyāt bar darāmad	income tax	مالیات بر در آمد
māmān	Mum	مامان
mār	snake	مار
mārgārin	margarine	مارگارین
mārs	March	مارس
māshin	car	ماشین

māshin e lebās shuyi	washing machine	ماشین لباسشویی
māshin gereftegi	travel sickness	ماشین گرفتگی
māsāzh	massage	ماساژ
māyo	bathing suit	مایو
ma'bad	temple	معبد
madrak e tahsili	qualifications	مدرک تحصیلی
madrese	school	مدرسه
maghāze	shop	مغازه
maghbare	shrine	مقبره
maghsad	destination	مقصد
magas	fly	مگس
mahall	location	محل
mahalli	local	محلی
mahall e tavallod	place of birth	محل تولد
mahall e bāzrasi	checkpoint	محل بازرسی
mahall e sukunat	accommodation	محل سکونت
mahdude	field	محدوده
mahrumiyyat	disadvantage	محرومیت
mahsus	sensible	محسوس
majalle	magazine	مجله
majjāni	free (of charge)	مجانی
majles	parliament	مجلس
majmu'e	series	مجموعه
majrā	opening	مجرا
makhlot kardan	to mix	مخلوط کردن
makhsus	special	مخصوص
malāfe	sheet (bed)	ملافه
malake	queen	ملکه
man	I	من

[man] be shomā zang mizanam
I'll give you a ring. (من) به شما زنگ می زنم

[man] eshtebāh mikonam
I'm wrong. (not right) (من) اشتباه می کنم

[man] sabzi khār am
I'm vegetarian. (من) سبزیخوارم

mantagheyi	regional	منطقه ای
marāsem	service (religious)	مراسم
mard	man	مرد
mardom	people	مردم
marg	death	مرگ
mariz	sick • ill	مریض
marizi	a sickness	مریضی
marja'	reference	مرجع
markaz e ettelā'āt o jahāngardi	tourist information office	مرکز اطلاعات و جهانگردی
markaz e shahr	city centre	مرکز شهر
marz	border	مرز
ma'shughe	lover	معشوقه
mashghul	busy (engaged)	مشغول
mashguliyat	engagement	مشغولیت
mashhur	popular, famous	مشهور
masā'el e jāri	current affairs	مسائل جاری
masihi	Christian	مسیحی
masir	path, track	مسیر
masirhā ye piyāderavi	hiking routes	مسیرهای پیاده روی
masjed	mosque	مسجد

maskhare kardan
to make fun of مسخره کردن

masno'i	synthetic	مصنوعی
mast budan	to be drunk	مست بودن
maz-hab	religion	مذهب
maz-habi	religious	مذهبی
mazre'e	farm	مزرعه
me'de	stomach	معده
me'mār	architect	معمار
me'māri	architecture	معماری
medād	pencil	مداد
mediteyshen	meditation	مدیتیشن
meh	May	مه
mehmuni	party	مهمانی
mehrabun	caring • kind	مهربان
mekāniki	garage	مکانیکی
meliyyat	nationality	ملیت

mesāl	example	مثال
mesvāk	toothbrush	مسواک
metr	metre	متر
meydun	court • square	میدان
meydun e asli	main square	میدان اصلی
meydun e tenis	tennis court	میدان تنیس
meymun	monkey	میمون

mifahmam — می فهمم
I see. [understand]

migren	migraine	میگرن

mikhāyim be ... berim
We'd like to go to ...
می خواهیم به ... برویم

mikhā ye chādor	tent pegs	میخ های چادر
milimetr	millimetre	میلی متر

mishe be man ... bedin?
Could you give me ...?
می شود به من ... بدهید؟

mishe ye aks begiram?
Can (May) I take a photo?
می شود یک عکس بگیرم؟

mitunin ruye naghshe be man neshun bedin?
Can you show me on the map?
می توانید روی نقشه به من نشان بدهید؟

mive	fruit	میوه
mive chini	fruit picking	میوه چینی
miz	table	میز
mizān e hoghugh	rate of pay	میزان حقوق
mo'āmele kardan	to deal (trade)	معامله کردن
mo'allem	teacher	معلم
mo'tād	addict	معتاد

mobārak e!
Congratulations!
مبارک است

moch e pā	ankle	مچ پا

modir	director • manager	مدیر
mofid	useful	مفید
moghābel	against	مقابل
mogarrarāt	rules	مقررات
mohāfezekār	conservative	محافظه کار
mohāfezat kardan	to protect	محافظت کردن
mohājerat	immigration	مهاجرت
mohandes	engineer	مهندس
mohandesi	engineering	مهندسی
mohemm	important	مهم

mohemm nist
It's not important.
مهم نیست

mohemm e
It's important.
مهم است

mohit	environment	محیط
moj	tide, wave	موج
mojarrad	single (person)	مجرد
mojassame	statue	مجسمه
mojavvez	permit	مجوز
mojri	presenter (TV, etc)	مجری
mokhālef	opposite	مخالف
molayyen	laxatives	ملین
momken	possible	ممکن

momken nist
It's not possible.
ممکن نیست

momken e
It's possible.
ممکن است

monshi	secretary	منشی
morāghebat kardan	to look after	مراقبت کردن
morabba'	square (shape)	مربع
morabbi	coach (trainer) (holiday)	مربی
morakhkhasi	dismissal	مرخصی
mordan	to die	مردن
morde	dead	مرده
morgh	hen	مرغ
moshābe	similar	مشابه
moshkel	difficult	مشکل

mosābeghe	match • race (sport) • game show	مسابقه
mosāfer	passenger • traveller	مسافر
mosāferat	journey	مسافرت
mosāhebe	interview	مصاحبه
mosāvi	same	مساوی
mosakken	painkiller	مسکن
mosalmun	Muslim	مسلمان
mostaghim	direct • straight	مستقیم

mostaghim berin مستقیم بروید
Go straight ahead.

mostamerri begir	pensioner	مستمری بگیر
mostanad	documentary	مستند

mota'assefam متأسفم
I'm sorry.

motafāvet	different	متفاوت
motakhasses	specialist	متخصص

motashakkeram متشکرم
Thank you.

motor	engine	موتور
motorsiklet	motorcycle	موتور سیکلت
movāfegh budan	to agree	موافق بودن

movāfegh nistam موافق نیستم
I don't agree.

movāzeb bāshin! مواظب باشید
Careful!

movaffagh bāshin! موفق باشید
Good luck!

movaffaghiyyat	success	موفقیت
mozāhem	pain in the neck	مزاحم
mu	hair	مو
mundan	to stay (remain)	ماندن
murche	ant	مورچه
murmur	creep (col)	مورمور

mush	rat	موش
musighi	music	موسیقی
musighi dān	musician	موسیقی دان
muze	museum	موزه

N

nā āmn	unsafe	نا امن
nā mādari	stepmother	نامادری
nā pedari	stepfather	ناپدری
nābarābari	inequality	نابرابری
nābinā	blind	نابینا
nāhār	lunch	ناهار
nāme	letter	نامه
nāmzad	fiancé(e)	نامزد
nāmzadi	engagement	نامزدی
nārenji	orange (colour)	نارنجی
nāshenavā	deaf	ناشنوا
nātavān	disabled	ناتوان
nāzok	thin (things)	نازک
nafas keshidan	to breathe	نفس کشیدن
naft	oil (crude)	نفت
naghghāsh	painter	نقاش
naghghāshi	painting (the art)	نقاشی
naghghāshi kardan	to draw (a drawing)	نقاشی کردن
naghshe	map	نقشه
naghshe ye jādde	road map	نقشه جاده
nakh e dandun	dental floss	نخ دندان
nakhost vazir	prime minister	نخست وزیر
namāyesh	a show	نمایش
namāyeshgāh	exhibition	نمایشگاه
namāyeshnāme	play (theatre)	نمایشنامه
namak	salt	نمک
nanu	hammock	ننو
narde	fence	نرده
navākhtan	to play (music)	نواختن
navār	cassette	نوار

navār behdāshti	sanitary napkins	نوار بهداشتی
navār e vidiyo	video tape	نوار ویدیو
navad	ninety	نود
nave	grandchild	نوه
nazdik	near	نزدیک
nazdik be	next to	نزدیک به
negāh kardan	to look	نگاه کردن
negahbun	curator	نگهبان
negahdāri ye bachche	childminding	نگهداری بچه
negarān	worried	نگران
nejāt dādan	to save	نجات دادن
nemidunam	I don't know.	نمی دانم
nerkh e arz	exchange rate	نرخ ارز
nerkh	price	نرخ
neshastan	to sit	نشستن
neshun dādan	to exhibit • show	نشان دادن
nesf	half	نصف
nevesht afzār furushi	stationers	نوشت افزار فروشی
neveshtan	to write	نوشتن
nevisande	writer	نویسنده
nezhād	race (ancestry)	نژاد
nezhād parasti	racism	نژاد پرستی
nezām e tabaghāti	class system	نظام طبقاتی
nim litr	half a litre	نیم لیتر
nime shab	midnight	نیمه شب
nish	bite (insect)	نیش
noghreyi	of silver	نقره ای
noghte	point (tip)	نقطه
noghte ye chesm andāz	lookout point	نقطه چشم انداز
noh	nine	نه
nohom	ninth	نهم
nokhā'	spine	نخاع
novāmr	November	نوامبر
nozād	baby	نوزاد
nun	bread	نان

nunavāyi	bakery	نانوایی
nun e tost	toast (bread)	نان توست
nur	light (sun/lamp)	نور
nur sanj	light meter	نورسنج
nush e jān! Bon appetit!		نوش جان
nushābe	a drink	نوشابه
nushidan	to drink	نوشیدن
nuzdah	nineteen	نوزده
nyuziland	New Zealand	نیوزیلند

O

oghāb	eagle	عقاب
oghyānus	ocean	اقیانوس
oj	peak	اوج
ojāgh	stove	اجاق
oksizhen	oxygen	اکسیژن
oktobr	October	اکتبر
olād	descendent	اولاد
operā	opera	اوپرا
operātor	operator	اوپراتور
ordak	duck	اردک
orkestr	orchestra	ارکستر
ostukhun	bone	استخوان
otāgh	room	اتاق
otāgh e do khābe	double room	اتاق دو خوابه
otāgh e entezār	waiting room	اتاق انتظار
otāgh e ghazākhori	dining room (in a home)	اتاق غذا خوری
otāgh e taki	single room	اتاق تکی
otāgh khāb	bedroom	اتاق خواب
overkot	overcoat	اورکت
ozv	member	عضو

P

pā	foot	پا
pākat	envelope	پاکت
pālto	coat	پالتو

P

pārk	a park	پارک
pārk e melli	national park	پارک ملی
pārk kardan	to park	پارک کردن
pārsāl	last year	پارسال
pāyin	low	پایین
pāyiz	autumn/fall	پاییز
panāhande	refugee	پناهنده
panāhgāh	mountain hut	پناهگاه
panbe	cotton	پنبه
panchari	puncture	پنچری
panir	cheese	پنیر
panj	five	پنج
panjere	window	پنجره
panj shanbe	Thursday	پنج شنبه
panke	fan (hand-held)	پنکه
parande	bird	پرنده
parastār	nurse	پرستار
parcham	flag	پرچم
pardākht	payment	پرداخت
pardākhtan	to pay	پرداختن
paridan	to jump	پریدن
pariruz	day before yesterday	پریروز
parkhāshgar	aggressive	پرخاشگر
parvāne	butterfly	پروانه
parvāz	flight	پرواز
pas dādan	to refund	پس دادن
pas fardā	day after tomorrow	پس فردا
pashimun shodan	to regret	پشیمان شدن
pashm	wool	پشم
patu	blanket	پتو
paziresh	check-in (desk)	پذیرش
paziroftan	to accept • admit	پذیرفتن
pedar	father	پدر
pedar bozorg	grandfather	پدر بزرگ
pedar o mādar	parents	پدر و مادر
pedar shohar	father-in-law (man's)	پدر شوهر
pedar zan	father-in-law (woman's)	پدر زن

pelāstik	plastic	پلاستیک
penisilin	penicillin	پنی سیلین
periyod	menstruation	پریود
pesar	boy/son	پسر
pestun	breast	پستان
pestunak	dummy/pacifier	پستانک
peydā kardan	to find	پیدا کردن
peyghām	message	پیغام
peykar tarāsh	sculptor	پیکر تراش
peykare	sculpture	پیکره
pinkponk	table tennis	پینگ پونک
pip	pipe	پیپ
pirhan	shirt	پیراهن
pish az in	already	پیش از این
pishband	bib	پیش بند
pishnahād kardan	to recommend	پیشنهاد کردن
piyāde ravi	hiking	پیاده روی
piyāde ravi kardan	to hike	پیاده روی کردن
pokhtan	to cook	پختن
poker	poker	پوکر
pol	bridge	پل
polis	police	پلیس
poliver	jumper • sweater	پولیور
por	full	پر
por kardan	to fill	پر کردن
por sar o sedā	noisy	پر سر و صدا
porozhoktor	projector	پروژکتور
porsidan	to question • ask	پرسیدن
porteghāl	orange (fruit)	پرتقال
posht	back (of body)	پشت
post	mail	پست
post e ...	... mail	پست ...
havāyi	air	هوایی
sari' osseyr	express	سریع السیر
sefāreshi	registered	سفارشی
zamini	surface	زمینی
pudr e bachche	baby powder	پودر بچه
pul	money	پول
pushak	nappy	پوشک

D I C T I O N A R Y

237

pushidan	to wear	پوشیدن
pust	skin • shell	پوست
puster	poster	پوستر
putin (e piyāderavi)	(hiking) boots	پوتین (پیاده روی)

R

rābete	relationship	رابطه
rādiyātor	radiator	رادیاتور
rāh	way	راه
rāh e dur	long distance	راه دور
rāh e kuhestāni	mountain path	راه کوهستانی
rāh pelle	stairway	راه پله
rāh raftan	to walk	راه رفتن
rāhāhan	railroad	راه آهن
rāhat	comfortable	راحت
rāheb	monk	راهب
rāhebe	nun	راهبه
rāhnamā	guide (person/ audio) • indicator	راهنما
rānandegi kardan	to drive	رانندگی کردن
rāst	right (not left)	راست
radd e pā	footpath • track (footprints)	رد پا
raft o āmad	traffic	رفت و آمد
raftan	to go	رفتن

raftan be ... cheghadr kharj dāre?
How much does it cost to go to ...?
رفتن به ... چقدر خرج دارد؟

rag	vein	رگ
rag be rag shodegi	a sprain	رگ به رگ شدگی
raghs	dancing	رقص
raghsidan	to dance	رقصیدن
ragbār	shower	رگبار
rahbar	leader	رهبر
rahmat kardan	to bless	رحمت کردن

ra'is	president	رئیس
rakhtkan	cloakroom	رختکن
rang	colour	رنگ
rang kardan	to paint	رنگ کردن
rangi	colour (film)	رنگی
ranj bordan	to suffer	رنج بردن
ra'y dādan	to vote	رای دادن
refāh e ejtemāyi	social welfare	رفاه اجتماعی
refāh	welfare	رفاه
reshte kuh	mountain range	رشته کوه
reshve	a bribe	رشوه
reshve dādan	to bribe	رشوه دادن
resid	receipt	رسید
residan	to arrive	رسیدن
residegi kardan	to deal with	رسیدگی کردن
resturān	restaurant	رستوران
rezerv kardan	to reserve	رزرو کردن
rish tarāsh	razor	ریش تراش
rismun	string	ریسمان
roghan	oil (cooking)	روغن
roghan e āftābgardān	sunflower oil	روغن آفتابگردان
roghan e zeytun	olive oil	روغن زیتون
romān	novel (book)	رمان
roshan	light (clear)	روشن
rozh e lab	lipstick	روژ لب
ruye	over, aboard	روی
rubāh	fox	روباه
rubāleshi	pillowcase	روبالشی
rudkhune	river	رودخانه
rusari	scarf	روسری
rustā	village	روستا
ruz	day	روز
ruz e kirismas	Christmas Day	روز کریسمس
ruz e sāl e no	New Year's Day	روز سال نو
ruz e tavallod	birthday	روز تولد
ruzāne	daily	روزانه
ruznāme	newspaper	روزنامه

ruznāme furushi	news-agency	روزنامه فروشی
ruznāme negār	journalist	روزنامه نگار
ruznāmehā ye ingilisi	English-language newspapers	روزنامه های انگلیسی

SH

Remember that s comes after sh

shād	happy	شاد
shāh	king	شاه
shākh	horn	شاخ
shākhe	branch	شاخه
shām	dinner	شام
shāmel budan	to include	شامل بودن
shāmpāyn	champagne	شامپاین
shāmpu	shampoo	شامپو
shāns	luck	شانس
shāyad	maybe	شاید
shab	evening • night	شب
shab bekheyr		شب بخیر
Good evening/night.		
shahāb sang	meteor	شهاب سنگ
shahr	city • town	شهر
shahr dār	mayor	شهردار
shahr e ghadimi	old city	شهر قدیمی
shakhsiyat	personality	شخصیت
shalvār	trousers	شلوار
shalvārak	short	شلوارک
sham'	candle	شمع
shamshir	sword	شمشیر
shamshir bāzi	fencing	شمشیر بازی
shanbe	Saturday	شنبه
sharāb	wine	شراب
sharāb sāzi	winery	شراب سازی
shargh	east	شرق
sharh e hāl	biography	شرح حال
sharh e vazāyef	job descrption	شرح وظایف

shart	a bet	شرط
shatranj	chess	شطرنج
she'r	poetry	شعر
shekāyat	petition	شکایت
shekar	sugar	شکر
shekastan	to break	شکستن
shekaste	broken	شکسته
shekl	shape	شکل
shen	sand	شن
shenā	swimming	شنا
shenā kardan	to swim	شنا کردن
shenākhtan	to know (someone) • to recognise	شناختن
shenāsnāme	birth certificate	شناسنامه
shenidan	to hear	شنیدن
shepesh	lice	شپش
sherkat	company	شرکت
shir	milk	شیر
shirin	sweet	شیرین
shishe	glass	شیشه
shishe ye morabbā	jar	شیشه مربا
shishe ye jelo	windscreen	شیشه جلو
sho'bade bāz	magician	شعبده باز
shoghl e āzād	self-employment	شغل آزاد
shoghl	job	شغل
shohar	husband	شوهر
shojā'	brave	شجاع
shokolāt	chocolate	شکلات
shol	loose	شل
shoma ... dārin?		شما ... دارید؟
Do you have ...?		
shomā	you	شما
shomāl	north	شمال
shomāre ye otāgh	room number	شماره اتاق
shomāre ye pāsport	passport number	شماره پاسپورت
shomordan	to count	شمردن
shostan	to wash	شستن

shukhi kardan	to joke	شوخی کردن
shulugh	busy (crowded)	شلوغ
shune	comb • shoulder	شانه
shuru' kardan	to begin	شروع کردن
shuru' e mosābeghe	kick off	شروع مسابقه

S

Remember that sh comes before s

sā'at	watch	ساعت
sā'at chand e?		ساعت چند است؟
What time is it?		
sā'at e divāri	clock	ساعت دیواری
sā'at e zangdār	alarm clock	ساعت زنگ دار
sābeghe ye kār	résumé	سابقه کار
sābun	soap	صابون
sāde	plain • simple	ساده
sāf	flat (land, etc)	صاف
sāgh e pā	leg	ساق پا
sāheb	owner	صاحب
sāhel	beach • coast	ساحل
sākhtan	to build	ساختن
sāket	quiet (adj)	ساکت
sāl	year	سال
sāl e ba'd	next year	سال بعد
sālgārd e arusi	wedding anniversary	سالگرد عروسی
sāliyāne	annual	سالیانه
sālon e entezār	transit lounge	سالن انتظار
sālon e varzeshi	gym	سالن ورزشی
sāniye	second (n)	ثانیه
sāntimetr	centimetre	سانتیمتر
sāye	shade • shadow	سایه
sabad	basket	سبد
sabk	style	سبک
sabok	light (adj)	سبک

sabr kon!		صبر کن
Wait!		
sabur	patient (adj)	صبور
sabz	green	سبز
sabzi	vegetable	سبزی
sabzi khār	vegetarian	سبزیخوار
sabzi furush	greengrocer	سبزی فروش
sad	a hundred	صد
saf	queue	صف
safar	trip	سفر
safar be kheyr!		سفر بخیر
Bon voyage!		
safar e por zahmat	trek	سفر پر زحمت
safar kardan	to travel	سفر کردن
safarnāme	itinerary	سفرنامه
safhe kelid	keyboard	صفحه کلید
safhe	screen • sheet (of paper)	صفحه
safhe ye shatranj	chessboard	صفحه شطرنج
safir	ambassador	سفیر
sag	dog	سگ
sag e rāhnamā	guide dog	سگ راهنما
sahar	dawn	سحر
sahne	stage	صحنه
sakhre	cliff • rock	صخره
sakhre navardi	rock climbing	صخره نوردی
sakht	hard	سخت
sakku	platform	سکو
salām	Hello.	سلام
salāmati	health	سلامتی
salib	cross (religious)	صلیب
sam'ak	hearing aid	سمعک
san'at	industry	صنعت
sanāye' e dasti	crafts • handicrafts	صنایع دستی
sandali	chair • seat	صندلی
sandali ye charkh dār	wheelchair	صندلی چرخدار

sandogh e post	mailbox	صندوق پست
sandugh	cash register	صندوق
sandughdār	cashier	صندوقدار
sang	stone	سنگ
sangin	heavy	سنگین
sar	head	سر
sar o sedā	noise	سروصدا
sar'i	epileptic	صرعی
sarāziri	steep	سرازیری
sarbālāyi	uphill	سربالایی
sard	cold (adj)	سرد
sardabir	editor (in chief)	سردبیر
sardard	a headache	سردرد
sard e It's cold.		سرد است
sargarm konande	entertaining	سرگرم کننده
sargarmi	fun	سرگرمی
sariy'	express	سریع
sarmā khordan	to have a cold	سرما خوردن
sarmā khordegi	a cold	سرما خوردگی
sath e zendegi	standard of living	سطح زندگی
satl	bucket	سطل
savār shodan	to board (ship, etc)	سوار شدن
savāri kardan	to ride (a horse)	سواری کردن
sa'y kardan	to try (attempt)	سعی کردن
sayyāre	planet	سیاره
sāyz	size (clothes, shoes)	سایز
se chāhārom	three-quarters	سه چهارم
seda	sound	صدا
sefārat	embassy	سفارت
sefāresh	order	سفارش
sefid	white	سفید
sefr	zero	صفر
seft	tight	سفت

seght	miscarriage • abortion	سقط
sekke	coin	سکه
self servis	self-service	سلف سرویس
senn	age	سن
septāmr	September	سپتامبر
serāmik	ceramic	سرامیک
servatmand	rich (wealthy)	ثروتمند
se shanbe	Tuesday	سه شنبه
setāregān	stars	ستارگان
setāre shenās	astronomer	ستاره شناس
sevvom	third	سوم
shirni	candy	شیرینی
si	thirty	سی
sidi	CD	سی دی
sigār	cigarettes	سیگار
sigār keshidan	to smoke	سیگار کشیدن
sim	wire	سیم
sine	chest	سینه
sinemā	cinema	سینما
sirk	circus	سیرک
siyāh	black	سیاه
siyāh o sefid	B&W (film)	سیاه و سفید
siyāsat	politics	سیاست
siyāsathā ye hezbi	party politics	سیاست های حزبی
siyāsatmadār	politician	سیاستمدار
sizdah	thirteen	سیزده
so'āl	question	سوال
sob	morning	صبح
sobhune	breakfast	صبحانه
sob bekheyr Good morning.		صبح بخیر
sofāl gari	pottery	سفال گری
sohbat kardan	to speak	صحبت کردن
sokhanrāni ye siyāsi	political speech	سخنرانی سیاسی
solh	peace	صلح
some'e	convent • monastery	صومعه
sorang	syringe	سرنگ

T

sor'at	speed	سرعت
sor'at e film	film speed	سرعت فیلم
sorb dār	leaded (petrol/gas)	سرب دار
sorfe	a cough	سرفه
sosyāl-domokrāt	social-democratic	سوسیال دمکرات
sosyālist	socialist	سوسیالیست
sot	voice	صوت
sud	profit	سود
sud dehi	profitability	سود دهی
su' e hāzeme	indigestion	سو هاضمه
surat hesāb	bill (shopping)	صورت حساب
surati	pink	صورتی
susk	cockroach	سوسک
suzan	needle (sewing/syringe)	سوزن

T

tā (zhu'an)	until (June)	تا (ژوئن)
tābe'iyyat	citizenship	تابعیت
tābestun	summer	تابستان
tājer	businessperson	تاجر
tākestān	vineyard	تاکستان
tārik	dark (light)	تاریک
tārikh	date (time)	تاریخ
tārikh e tavallod	date of birth	تاریخ تولد
tāval	a blister	تاول
tāyp kardan	to type	تایپ کردن
tāze	new	تازه
ta'ajjob	a surprise	تعجب
tab	fever	تب
tabaghe	class • floor (storey)	طبقه
tabdil	exchange	تبدیل
tabdil kardan	to exchange	تبدیل کردن
tab e yonje	hayfever	تب یونجه
tabi'at	nature	طبیعت
tab'iz	discrimination	تبعیض

tabl	drum	طبل
tadris	teaching	تدریس
tafrih kardan	to have fun	تفریح کردن
taghallob	a cheat	تقلب
taghriban	almost	تقریباً
taghsir	fault (someone's)	تقصیر
taghsir e man e ast I'm wrong. (my fault)		تقصیر من است
taghvim	calendar	تقویم
taghyir dādan	to change	تغییر دادن
tah	[at the] bottom	ته
tahavvo'	nausea	تهوع
tahsin kardan	to admire	تحسین کردن
tahvil giri ye bār	baggage claim	تحویل گیری بار
tajāvoz	rape	تجاوز
tak	single (unique)	تک
takhfif	discount	تخفیف
ta'khir	delay	تاخیر
takht e do khābe	twin beds	تخت دو خواب
takhte nard	dice • die	تخته نرد
takhte ye moj savāri	surfboard	تخته موج سواری
takhtkhāb	bed	تختخواب
talāyi	of gold	طلایی
tamām shodan	to end	تمام شدن
tamām	whole	تمام
tamāshā kardan	to watch	تماشا کردن
tambr	stamp	تمبر
ta'min e ejtemāyi	social security	تامین اجتماعی
tamiz	clean	تمیز
tamiz kardan	cleaning	تمیز کردن
tamrin	workout	تمرین
tanāb	rope	طناب
tanbāku	tobacco	تنباکو
tanbal	lazy	تنبل
tanbali	laziness	تنبلی

tanbih kardan	to punish	تنبیه کردن
tanhā	alone	تنها
tanzim	tune	تنظیم
tappe	hill	تپه
tarāshidan	to shave	تراشیدن
taraf	side	طرف
tarh	design • proposal	طرح
tarjih dādan	to prefer	ترجیح دادن
tarjome kardan	to translate	ترجمه کردن
tark kardan	to depart (leave) • to quit	ترک کردن
tars	fear	ترس
tarsidan az	to be afraid of	ترسیدن از
tashakkor kardan	to thank	تشکر کردن
tasādof	accident	تصادف
tasfiye shode	filtered	تصفیه شده
tasmim gereftan	to decide	تصمیم گرفتن
ta'tilāt	holidays • vacation	تعطیلات
tavāghghof kardan	to stop	توقف کردن
tavānestan	able (to be); can	توانستن
ta'yiyd kardan	to confirm (a booking)	تایید کردن
tazāhorāt e khiyābāni	street demonstration	تظاهرات خیابانی
tazāhorāt	demonstration	تظاهرات
tazrigh	injection	تزریق
tazrigh kardan	to inject	تزریق کردن
te'ātr	theatre	تئاتر
te'ātr e sonnati	classical theatre	تئاتر سنتی
tejārat	business	تجارت
tekrār kardan	to repeat	تکرار کردن
telefon	telephone	تلفن
telefon e hamrāh	mobile phone	تلفن همراه

telefon kardan	to telephone	تلفن کردن
teleskop	telescope	تلسکوپ
telgerāf	telegram	تلگراف
televiziyon	television	تلویزیون
tenis	tennis	تنیس
termināl	bus station	ترمینال
teshne	thirsty	تشنه
test	test	تست
tigh e rishtarāshi	razor blades	تیغ ریش تراشی
tikke	piece	تکه
tim	team	تیم
tir andāzi kardan	to shoot (gun)	تیر اندازی کردن
tire	dark (colour)	تیره
tishert	T-shirt	تی شرت
to	you (sg, inf)	تو
tohin	offence	توهین
tolid kardan	to produce	تولید کردن
tolid konande	producer	تولید کننده
tolombe	pump	تلمبه
tond	fast • spicy (hot) • quick	تند
tormoz	brake	ترمز
toshak	mattress	تشک
tosye	advice	توصیه
tozi' konande	distributor	توزیع کننده
tufān	storm	طوفان
tule sag	puppy	توله سگ
tulu'	sunrise	طلوع
tup	ball	توپ
tur	net	تور
tuvālet	toilet	توالت
tuvālet e umumi	public toilet	توالت عمومی

U

u	he • she	او
ulum e ejtemāyi	social sciences	علوم اجتماعی
umadan	to come	آمدن

tavallodet mobārak!
Happy birthday! تولدت مبارک

umumi	general	عمومی

un chi mige?
What's he saying? اوچه می گوید؟

un key harekat mikone?
When does it leave? آن کی حرکت می کند؟

un mojāz e
It's allowed. آن مجاز است

un mojāz nist
It's not allowed. آن مجاز نیست

unhā	they	آنها

unhā kiyand?
Who are they? آنها کی هستند؟

urupāyi	European	اروپایی
ut	August	اوت
utubān	tollway	اتوبان
utubus	bus	اتوبوس
utubus e beyn e shahri	long-distance bus	اتوبوس بین شهری

vāksināsyon	vaccination	واکسیناسیون
vānet	van	وانت
vāred shodan	to enter	وارد شدن
vāzeh	obvious	واضح
va	and	و
va'de	promise	وعده
vafādār	loyal	وفادار
vaghfe	intermission	وقفه
vaght e nāhār	lunchtime	وقت ناهار
vaght	time	وقت
vahshatnāk	awful • horrible terrible	وحشتناک
vakil	lawyer	وکیل
varagh	playing cards	ورق
varagh bāzi kardan	to play cards	ورق بازی کردن
varzesh	sport	ورزش
varzeshkār	sportsperson	ورزشکار
vasāyel e charmi	leathergoods	وسایل چرمی

vasi'	wide	وسیع
vasile	equipment	وسیله
vasile ye ghavvāsi	diving equipment	وسیله غواصی
vaz'iyat e ta'ahhol	marital status	وضعیت تأهل
vazagh	toad	وزغ
vazn	weight • rhythm	وزن
vazn kardan	to weigh	وزن کردن
virāstār	editor	ویراستار
virus	virus	ویروس
vitāmin	vitamin	ویتامین
vizā	visa	ویزا
vurud	arrivals	ورود

yā	or	یا
yād gereftan	to learn	یاد گرفتن
yāzdah	eleven	یازده
yahudi	Jewish	یهودی
yakh	ice	یخ
yakhchāl	refrigerator	یخچال
ye bār	once • one time	یک بار
ye daghighe	a minute	یک دقیقه

ye daghighe sabr konin
Just a minute.

یک دقیقه صبر کنید

ye milyon	one million	یک میلیون
ye sare	one-way (ticket)	یک سره
ye zarre	a little bit	یک ذره
yek shanbe	Sunday	یک شنبه
yeylāgh	countryside	ییلاق
yubusat	constipation	یبوست
yubusat dāshtan	to be constipated	یبوست داشتن

zhānviye	January	ژانویه
zhu'an	June	ژوئن

Z

Remember that zh comes before z

zānu	knee	زانو
zabānhā	languages	زبان ها
zabt	recording	ضبط
za'if	weak	ضعیف
zakhim	thick	ضخیم
zakhire	reservation	ذخیره
zakhm	injury • wound	زخم
zamime	appendix (written)	ضمیمه
zamin	earth (soil) • land	زمین
zan	wife • woman	زن
zanbur	bee	زنبور
zang	dial tone • ring (of phone) ring (sound)	زنگ
zard	yellow	زرد
zedd e āftāb	sunblock	ضد آفتاب
zedd e aragh	deodorant	ضد عرق
zedd e hāmelegi	contraceptives	ضد حاملگی
zedd e haste yi	antinuclear	ضد هسته ای
zedd e ufuni konande	antiseptic	ضد عفونی کننده
zehn	mind	ذهن

zelzele	earthquake	زلزله
zemestun	winter	زمستان
zende bād ...!	Long live ...!	زنده باد ... !
zende māndan	to survive	زنده ماندن
zendegi	life	زندگی
zendegi ye giyāhi	vegetation	زندگی گیاهی
zendigi kardan	to live (somewhere)	زندگی کردن
zendun	jail • prison	زندان
zenduni	prisoner	زندانی
zeytun	olives	زیتون
zibā	pretty	زیبا
zin	saddle	زین
zir nevis	subtitles	زیرنویس
zir sigāri	ashtray	زیرسیگاری
zir	below	زیر
ziyād	a lot	زیاد
zobāle ye sammi	toxic waste	زباله سمی
zohr	noon	ظهر
zoj	pair (a couple)	زوج
zud	early	زود
zud e	It's early.	زود است

مندرجات

F
I
N
D
E
R

252

SUSTAINABLE TRAVEL

As the climate change debate heats up, the matter of sustainability becomes an important part of the travel vernacular. In practical terms, this means assessing our impact on the environment and local cultures and economies – and acting to make that impact as positive as possible. Here are some basic phrases to get you on your way …

COMMUNICATION & CULTURAL DIFFERENCES

I'd like to learn some of your local dialects.

man mikhām ba'zi az	من می خواهم بعضی از
lahjehāye mahalliye shomā	لهجه های محلی شما
ro yād begiram	.را یاد بگیرم

Would you like me to teach you some English?

| mikhāhin be shomā | می خواهید به شما |
| kami ingilisi yād bedam? | کمی انگلیسی یاد بدهم؟ |

Is this a local or national custom?

| in yek rasme mahalli | این یک رسم محلی |
| hast yā beynolmelali? | هست یا بین المللی؟ |

I respect your customs.

| man be rusume shomā | من به رسوم شما |
| ehterām mizāram | .احترام می گذارم |

COMMUNITY BENEFIT & INVOLVEMENT

What sorts of issues is this community facing?

| in jāme'e bā che | این جامعه با چه |
| masā'eli ruberu hast? | مسائلی روبرو هست؟ |

economic sanctions	tahrime eghtesādi	تحریم اقتصادی
illiteracy	bisavādi	بیسوادی
inflation	tavarrom	تورم
media	madudiyate	محدودیت
restrictions	resānehā	رسانه ها
political unrest	nāārāmiye siyāsi	نا آرامی سیاسی
poverty	faghr	فقر
unemployment	bikāri	بیکاری

I'd like to volunteer my skills.

man mikhām dāvtalabāne
mahārathāyam ro dar
ekhteyāre shomā bezāram

من می خواهم داوطلبانه
مهارت هایم را در
.اختیار شما بگذارم

Are there any volunteer programs available in the area?

hich barnāmeye
dāvtalabāne dar
mantaghe vujud dārad?

هیچ برنامه
داوطلبانه در
منطقه وجود دارد؟

TRANSPORT

Can we get there by public transport?

mitunim be unjā bā
vasāyele naghliyeye
umumi berim?

می توانیم به آنجا با
وسایل نقلیه
عمومی برویم؟

Can we get there by bike?

mitunim be unjā bā
docharkhe berim?

می توانیم به آنجا با
دوچرخه برویم؟

I'd prefer to walk there.

man tarjih midam be
unjā piyāde beram

من ترجیح می دهم به
.آنجا پیاده بروم

ACCOMMODATION

I'd like to stay at a locally run hotel.

man mikhām dar yek
hotele mahalli bemunam

من می خواهم در یک
.هتل محلی بمانم

Can I turn the air conditioning off and open the window?

mitunam tahviyeye matbu'
ro khāmush konam va
panjare ro bāz konam?

می توانم تهویه مطبوع
را خاموش کنم و
پنجره را باز کنم؟

There's no need to change my sheets.

lāzem nist malāfehām
avaz beshan

لازم نیست ملافه هایم
.عوض بشوند

SHOPPING

Where can I buy locally produced goods?
az kojā mitunam vasāyele
tolide dākheli bekharam?

از کجا می توانم وسایل
تولید داخلی بخرم؟

Where can I buy locally produced souvenirs?
az kojā mitunam soghātihāye
tolide dākheli bekharam?

از کجا می توانم سوغاتی
تولید داخلی بخرم؟

Is this made from animal skin?
in az puste heyvānāt
dorost shode?

این از پوست حیوانات
درست شده؟

FOOD

Do you sell …?	shomā … mifurushin?	شما ... می فروشید؟
locally produced food	ghazāye tolide dākheli	غذای تولید داخلی
organic produce	tolidāte tabiyi	تولیدات طبیعی

Can you tell me what traditional foods I should try?
mitunin be man begin che
ghazāhāye mahalli ro
bāyad emtehān konam?

می توانید به من بگوئید چه
غذاهای محلی را
باید امتحان بکنم؟

SIGHTSEEING

Does your company ...?	sherkate shomā ...?	شرکت شما ...؟
donate money to charity	be kheyriye pul midahad	به خیریه پول می دهد
hire local guides	rāhnamāye mahalli migirad	راهنمای محلی می گیرد
visit local businesses	az tejārathāye mahalli bāzdid mikonad	از تجارت های محلی بازدید می کند

Does the guide speak any local dialects?
in rāhnamā hich lahjeye mahalliyi rā sohbat mikonad? این راهنما هیچ لهجه محلی ای را صحبت می کند؟

Are cultural tours available?
turhāye farhangi dārin? تورهای فرهنگی دارین؟